P9-DMD-167

DATE DUE

BRODART, CO.   Cat. No. 23-221-003

TO CONVEY INTELLIGENCE

052.09421
C598C

TO CONVEY INTELLIGENCE

The Spectator
1928–1998

Simon Courtauld

P
PROFILE BOOKS

First published in Great Britain in 1999 by
Profile Books Ltd
58A Hatton Garden
London EC1N 8LX

Copyright © The Spectator (1828) Ltd, 1999

All rights reserved. Without limiting the rights under copyright reserved above,
no part of this publication may be reproduced, stored or introduced into a retrieval system,
or transmitted, in any form or by any means (electronic, mechanical, photocopying, recording
or otherwise), without the prior written permission of both the copyright owners and the
publisher of this book.

Typeset in Times by MacGuru
macguru@pavilion.co.uk

Printed in Great Britain by
St Edmundsbury Press, Bury St Edmunds

A CIP catalogue record for this book is available from the British Library.

ISBN 1 86197 127 3

CONTENTS

ACKNOWLEDGMENTS

Charles Seaton died little more than a year before I started researching and writing this book. I know how he would have enjoyed producing (mostly from memory) the facts and figures of *The Spectator*'s history with which he was uniquely familiar and chiding me for the errors I made. Alas, *The Spectator*'s librarian and archivist for more than 40 years left me to rely on memories less encyclopaedic.

The history of *The Spectator*'s first hundred years was published by Methuen in 1928. It was begun several years earlier, and its author was Sir William Beach Thomas, who for many years wrote a weekly Country Life column for the magazine. A prefatory note, however, pays tribute to Miss K.S. Leaf for having started writing the book; 'and the greater share, especially in the work of research, is hers'. (Miss Leaf, later Mrs Douglas West, was the mother of Richard West, who wrote regularly for *The Spectator* during Alexander Chancellor's editorship.)

For whatever reason, the Beach Thomas history is not entirely satisfactory: the Townsend/Hutton years (1861–97) are only sketchily treated. I have written a foreword covering not only the first hundred years of *The Spectator* but also its previous incarnation in the early 18th century in the hands of Addison and Steele.

While I can claim a very tenuous link with the 19th-century *Spectator*, through my cousin by marriage and godfather Rab Butler, who was related to Meredith Townsend, my more relevant qualifications for writing this book consist of an association with the magazine which lasted, on and off, for 20 years. I joined when Henry Keswick bought it in 1975, and was deputy editor to Alexander Chancellor from 1980 to 1984. References to myself in the text have been, I hope, kept to a minimum.

For the sake of consistency, I have referred to *The Spectator* throughout as a magazine, although it was, at least until the 1970s, more commonly described as a paper. Today, largely because of its greater bulk (the number of pages is often twice what it was in the 1970s), better-quality newsprint and colour advertising, it can no longer be thought of as a weekly paper. Although several of the dramatis personae have been knighted, or elevated to the peerage, during the course of the story, I have usually continued to refer to them by their surnames.

My thanks are due to a large number of people who have helped, in greater or smaller ways, with this book. I am especially grateful to Luis Dominguez who first proposed that I should write it and to Algy Cluff who gave me the commission; to Michael Heath for the book's jacket and for his help in selecting the illustrations; to John Taplin, Ian Gilmour (Lord Gilmour of Craigmillar), Jean Hamilton, Alexander Chancellor, James Knox and Jenny Naipaul who, apart from giving freely of their time, also provided much useful documentary material. And to the following, without whose valuable insights, recollections and assessments this book could not have been written: Peter Ackroyd, Larry Adler, Mark Amory, Anne Applebaum, Clare Asquith, Conrad Black, Sir Richard Body, Christopher Booker, Fred Brenchley, Roland Brown, Ian Buruma, Robert Conquest, Patrick Cosgrave, Maurice Cowling, Harry Creighton, Dan Colson, Bill Deedes (Lord Deedes of Aldington), Stephen Fay, Christopher Fildes, Kimberly Fortier, Christopher Frere-Smith, Timothy Garton Ash, Sir Philip Goodhart, Cecilia Goodlad, Germaine Greer, Trevor Grove, Dennis Hackett, Juliette Harrison, Anthony Hartley, Simon Heffer, E.C. Hodgkin, Christopher Hudson, James Hughes-Onslow, Pamela Hutchinson, Ruth Inglis, Richard Ingrams, Eric Jacobs, Frank Johnson, Paul Johnson, Henry Keswick, Rory Knight Bruce, Sheila Lawlor, Dominic Lawson, Nigel Lawson (Lord Lawson of Blaby), Bernard Levin, the Earl of Longford, John McEwen, Baroness Macleod of Borve, Hugh Macpherson, Patrick Marnham, Karl Miller, Hugh Montgomery-Massingberd, Charles Moore, Ferdinand Mount, Julia Mount, Jennifer Paterson, Peter Paterson, David Potton, Isabel Quigly, Malcolm Rutherford, Rae Sebley, Lorraine Sherry, Jim Slater, Xan Smiley, Sir John Smith, Hilary Spurling, Gavin Stamp, Taki Theodoracopulos, John Thompson, Sally Vincent, Alan Watkins, Auberon Waugh, Richard West, Geoffrey Wheatcroft, Katharine Whitehorn, A.N. Wilson, Sir Peregrine Worsthorne, Michael Wynn Jones.

PREFACE

Joseph Addison and Richard Steele had collaborated in publishing the *Tatler* before they started *The Spectator*, which appeared every weekday between March 1711 and December 1712. They were both Whigs, and both in their thirties. It may have been a short-lived publication, but was widely read at the time. Estimates of its daily sale vary from 2,000 to 20,000 on occasion. Abstaining from politics, *The Spectator* consisted of humorous and satirical essays and sketches, often of manners and human eccentricities, though sometimes rising to a more serious literary and moral plane. The 'speculations' of Mr Spectator often provided what would today be called talking-points, none more successful than on the subject of women. 'I shall take it for the greatest Glory of my Work,' Steele wrote, 'if among reasonable Women this Paper may furnish Tea-Table Talk.' Numerous letters from women produced something akin to an agony column; it was an early example of successful modern journalism. *The Spectator* also formed a club in its pages, of whose seven members Addison's most memorable creation was Sir Roger De Coverley, 'a whimsical Country Knight'.

The Spectator folded after 555 issues, prompting one reader to regret the loss of 'so Elegant and Valuable Entertainment. And we could not without Sorrow reflect that we were likely to have nothing to interrupt our Sips in a Morning, and to suspend our Coffee in mid-air, between our Lips and Right-Ear, but the ordinary Trash of Newspapers.' Addison and Steele were certainly not lacking in journalistic enterprise: within three months they had started the *Guardian*, and in 1714 Addison briefly revived *The Spectator* (for another 80 numbers) with his cousin, Eustace Budgell, who died a lunatic.

The Spectator title was not taken up again until 1828, when a Scots newspaperman, Robert Rintoul, who had edited the *Dundee Advertiser*, and briefly the *Atlas*, founded a 'new London weekly paper' which has continued without interruption to this day. It is the only one that has: quite a number of magazines were around in the first decades of the 19th century, most of them with Scottish connections, when Rintoul elected to throw his hat into the ring. Apart from the *Edinburgh Review* and *Blackwood's Magazine*, the *London Magazine*, the *Quarterly Magazine*, *Fraser's Magazine* and the *Spy* were all edited by Scotsmen. (the *Athenaeum* was started in the same year as *The Spectator*, and absorbed by the *New Statesman* a century later; *Punch* began in 1841.)

In his first issue, which appeared on 6 July, Rintoul declared his purpose: 'to convey intelligence. It is proposed in *The Spectator* to give the first and most prominent place to a report of all the leading occurrences of the week.' (In one early issue, he even published illustrations to accompany an article on murder.) But this was only part of it: a liberal-radical in outlook, and belonging to no political party, Rintoul was outspoken in his support for parliamentary reform, demanding 'the Bill, the whole Bill, and nothing but the Bill' before its passage in 1832. He campaigned for repeal of the corn laws and espoused other social reforms over the next 30 years. He gave short shrift to Lord Melbourne and ridiculed the extravagance of the Queen's coronation and the Great Exhibition.

Through his friendship with Edward Gibbon Wakefield, Rintoul gave *The Spectator*'s support to what amounted to a revolution in British colonial policy. Wakefield, who had done three years in Newgate prison for having abducted a 16-year-old heiress, persuaded Rintoul that *The Spectator* should propagate his ideas for selling land in the colonies and using the proceeds as an emigration fund, to settle labourers and young married couples in Australia and New Zealand. It was in large measure because of Wakefield's and Rintoul's enlightened imperialism that Canada was granted self-government in 1840.

Rintoul's *Spectator* must have enjoyed a reasonable commercial success, if only because — uncharacteristically for a Scot — he was very generous to his contributors, sometimes paying as much as £10 for an article (worth well over £500 in 1998). With his family he lived 'above the shop', at 1 Wellington Street, at the corner of the Strand and what is now Lancaster Place, which housed not only the editorial offices but also the printing presses. Among the regular visitors to the building in Rintoul's day were the Rossetti brothers; Rintoul's daughter, Henrietta, set her sights unsuccessfully at Dante Gabriel.

When Rintoul retired in 1858, he accepted an annuity from a Mr John Scott of Stourbridge, Worcestershire, in part payment for the magazine — and died four months later. Nothing is known of Mr Scott, but it appears, from an indenture dated January 1859, that he sold *The Spectator* to Thornton Hunt for £3,000. Hunt had been a regular contributor to *The Spectator* since 1840, but there is no reference in the *Dictionary of National Biography* (*DNB*) to his having owned the magazine. According to the *DNB*, at the relevant time he was a political writer for the *Daily Telegraph* 'and practically editing it'. At any rate *The Spectator* passed in 1861, for the sum of £1,000, to Meredith Townsend, who had spent ten years editing journals in India and who ran it almost until the end of the century in partnership with a theologian, Richard Holt Hutton. Though Townsend retained ultimate control, it was usually thought of, at least in the early years, as Hutton's *Spectator*. He said it was 'one of the few papers which are written in the fear and love of God'.

John Buchan, who worked at *The Spectator* during Townsend's later years, described him as a holy man, a sort of guru, who took snuff and to whom the flavour of the East still clung. Townsend began one of his leading articles: 'Recent events have shown us that God not only reigns but governs.' He was acknowledged as the finest leader writer of his day. *Spectator* writers today would do well to note the characterisation of his prose style by his successor as proprietor/editor, John St Loe Strachey:

> He used no literary artifice, no rhetorical emphasis, no elaboration of language, no finesse of phrase. His style was easy but never eloquent or precious or ornamented. It was familiar without being commonplace, free without discursiveness, and it always had in it a note of distinction.

For many years Townsend also wrote a weekly political article for the *Economist*. Walter Bagehot introduced him to Hutton, and they enjoyed what Townsend described as 'a literary alliance which at once in its duration and completeness is probably without a precedent'. Townsend generally looked after the front half, writing frequently on foreign politics and always giving prominence to Indian affairs; while Hutton supervised the literary and other pages. He was a good critic, but his high moral tone and the opaqueness of his prose could be off-putting. It was said of his sentences that they 'went tottering on, bent double under their burden of thought'. When Townsend took on an assistant editor in the 1880s, he encouraged him to lighten *The Spectator*'s 'incorrigible seriousness'.

Theological questions were a favourite subject for Hutton's pen (he was a sometime unitarian, who subsequently became an admirer of Cardinal Newman and regularly heard Mass in his last years); and he campaigned against the practice of vivisection. In the literary pages he condemned Tennyson for frivolity but was a fan of Scott and Shelley; and the novelist Mrs Oliphant provided a diverting 'Commentary from an Easy Chair' for some years.

Following the interregnum between Rintoul and Townsend/Hutton, *The Spectator* had forfeited much of its *succès d'estime*, which declined further when it gave early support to the Union cause in the American Civil War. Slavery was the principal reason for *The Spectator* taking this stance, in opposition to most of the English middle classes and almost every other English journal. But as the two editors continued to urge and anticipate victory over the confederacy, and were proved right, so the fortunes of *The Spectator* took a turn for the better. A decade later, the magazine poured scorn on Disraeli — it had never liked him, and even refused to acknowledge his talents as a novelist — for his handling of the Bulgarian atrocities question; and in 1886 it deserted Gladstone, in spite of Hutton's friendship with him, over Irish home rule, becoming the leading supporter in the press of the Liberal Unionist party.

Around this time a future Liberal prime minister, H.H. Asquith (later to become the Earl of Oxford and Asquith), gave up writing leaders for *The Spectator*, where he had been supplementing his income from the Bar, to go into politics, and was replaced by John St Loe Strachey (who started off with a sustained attack on Cecil Rhodes for giving his support to Irish home rule and, in particular, £10,000 to Charles Parnell). Hutton retired, and Strachey was given to understand by Townsend that the succession, as owner/editor, would be his in due course.

The time came in 1897, and for the next quarter-century Strachey not only presided over *The Spectator* but was its general manager, chief leader writer and regular reviewer. Readers were often outraged by his vigorously expressed opinions, but they bought the magazine in steadily increasing numbers, 'to see what Strachey had to say'. His son John, in a tribute written a year after his father's death, described him as 'surely the worst "party man" imaginable', liberal and conservative by several turns. (John, who opted for a political career, hardly distinguished himself by his consistency. Having edited a Conservative journal at Oxford, where he played cricket for Magdalen wearing a French peasant hat hung with pink ribbons, he joined the International Labour party, was closely associated with Oswald Mosley, turned to Communism, then became a Labour MP and subsequently War Minister.)

The two things that Strachey cared about most passionately in politics — free trade and the Union — were championed by opposite parties. Like Rintoul before him, Strachey was a fierce opponent of tariffs, having been since university a supporter of free trade, free exchange and free markets; and following the tariff reform controversy he advised *Spectator* readers to vote Liberal in the 1906 election. But he turned against what he saw as the interventionist, social left-wingery of the administration led by his predecessor as *Spectator* political columnist, Asquith. Honesty of mind, together with moral and intellectual candour, were the virtues most often attributed to Strachey.

By this time the circulation of *The Spectator* was falling, and continued to fall during the war when Strachey tried to do too much war work, as High Sheriff of Surrey devoting himself to recruitment and to compiling a register of ex-soldiers who could be called up. In 1916 he became seriously ill. His greatest wartime achievement was to arrange weekly 'American tea-parties' at his house in Queen Anne's Gate, bringing a Cabinet minister to give an informal briefing to American newspaper correspondents who had hitherto been starved of news of the war.

The cause of Anglo-American relations was the strongest link between Strachey and Evelyn Wrench, who came to *The Spectator* in 1922 and agreed two years later to pay £25,000 for a controlling interest in the magazine, which at the time was making a profit of around £2,000 a year. The deal was completed in July 1925. Strachey had not really exercised effective control since 1914; from the time of Wrench's arrival circulation rose swiftly, from a low point of 13,500 to over 22,000 in 1928, the same figure attained under Strachey 15 years earlier. Strachey published two books after handing over to Wrench, and continued to write for *The Spectator*. His last article appeared in 1927, six months before he died.

EDITORS
AND
PROPRIETORS

Editors

1925–32 Evelyn Wrench

1932–53 Wilson Harris
1953–54 Walter Taplin
1954–59 Ian Gilmour
1959–62 Brian Inglis
1962–63 Iain Hamilton
1963–65 Iain Macleod
1966–70 Nigel Lawson
1970–73 George Gale
1973–75 Harold Creighton
1975–84 Alexander Chancellor

1984–90 Charles Moore
1990–95 Dominic Lawson
1995– Frank Johnson

Proprietors

1925–54 Evelyn Wrench (from *c.* 1930 jointly with Angus Watson)

1954–67 Ian Gilmour

1967–75 Harold Creighton

1975–81 Henry Keswick
1981–85 Algy Cluff
1985–88 Fairfax
1988– The Telegraph

1

THE HARRIS YEARS

In 1928 Stalin introduced his first Five Year Plan, Herbert Hoover became president of the United States and Germany signed the Kellogg-Briand pact for the renunciation of war. Professor Alexander Fleming discovered penicillin, and Britons were declared the greatest cigarette smokers in the world. Amelia Earhart became the first woman to fly the Atlantic, and Thomas Hardy died. In parts of South Wales unemployment levels rose to 40 per cent; one of the worst-hit towns was Aberdare which, towards the end of that year, *The Spectator* decided to 'adopt'. An appeal to readers, for the relief of the people of Aberdare, was published in the first week of December; by the end of February 1929 more than £12,000 (worth over £400,000 in 1998) had been donated, together with countless blankets, items of clothing and food. It was said that during that winter in Aberdare faces would light up when *The Spectator* was mentioned. The town decided to present its benefactors with a statuette of an Aberdare miner, pick and shovel over one shoulder, a lamp in his other hand. It was inscribed 'From the Townsfolk of Aberdare in Grateful Recognition: "The Greatest of These is Love"', and it stands on the mantelpiece of the editor's office today.

The proprietor/editor in 1928, who had been moved to make the appeal by accounts of the misery in South Wales, was Evelyn Wrench. While he and the people of Aberdare were amazed at the scale of the response, it was entirely in character for *The Spectator* and its readership to show their concern for the underprivileged. William Beach Thomas, the historian of *The Spectator*'s first hundred years, described its political position as combining 'an intellectual admiration for tradition' with 'a deep sympathy for "those who live in small houses"'. And, as the magazine's long-time Country Life columnist, he went on to include, as also deserving of editorial sympathy, 'those lesser animals who suffer needless pain, those who live in burrows and nest in trees, as well as those who barely exist in slums'.

At this time *The Spectator* was still discharging the duty laid upon it a century before by its founder, Robert Rintoul, which was 'to give the first and most prominent place to a report of all the leading occurrences of the week'. The first three pages of the magazine were devoted to News of the Week paragraphs, 15 or 20 of them, which not only gave the news but made clear what *The Spectator* thought of it. Wrench, who had started contributing a weekly column of notes on imperial affairs in 1922, saw no reason to alter the practice. The wireless offered no more than two or three daily bulletins on one channel, news from abroad did not travel fast, and quite a number of *The Spectator*'s 22,000 readers resided in corners of the empire out of the BBC's range. (The BBC began its broadcasts to listeners abroad, known as the Empire Service, at the end of 1932.)

Wrench, an Irishman, had been chairman and editor of *The Spectator* since 1925, following John St Loe Strachey's 28-year reign as proprietor/editor before him. At Strachey's invitation, Wrench had joined the magazine as business director. During the first two decades of the century he had started a picture postcard business, highly successful for a time, then founded the Overseas League and the English-Speaking Union. When Strachey came to retire, he was concerned at what might happen to *The Spectator* if it was inherited by his alarmingly left-wing children, Amabel and John (both were Communist sympathisers, and he was seeking election as a Labour MP). So he resolved to sell the bulk of his shareholding to Wrench, while retaining a small parcel of preference shares for the family.

Wrench, whose political outlook, like Strachey's, could be described as left-centre, is remembered as courteous, fastidious and dapperly dressed, often in a wing collar and bow-tie. His liking for coloured waistcoats was copied by several members of the staff. At home he used to sit with a Persian cat on his lap. In addition to *The Spectator*, he was devoting much of his time to his twin causes of promoting Commonwealth unity and Anglo-American cooperation, and to the writing of his first book, *Uphill*, which was followed a year later by *Struggle* (and some years afterwards by a biography of Geoffrey Dawson). Perhaps because of his other commitments, Wrench sold more than half of his shareholding to Angus Watson, an obsessive teetotaller and nonconformist Liberal, who ran a successful business from Newcastle-on-Tyne, supplying Norwegian brisling, which he called Skipper Sardines, to the nation. But Wrench, who gave up the editorship in 1932, remained chairman, not only throughout the period when he was co-proprietor (he and Watson sold *The Spectator* in 1954), but until his death in 1966.

To mark the magazine's centenary year, Wrench took steps, as he put it, 'to ensure its future political independence, in the national interest'. A Special Resolution was passed and a committee established to vet future transfers of more than 50 per cent of *The Spectator*'s shares. Wrench was determined to protect the magazine from the depredations of press barons, however public-spirited they might appear to be. Its ownership, he declared, should 'never be regarded as a mere matter of commerce, to be transferred to the highest bidder'. The committee which he appointed was to comprise the Lord Mayor of London, the president of the Royal Society, the president of the Royal Historical Society, the president of the Law Society, the president of the Institute of Chartered Accountants and the chairman of the Headmasters' Conference. In deciding on the suitability of a future proprietor, these august gentlemen were required to

> have regard to the importance of:
> (a) Maintaining the best traditions and political independence of *The Spectator* newspaper and national rather than personal interests, and
> (b) Eliminating as far as reasonably possible questions of personal or commercial profit.

While these criteria may cause mild amusement today — the committee only sat twice, to approve Ian Gilmour and Harry Creighton — their spirit has been followed in more recent years, when the blandishments of both James Goldsmith and Rupert Murdoch were resisted.

However, Wrench did show he was not immune to considerations of commercial profit when he published, on 3 November 1928, a centenary issue, appropriately containing 100 pages of advertisements. In the spring of 1929 *The Spectator* moved offices, from York Street, Covent Garden, to 99 Gower Street, in Bloomsbury, hard by University College Hospital. Throughout its 170 years *The Spectator* has had offices in the West Central district of London. Having spent almost 100 years in Wellington Street, south of the Strand, *The Spectator* moved a few hundred yards north, to

13 York Street, in 1920. (This address is now 15 Tavistock Street, the premises of Luigi's Restaurant.) Between the Strand and Tavistock Street further *Spectator* associations are to be found: at 21 Wellington Street (the Lyceum Ballroom, now Theatre), where its 150th anniversary ball was held in 1978, and at no. 18, Christopher's Restaurant, which belongs to a son of Ian Gilmour, *The Spectator*'s proprietor from 1954 to 1967.

Having left Covent Garden, *The Spectator* has resided in Bloomsbury for the past 70 years. A previous occupant of 99 Gower Street, known as Angel Anna, once ran a hotel-cum-brothel there. She apparently had American ancestry, although she claimed to be the illegitimate daughter of the mad King Ludwig of Bavaria and the Spanish dancer, Lola Montez. Anna's house of ill fame became so notorious that her subsequent prosecution at the Old Bailey was conducted by Sir Edward Carson, and she was sent down for seven years. *The Spectator* moved in shortly before a Labour government was returned to power for the second time, under Ramsay MacDonald. When it moved out, after 46 years, Margaret Thatcher was leader of the Conservative party.

Peter Fleming wrote for *The Spectator* for almost the whole of that period, from his appointment as assistant literary editor, aged 23, in April 1931, until shortly before his death in 1971. Fleming occupied one of a row of cubicles at Gower Street which, as he described them, had surely been 'designed either as oubliettes for very minor poets or as ferret-hutches for very large ferrets'. After only a few months he wangled an invitation to attend a conference of the Institute of Pacific Relations in Shanghai (on behalf of Chatham House, not *The Spectator*). He travelled across Russia on the Trans-Siberian railway, having left the country on the day that Britain went off the gold standard. As he wrote later, 'In the ensuing economic blizzard *The Spectator*'s small staff was drastically reduced. But they couldn't sack me, because no one knew where I was. When I returned early in 1932 to the half-empty offices everybody was nonplussed and in the confusion I was appointed literary editor.' He succeeded Celia Simpson, who had left and would marry John Strachey the following year. Anxious to make an impression, Fleming asked T.E. Lawrence to review a book by the Arabian explorer Bertram Thomas, only to receive a courteous note from Lawrence pointing out that he could hardly accept the commission as he had written a preface to the book. Fleming also became theatre critic — this was the heyday of Noel Coward, and of John Gielgud and Peggy Ashcroft playing Shakespeare — and wrote a weekly pseudonymous essay.

One day in May 1932 Fleming was coming out of the Gower Street office when he ran into an acquaintance and fellow old Etonian, Roger Pettiward, a red-haired artist best remembered for a collection of drawings entitled 'The Last Cream Bun'. Fleming at once asked him to join his expedition to the Mato Grosso in Brazil, to ascertain the fate of Colonel Fawcett (after a couple of days, Pettiward agreed). He was to be away from *The Spectator* for a few months, but before setting off on his Brazilian adventure he arranged for the then Frank Pakenham to keep his Gower Street chair warm for him. At the age of 92, Lord Longford remembered Fleming telling him that Wrench had said he would make him editor on his return. But when Fleming came back from Brazil he found the political editor, Wilson Harris, firmly installed in the editor's chair. Harris told Fleming he valued his writing more than his administrative ability. He made Derek Verschoyle literary editor and got rid of Frank Pakenham. Twenty years later, however, when Harris was removed from the editorship, both Pakenham and Fleming would attend his farewell dinner at the Travellers' Club.

Lord Longford remembered Harris to be 'an old-fashioned, non-conformist type, a League of Nations liberal. He was tall, balding and wore pince-nez, rather like President Wilson' (who was the subject of Harris's first book, published in 1917). As editor, he could be something of a disciplinarian, but he had an engaging habit of making dry jokes with a solemn face. From the evidence of his prose style, Harris appeared priggish and ponderous, but he was not above sending the young Pakenham down to Eton to investigate a story of drunkenness among the boys. Pakenham went to see his old headmaster, the Very Revd C.A. Alington (the future father-in-law of the Earl of Home), to be told: 'It's always a pleasure to see you, Frank, but if you wish to betray your old school this is where we must part company.'

From his Quaker upbringing in Plymouth, Harris went on to Cambridge, and a short spell as a schoolmaster, before joining the *Daily News*, where he worked first as sub-editor, then as leader writer throughout the first world war, and afterwards as diplomatic correspondent. For most of the 1920s he worked with the League of Nations Union and edited its journal.

He was more than twice Fleming's age in 1932, and one may reasonably surmise that they had little in common. Fleming used to treat Harris like his commanding officer, calling him 'Sir', but this may have been done in order to embarrass his editor rather than out of deference towards him. Both Fleming and Verschoyle were responsible for bringing to *The Spectator* a sense of fun and a slightly anarchic streak which have characterised the magazine in more recent years. Together they edited *Spectator's Gallery* in 1933, an anthology of *Spectator* articles which Harris would have thought rather too light-hearted to be put together as representing *The Spectator*. (Harris knew nothing of the book until he saw it for sale in a shop.) Fleming certainly incurred Harris's displeasure when, in January 1932, he wrote, under the pseudonym of 'Moth':

> The task of producing a weekly paper is a formidable one…the duties of the editorial staff subject its personnel to an intellectual strain of the most frightful severity. By their exertions alone, thousands of readers are provided, Friday after Friday, with a fresh, clean copy of *The Spectator*, profound, witty, intensely grammatical, and always differing, however slightly, from the one they read the week before. It is the proud boast of the editorial staff that no two issues of *The Spectator* have ever been proved identical. Sometimes it is the phraseology that is different, sometimes the order or titles of the articles are changed. If the same thing is said, it is said in a different way. If the same words are used, they are used of something else. That has always been the tradition. If not variety, then at least divergence. Semper idem, sed nunquam verbatim.

Though Fleming's wit and style must sometimes have seemed alien to Wrench and Harris, they kept him on and he continued to write regularly, whether under his own name or one of several pseudonyms, during the Harris years. Having gone off to war for the duration, Fleming returned to *The Spectator* as Strix, the alter ego which he adopted for the next 25 years. To his credit, Harris recognised Fleming's talent for the incisive writing which he, and *The Spectator*, often lacked. A leading article, written by the editor in the issue of 12 August 1938, a few weeks before Munich, began:

> A number of circumstances, which it would be laborious and unnecessary to enumerate in any completeness, and which may, in fact, be less intrinsi-

cally significant than they appear, suggest that the second half of this month may be a particularly critical period in European affairs.

It was the sort of pronouncement which, under his predecessor St Loe Strachey, was mockingly referred to as 'spectatorial'.

Harris was remembered by another colleague as a kindly man, but 'a bit of an ass, who waffled a lot'. An occasional contributor to *The Spectator*, Honor Croome, once pointed out that removing the last sentence of any article written by Harris subtracted nothing at all from its sense or argument. E.C. Hodgkin, who worked at *The Spectator* during the last years of Harris's editorship, confirmed this to be so, saying that the last sentence of his articles was 'more like an amen or an embroidered full stop'. He would write his articles in a small, neat hand and carry them round with him, according to Fleming, as gingerly as if they had been sackfuls of ferrets.

Although he was a good Quaker and a member of the Reform Club, Harris enjoyed speculating on the stock market and would telephone his broker almost every morning. Anecdotal evidence suggests a repressed sexuality. Graham Greene, when literary editor in the 1930s, noticed that several books with suggestive titles were disappearing from his office. Suspecting Harris, he sent him a condom filled with sugary sweets for his birthday. Another literary editor, James Pope-Hennessy, told the less likely story of having once found pornographic photographs in the Bible in Harris's desk drawer. Graham Watson, son of the co-proprietor, remembers being asked, with his sister, to naked swimming parties at Harris's cottage near Dorking in the 1930s. Like Strachey, Harris listed his recreation as 'motoring'.

Whatever the truth of these stories, Harris gave *The Spectator* a moral authority for which it had also been renowned in the 19th century. Politically, he carried on the left-centre tradition of Strachey, whom he much admired, and of Townsend and Hutton before him. Since Harris had, at different times, voted for all three principal parties, he was happy to adopt the moderate political line of his chairman, who would be classified today as a Tory 'wet'. Harris took the view, which has not always been followed by subsequent editors, that the same political stance should be maintained throughout the magazine. There was no place in *The Spectator*, he wrote, for 'current literature discussed from the point of view of fellow-travellers.

If it is to stand for anything it must be a unity from beginning to end.' He was not apparently concerned at the disunity of prose style between the front and back halves of the magazine.

A typical issue of *The Spectator*, in the early months of Harris's editorship, ran to 40 pages, with the cover page taken up by an advertisement. The bold headline 'Rejuvenation' sits oddly, on the front page of one issue, immediately below the masthead and above a photograph of a wing-collared gentleman attesting to the fortifying properties of Phyllosan tablets, for 'men and women of all ages — especially those over 40'. The editorial began with News of the Week, consisting of short items of news and comment, most of them of approximately 200 words, followed by two leading articles, each of page-length. Then came A Spectator's Notebook, the 'middles', consisting of four or five signed articles, perhaps one or two theatre reviews and Beach Thomas's page of Country Life. Three or four pages of Letters to the Editor came next, sometimes preceded by a much longer letter on an important topic of the day, under the separate heading of Correspondence. There followed book reviews, motoring and financial columns, and a crossword, which was one of Harris's modest innovations. A memorable letter appeared in the correspondence columns on 8 October 1932, from A Lifelong Reader of *The Spectator*:

> Sir — Low indeed has *The Spectator* fallen! It is hard to believe the footnote on page 366 of the 24 September issue of that once revered and beloved paper; it runs, '*The Spectator* will, from next week onward, provide its readers with crossword puzzles.' May I be one of the thousands of readers to protest against this vulgarising of a paper hitherto holding a high standard?

The issue dated 7 April 1933, in its News of the Week, referred to the boycott of Jews in Germany and the nature of the new regime, commenting that Hitler had 'given no evidence so far of any large capacity for government himself'. Other items included Lord Clydesdale's flight over Mount Everest and the second reading of a bill to allow hotels and restaurants an extension of an hour for the serving of alcohol with dinner. The purpose of the licensing laws, *The Spectator* declared, was to avoid intoxication on public premises, not 'to prevent a man taking a late meal from drinking a glass of beer or wine with it. But it is quite essential that the meal shall not be merely a pretext for evasion of the law which limits drinking pure and simple to certain hours.' (For many years Harris was a teetotaller, and Watson never touched a drop.) There was a leader on the trial of British employees of the Metropolitan-Vickers company in Moscow, and a piece 'By a Legal Correspondent', arguing for greater protection for children under civil law.

The Rt Hon. Leo Amery was writing about imperial preferences following the Ottawa Conference, and another MP considered the case for economic orthodoxy, answering the expansionist case put forward the previous week by Captain Harold Macmillan. There was an informative essay on carp, and a less than enthusiastic review of *The School for Scandal*, with Malcolm Keen, Peggy Ashcroft, Roger Livesey and Alastair Sim. Beach Thomas was reflecting on the habits of swifts and rooks. The letters included one from A. Munthe of Potsdam in defence of modern Germany, 'this peaceful, orderly, kindly country', prompting a sharp retort from the editor on the matter of intimidation by the Nazi party: '*The Spectator* has consistently shown itself a friend of Germany, but it is a friend of freedom first.' Lord Tavistock took Maynard Keynes to task for wanting to increase the burden of debt, while another correspondent wrote in praise of the Prince of Wales's ideas for tackling unemployment.

Books on economics, young writers and Asia were reviewed by Pakenham, Edmund Blunden and Fleming respectively; a batch of new novels, including one by Daphne du Maurier, was considered by Graham Greene. Following a column on the budget, reports of company meetings — from the National Bank of India, Vickers, the Cunard Steam Ship Company and Associated Portland Cement — occupied three pages. In 1933 *The Spectator* cost 6d; according to contemporary advertisements, a packet of 20 cigarettes cost 1s 4d, boiling fowl 10d per pound and 'fat, tender geese' 6s 6d each. Blue Star Line was offering two-week cruises, to Casablanca, Las Palmas and Madeira, from 21 guineas. In the Classified section, the British Sexological Society announced a lecture on bisexuality, and Emkolene ointment was recommended for haemorrhoids, promising 'instant and lasting relief'.

One curious feature of the 1930s *Spectator* was a weekly column written alternately in French and German. The articles might be on the political, social or artistic affairs of the country, but it was not clear why they were not published in English. Nor did *The Spectator*'s staff seem very sure how the anonymous writers should be described in their respective languages. The column would appear '*von einem deutschen Korrespondenten*' one week, '*von einem deutschen Korrespondent*' another. And the French '*correspondant*' was sometimes spelt 'correspondent'. The columns continued until the outbreak of war; the final article in German, on Danzig, was published in the issue dated 1 September 1939, signing off with a comment of no great prescience: 'However the future turns out, it will hardly be a happy one.' The following year Sir Evelyn Wrench (knighted in 1932) published a book entitled *I Loved Germany*; but the German language was no longer acceptable in *The Spectator*. One might express surprise that it had been tolerated for so long.

One of the critical events of the 1930s for Harris, as a passionate League of Nations man, was Mussolini's invasion of Abyssinia in October 1935. The previous month, under the heading, 'Britain's Lead to the World', *The Spectator* had been fulsome in its praise of the Foreign Secretary, Sir Samuel Hoare, for his 'conspicuous wisdom and ability'. His speech to the League of Nations Assembly in Geneva, promising resistance to all acts of unprovoked aggression, had 'lifted him to a high place among the more notable occupants of his office'. By the first week of December 'Slippery Sam' Hoare had made a squalid pact with his French counterpart, Pierre Laval, to cede nearly two-thirds of Abyssinian territory to the Italian aggressor. It must have been a terrible shock to Harris, yet one does not find him condemning Hoare and Baldwin with the vehemence which they deserved. (The government never applied the oil sanctions against Italy which the League had imposed.) Perhaps it was his natural courtesy, or deference towards the Establishment, that prevented him from going further than he did. True, he called the Hoare-Laval pact 'the greatest political blunder of recent years'. But it was more than that: it was a betrayal — of the League, of Abyssinia, of all that Hoare had declared the government stood for 12 weeks earlier. Harris instead chose to write that Hoare 'by his resignation, has done what he can to atone for his mistake, and all who have watched his past career will be more disposed to sympathise than to castigate'. To which many readers would surely have replied. 'Oh, no, they won't!'

1936 was a critical year: Hitler invaded the Rhineland, the Spanish civil war began, F.D. Roosevelt was re-elected and King Edward VIII abdicated. *The Spectator* stuck to the non-interventionist line during Spain's war. When the king was about to abdicate, Harris was statesmanlike in his leading articles, expressing sympathy for the king and admiration for Baldwin's handling of the affair. But it is hard to read some of his comments today without a sense of irony. 'None would willingly intrude for a moment,' Harris wrote of King Edward, 'into such privacy as the exigencies of his station leave him.' Of George V he wrote of the 'unexampled hold on the loyalty and devotion of his subjects [which] sprang before all things from their admiration of a family life which the highest and the lowest of his people could with advantage take as model.'

The Spectator adopted a more sceptical attitude to Hitler's flagrant violation of the Treaty of Locarno — 'Does Germany Mean Peace?' — than did the daily papers. The *Times*, only a day after 30,000 German troops had crossed the Rhine, headed its leading article 'A Chance to Rebuild', while both the *Daily Herald* and *News Chronicle* supported Hitler's new peace proposals. Harris did not follow Geoffrey Dawson of the *Times* down the appeasement road, though he gave his magazine's support to Neville Chamberlain at the time of the Munich crisis, believing, as he wrote later, that 'having regard to both our own and France's glaring unpreparedness... even the most desperate attempt to save the peace was worthwhile'. In the week that the Munich agreement was signed, Harris heaped praise on the prime minister, opining that 'the jury which awards the next Nobel Peace Prize will hardly need to meet'. But *The Spectator* was less optimistic than most of the press that the peace would last. An article by R.C.K. Ensor, published in the issue of 7 October, explained how for the past five years he had been predicting that Germany would be ready to make war in Europe in September 1938. He based his view on a reading of *Mein Kampf* (in German) and the number of conscript classes which had been trained since 1933. By August 1938, according to Ensor's calculations, the German army strength would be 50 per cent above normal, with the newest recruits having had at least ten months' training. In a letter the following week Ensor commented that Hitler, having achieved the hegemony of central Europe, could now do as he liked. 'France, demoralised as she is both politically and industrially, could without war be Fascised into his orbit.... If, however, the facts went to the Fuhrer's head, he might prefer to dispose of France earlier, and by war.' Years later, Hugh Trevor-Roper would recall how great an impression Ensor's predictions had made on him in 1938, when he was a research fellow at Oxford.

When Hitler took the Czech nation under his 'protection' in March 1939, Harris commented that a state of peace could only be said to exist in central Europe to the extent that 'the disparity between aggressor and victim is such that resistance would be suicide'. Harris had visited Berlin in 1936 and attended a ceremony at which his arm was the only one not to be raised in the Nazi salute as the Fuhrer entered the arena. The editor of *The Spectator* feared arrest for having made his point, but nothing happened to him. On another occasion Hitler took tea in Harris's hotel (where he might have been at greater risk had one of Hitler's henchmen noticed that his address was listed in the hotel register as Golders Green).

During the late 1930s Harris took on as art critic an incipient traitor, one Anthony Blunt, who made no attempt to hide his anti-Establishment bias in his reviews. Blunt's friend and admirer, Goronwy Rees, who was assistant editor, was also working for the KGB at this time, although he ceased to do so after the Soviet-Nazi pact of August 1939. If Rees did not already know that Blunt was a Soviet agent, he was told one night by a drunk Guy Burgess. One can only guess at the treacherous plots that may have been hatched in the Gower Street corridors in the name of Communism. (Reviewing a book on the Comintern in September 1938, Rees did not seek to conceal his sympathy for Communism which, he wrote, no longer spoke with the voice of a revolutionary sect but was now 'pledged to the defence of capitalist democracy'.) Graham Greene, who later struck up a friendly correspondence with Kim Philby after the latter defected to Moscow, was cinema critic and, after the outbreak of war, became literary editor when Verschoyle and H.E. Bates joined the RAF. Rees, who served in intelligence during the war, was hoodwinked by Verschoyle into authorising payment for vital information from an underground contact in Italy. The information was in fact invented by Verschoyle himself.

At the beginning of 1939 Harold Nicolson began to write a weekly column for *The Spectator*, which continued, under the heading Marginal Comment, until 1952. Harris described it as 'the dominant feature of the paper, and it marked out its writer as the outstanding essayist of the day'. By 1939 another distinguished contributor, Beach Thomas, had been writing his Country Life column for nearly 20 years. It was a delightful and often idiosyncratic amalgam of facts and comment on the flora and fauna of the countryside. In the first week of the war Beach Thomas recalled having flushed a covey of partridges in 1915 from a deserted gun carriage in Flanders, where he was serving as war correspondent for the *Daily Mail*. He had also seen a cock pheasant fly over his head into the desolation of the battlefield; 'and the tremendous bombardment which opened the Somme battle did not in the least alarm a family of quails that clucked all around me'.

Beach Thomas was third in the line of sportsmen-naturalists who wrote for *The Spectator*, preceded by Eric Parker (who later became editor of *The Field*) and, before him, C.J. Cornish, a classics master at St Paul's School. Beach Thomas's writing followed the tradition of treating natural history as news; it was full of quirky titbits of information and unusual observations on the countryside. He was also a learned gardener, knowledgeable farmer and enthusiastic beekeeper.

In 1940 it was announced that Beach Thomas wished to retire, to be replaced by Bates, who had already contributed an occasional country column and was now the literary editor. But Bates soon afterwards went off on active service and Beach Thomas agreed to return to his column, which he finally relinquished, at the age of 82, in 1950. (He reviewed Harris's memoirs, *Life So Far*, in *The Spectator* in 1954, and died in his 90th year. Harris's life lasted only a few months after the publication of his book.)

The literary editorship, having passed to Graham Greene for a short time until he left for West Africa, was then assumed by W.J. (Walter) Turner, an Australian poet and former music critic of the *New Statesman*, whom the editor's secretary, Joan Baylis, remembered as 'a Bohemian figure, with untidy, greying hair, rumpled clothes, gay scarlet flannel waistcoat, vivid ties — a figure I came to know and like'. He and Harris did not get on: Turner, impulsive and impatient, wanted to liven up the books pages, but Harris, the cautious Quaker, suspicious of his highly-strung temperament and Bohemian ways, would have none of it. Nevertheless, Turner stayed as literary editor until his death, from a cerebral haemorrhage, in 1946.

On the outbreak of war the chairman, Wrench, organised a Tobacco Fund with the Overseas League which he had founded in 1910. Every £1 contributed provided 1,000 duty-free cigarettes for the men at the front.

King George VI gave £25, according to a full-page advertisement in *The Spectator*, and the Secretary of State for War, Leslie Hore-Belisha, commented: 'Believe me, from my personal knowledge, there is nothing more appreciated at the front than a good supply of cigarettes.' A few months later, Wrench set off on a lecture tour of North America and Australasia, and thence to India, where from 1942 to 1944 he served as American relations officer to the government and wrote occasional articles for *The Spectator*, including one on Jinnah and an interview with Gandhi. The other principal shareholder of the magazine, Watson, became divisional food officer for the north of England.

Wartime restrictions on the use of paper meant that, for the duration, *The Spectator* was obliged to publish 24-page issues, on a more lightweight paper, having averaged 48 pages throughout 1939. But the daily newspapers were required to effect much more drastic reductions, both in issue sizes and print runs; so that while the magazine inevitably lost staff and advertising revenue during the war, its circulation in fact benefited from the paper controls. Assisted by arrangements made for sending it to forces overseas, sales doubled between 1939 and 1945; and *The Spectator* never missed a week throughout the war. (For the first time in its history, however, publication was suspended by the government, when all weeklies were affected for two weeks in February 1947, on grounds of 'fuel economy'. On the two Fridays when *The Spectator* did not appear, it was given the hospitality of the *Daily Mail*'s leader page.)

In the autumn of 1939 Harris removed *The Spectator*'s offices from Gower Street to Surrey, near Walton Heath; but the arrangement did not work and the staff soon returned to London. No. 99 was virtually untouched by bombs throughout the war; an incendiary once bounced through an office window into the stock room at a weekend, but the resulting fire was soon extinguished by an alert fire-watching party. Greater inconvenience was caused by unreliable telephone and postal services.

The quiet and decorum at 99 Gower Street was broken only occasionally by the sound of shattered glass or a blown-in door. In view of the frequent interruptions to the postal delivery, it was a surprise to find sometimes three pages of letters in a wartime *Spectator*. In the issue of 9 June 1944, Michael Foot was writing to argue with Captain Quintin Hogg over Chamberlain and Munich; and the cartoonist David Low was chiding Arnold Lunn for supposing that his character Colonel Blimp represented the Conservative party. The Revd W.E.J. Lindfield wrote from Worcester to relate the experience of a woman who had very reluctantly agreed to provide a billet for two American soldiers. Horrified to discover that they were both black, she awoke the next morning from a most uneasy sleep to hear the strains of negro spirituals below and to find that her unwanted guests had done all the housework and were waiting to prepare her breakfast.

At other times during the war, distinguished writers offered their experiences. Bates wrote about the people he met on train journeys round England in 1940; Julian Huxley told of the time he pursued a Grevy's zebra through Regent's Park the morning after the London Zoo had been bombed; and poems were published by such as Vita Sackville-West, Siegfried Sassoon and Freya Stark. Hogg wrote a piece on the Eighth Army and Gerald Hanley sent an article from Burma describing the Japanese retreat after Kohima. Strategicus (H.C. O'Neill) gave his regular military analysis, and Harold Nicolson's weekly Marginal Comment provided an absorbing running commentary on the state of the war, the wartime atmosphere in Britain and the sometimes mundane things that concerned people during those years. On occasion he would write a morale-boosting paragraph, looking ahead to the war's successful outcome. Shortly before Christmas 1941 he commented:

> How strange it was to be in London last week and to realise that the public (stunned as they were by our naval losses) seemed unaware that two decisive events had occurred. The fact that the United States have entered the war against all our enemies means in all certainty that Germany cannot win. The fact that Congress has almost in the first hour voted for the creation of an American expeditionary force means that Germany is certain to be beaten. It may be that for the next eight months we shall suffer bitterly; but when that grim period is past the road to victory stretches clear ahead.

In the autumn of 1944 an article appeared on education, at the time of the passage of R.A. Butler's Act, by Amabel Williams-Ellis. The theme of the article, the need for more textbooks and visual aids in education, was perhaps less interesting than the person who wrote it. Lady Williams-Ellis was the wife of Sir Clough, architect and creator of Portmeirion, daughter

THE SPECTATOR, May 4, 1945
119 GOWER STREET, W.C.1
Subscription 30s. a year
to any part of the world.

THE DAY OF DOOM

SPECTATOR

No. 6097. FRIDAY, MAY 4, 1945 Price 6d.

CONTENTS

JOLTS AT SAN FRANCISCO

WITH Germany dissolving in cataclysm and chaos, the San Francisco Conference (about whose fortunes the new German Foreign Minister, Count Schwerin von Krosigk, shows himself so strangely solicitous) has been getting into its stride amid the minor crises and dissensions which all familiar with the habits of international conferences will assess at their true value. Having listened to the broadcast speech of President Truman, the conference began last Friday to settle down to its work, which will be transacted partly by the steering committee, partly in plenary session, partly in commissions, and partly in private talks between the statesmen behind the scenes. Mr. Stettinius, Mr. Eden and Mr. Molotov stated in broad terms the politics of their respective countries, which lead to the common determination to create a strong international organisation for security, Mr. Eden stressing the point that the Conference should not attempt at one stroke to establish a complete new order, but should devote itself to the single task of agreeing upon the machinery for security which should be set up. Even under this limitation it was soon discovered that there was room enough for differences of opinion, and even differences about the procedure which should be adopted at the Conference itself. At an early meeting Mr. Molotov objected to the proposal that Mr. Stettinius should preside at the public sessions and in the main committees, and wanted the chairmanship to be taken in rotation; and it had to be left to a second meeting before this question was settled by a compromise. That was the first, though a minor, setback to the Russian delegation. Far more important was the question of the offer of a seat at the Conference to the Lublin Provisional Government, recognised only by the Soviet Government—an offer which it had been obvious beforehand could not be allowed by Britain and the United States, who take their stand on the Yalta agreement and the broadening of the basis of the Polish Government. Everyone knows that there is more in this question than the admission of Polish delegates to San Francisco. Poland presents a disturbing test case as to whether the Great Powers, appointed to work together on the Security Council, are capable of acting jointly within the proper sphere of joint action; if already one of them goes off, at a tangent insisting on unilateral action, what are the prospects of that future accord between the Great Powers which is the presupposition of collective security?

The refusal of the Conference to admit the Lublin Government constituted a second rebuff to the Russian view, and a third occurred when Mr. Molotov resisted the claims of Argentina to representation, and a majority of the Conference decided against him. This has been the one occasion up to now when the Russians probably had more sympathy than votes, for there is a great deal to be said for the view that Argentina's record in the war is scarcely one which qualifies her for a vote at San Francisco. Happily there was one Russian claim which could be and was readily accepted—that the Ukraine and White Russia should have separate seats, so that Russia will now be in a position of having three votes. Up to the present in the various meetings of the Conference it has fallen to Russia to raise points which became bones of contention, and it must earnestly be hoped that Mr. Molotov (or his successor, for he departs next week) will not always be found in the opposing minority camp. But perhaps it is not so astonishing that he should be supporting Sir Walter Citrine's demand that the World Trade Union Federation should have a place in the Conference as that Sir Walter Citrine himself should have lent his countenance to so strange a suggestion. In meeting which consists of representatives of governments only, why on earth should trade unionists be singled out for representation as if they were a separate Power, as if they were not already represented by their Governments? Of Sir Walter Citrine it can only be said that one would have thought he would have known better. Labour cannot have it both ways, either at home or abroad. It is organised for political purposes as the Labour Party, and the leader of that party is actually one of the two principal British delegates at San Francisco. It is organised industrially as the Trade Union Congress, and in that capacity it has direct representation on the International Labour Organisation. To admit trade unions as such to the United Nations Conference would be to double Labour representation quite illegitimately. The resolution of the Conference on Wednesday into four separate commissions marks the beginning of its detailed work. The first commission, it may be noted, sits under General Smuts' chairmanship to deal with the purposes and principles of the new organisation, and will no doubt produce in the end that general "charter" on which the South African statesman has for some days been working.

Russia and Her Friends

Russian procedure in approving the establishment of a so-called Provisional Government in Austria is another example of the Soviet Government's embarrassing practice of settling matters of common concern without consultation with its Allies. The objection in this case is not to the thing done—as in the creation of an unrepresentative Government in Poland—but to the fact that action was unilateral. Indeed, in one respect it might be thought that the

Three days before the German surrender, The Spectator *devoted its main article to* The Day of Doom *for 'a great empire in its death-throes' rather than the Allied victory.*

of St Loe Strachey, sister of the Labour politician, John Strachey, and a member of the board of *The Spectator*. Together the Williams-Ellises attracted a number of left-wing intellectuals to their Welsh idyll, among them the Communist historian Eric Hobsbawm and the peace campaigner E.P. Thompson. Her brother's wife, to whom she was politically very close, was said to have suffered a nervous breakdown after reading Arthur Koestler's *Darkness at Noon*. From the 1930s onwards, Lady Williams-Ellis was one of the Soviet Union's more significant fellow-travellers. Although she does not appear to have tried to influence *The Spectator*'s political stance, it was nevertheless unusual, to say the least, for such a committed socialist, and sometime Marxist, to be a director of *The Spectator*. (She had also been its literary editor in 1922–23.)

When war ended Harris was elected as Independent member for Cambridge University. It suited him to be free from any party allegiance, and he served as an MP, speaking occasionally in debates on education, journalism and broadcasting, until the university seats were abolished in 1950. For some years Harris had been running an Undergraduate Page, to attract young writers and young readers to *The Spectator*. In this he had some success; however, in the immediate postwar years the circulation began to slip back, and Wrench started to think that the magazine could do with a more youthful hand on the tiller. After all, Harris had passed his 65th birthday in 1948, and there was not too much young blood among his regular contributors.

But if some of the articles were inclined to be on the turgid side, there were plenty of bright sparks to enliven other pages of *The Spectator*. J.P.W. Mallalieu, the Labour MP for Huddersfield, had begun to contribute articles on sporting and other subjects. His description of a Durham miners' gala, published in 1951, has all the charm and the accomplished writing of the best sort of *Spectator* piece, of any era.

> Old Elvet is a gentle backwater of history. For most of the year, except perhaps on race-days, the world leaves it basking in memories or gazing with shaded eye at the cathedral. But on one day of the year the backwater becomes the main stream, with a quarter of a million men, women and children in its flood; for Old Elvet is a long narrow street leading from the heart of the city of Durham to the racecourse, and through it there flows once a year the gala of the Durham miners...
>
> The first banner floated away on the morning air. But the sound of the accompanying band could still be heard when a second banner and a second band appeared in Old Elvet; and from then until well after twelve there were never fewer than two banners and two bands with their marchers in the street at the same time. There is no organisation about the march. Bands, banners and marchers set off when they wish from their villages. Some come in by train or bus and march only from the station. Others march all the way, five, eight miles maybe. They arrive at Old Elvet's bottleneck in their own time — and each side of Old Elvet is packed with watchers fifteen deep...
>
> There were times when the speeches were the gala. Certainly the list of speakers through the years contains famous names — Charles Bradlaugh, Annie Besant, Prince Kropotkin, Havelock Wilson, MacDonald, Henderson, Snowden and many more...This Saturday it contained the names of Attlee, Morrison, Horner and Foot. But the speeches were only incidental. They mixed with the sounds of the fair, of late-arriving bands, of sandwich papers and of popping corks...

It was long after the meetings had ended that I saw the gala reach its height. The sun had come gloriously into the sky as the bands and banners and marchers began their return through Old Elvet; and Old Elvet seemed unwilling that anyone should leave...

Another band and another banner came to a stop outside the hotel, and suddenly there was silence. The colours still danced, but everything else was still. For the banner we now saw was draped in black. It carried a flag sent by the miners of Yugoslavia. It carried also the name of Easington Colliery. In that colliery, 52 days earlier, 83 miners had lost their lives. Through the silence the Easington band began to play. It played 'Gresford', the tune which a miner himself had written in sorrow for the great Gresford disaster. When the tune came to an end there was again stillness and silence until Old Elvet gently relaxed his hold and there was space to move. With the first movement the great crowd set up a storm of cheering that could be heard in Paradise, dancers cavorted again and the sunshine wiped away all thought of tears.

Long ago, in 1880, 164 men died entombed in a Durham pit. When at last the rescue workers found the bodies, they found also written on a roof plank the words, 'The Lord has been with us. We are ready for heaven. Bless the Lord. We have had a jolly prayer-meeting. Every man ready for glory. ½ past 2 o'clock. Thursday. Sign Ric Cole.' Miners rub shoulders with death. They know how to face death. Last Saturday I saw, too, that they will not let death spoil life.

In the late 1940s Harris recruited a fellow Quaker, Edward Hodgkin, from the *Manchester Guardian*, to join *The Spectator*'s staff as number three (Walter Taplin had arrived at Gower Street in 1946 and was deputy editor; Iain Hamilton joined from the *Manchester Guardian* in 1952, when Hodgkin moved to the *Times*). Hodgkin remembers Fleming driving to the office from Nettlebed in his Rolls-Royce shooting-brake (as station-wagons were then called). When asked why he needed all that space in the back, Fleming replied, 'I must have something I can put a stag in.' In those days of rationing a generous Canadian reader used to send a food parcel two or three times a year, when distributions of bacon, dried apricots and tea would be made from Harris's office.

Charged with sorting the numerous manuscripts submitted for the

Undergraduate Page, Hodgkin succeeded in getting five cousins into print for the first time (including David Cairns, later to become music critic, and two future ambassadors). While the literary editor, Pope-Hennessy, a protégé of Harold Nicolson, was engaged on his life of Queen Mary, Hodgkin introduced Olivia Manning as a book reviewer. A bright young man from Oxford, Kenneth Tynan, also wrote some theatre reviews for *The Spectator*. In his notice of *The Other Heart* at the Old Vic, by James Forsyth, he wrote, in April 1952: 'My vision was obscured by two interposed obstacles, which came and went, staying ever longer as the evening progressed, and which turned out to be my eyelids.'

Tynan went on to write of the unfortunate Mr Forsyth: 'If his intention really is to prostrate the spectator with fatigue, he must set about it more perniciously in the future. To bore people is not as easy as it seems; and, though Mr Forsyth occasionally makes it look deceptively simple, he often works quite hard and achieves no more than an effect of downright badness, which is not boring at all.'

In 1952 Wrench, having reached his 70th birthday, resolved that the editorial chair should no longer be held by someone only a year younger than himself. He remained happy with *The Spectator*'s political line — it was, for the most part, well disposed towards the Attlee government — but a certain personal animosity was developing between proprietor and editor. (Wrench even thought of resuming the editorial chair himself, an idea which Watson refused to countenance.) The magazine's finances were not as healthy as they had been, and the cover price had been increased to 7 pence. In the issue of 7 September 1951 *The Spectator* took the most unusual step of alluding to its deteriorating financial position: 'The last dividend was cut, allocations to reserve were suspended, various economies have been effected. The finances of the paper are on a thoroughly sound basis, but in order that they may be kept so it is essential to increase the cost of the paper by one penny a week (half the price of a cigarette) as from the issue of October 5th.'

Circulation continued to decline (from almost 50,000 in 1948 to 41,000 in 1952) and Harris's contract was terminated at the end of March 1953. One might have thought that, at this age, he would have been happy to retire gracefully. The board issued a statement referring to his retirement and recording 'their deep appreciation of [his] distinguished service. . . and a memorable editorship'; but it is clear from his autobiography that he left unwillingly and, as he put it, with 'some soreness of spirit'. The magazine's film critic, Virginia Graham, wrote to her friend, Joyce Grenfell, in South Africa. 'Wilson Harris has got the sack — did I tell you? Very badly managed, I gather, and a lot of hard feelings.'

In a letter published in *The Spectator* in April 1953, Harris thanked the readers who had written to him on 'my severance from 99 Gower Street'. Concluding his last Notebook, still under the quite inappropriate pseudonym of Janus, he wrote, with no insincerity and with more than a hint of bitterness: 'There are reasons for saying no more than simply Valedico. Parting, Juliet said, is such sweet sorrow. I deny the adjective and double-stress the noun.' Harris wrote nothing of the circumstances of his dismissal, but referred to the hundreds of letters he received, 'of sympathy, regret and in some cases of indignation'. Anthony Eden wrote to him, and so did several newspaper editors and bishops. Nicolson, who had finally given up his weekly Marginal Comment at the end of 1952, gave a dinner at the Travellers Club. (On his retirement from the column, Sir Harold had written: 'I do not believe that the history of journalism can show a more shining example of amicable cooperation as that which for all these years has existed between the Editor and myself.')

In his first issue the new editor, Taplin, wrote a personal appreciation of Harris and his editorship. Having referred to the typographical and other changes which he had introduced in the 1930s, and to the new literary luminaries — Graham Greene, V.S. Pritchett, Evelyn Waugh, William Plomer, Sean O'Faolain — who came to *The Spectator* at that time, Taplin went on to comment on Janus, Harris's alter ego and 'artistic creation', who wrote in his very first column, 'I sometimes fancy I am not a Conservative', and whose style and satiric humour were so different from Harris, the author of the leading article which preceded A *Spectator*'s Notebook. Taplin then set about describing the man whom he had worked with for seven years:

> I only know the man... who rose out of a cold bath at a remarkably early hour, drove a car in a mildly alarming fashion to 99 Gower Street, went swiftly up two flights of stairs with a characteristic but indescribable lope and disappeared into the editor's room . . . He has on countless occasions tripped over my electric fire, bumped his head on my electric light (which is not slung very low from the ceiling), sometimes acquiring wounds which

were visible for days, and perched himself on my window seat, always failing to make allowance for a bracket projecting from a wall into the middle of his back.... He is deeply interested in words, liking old ones and disliking new ones. He had a habit of disarming his colleagues and blunting their comments on the less pleasing unsolicited contributions by handing them over and saying, 'I expect you wish you could have written this'. The attitude of those colleagues to him changed by a process which is perhaps most usual in the case of boys observing a headmaster as they go through their school years. It began with awe, developed into respect and ended as a curious form of affection in which traces of the two former impressions still remained. But above all, to those who have worked with him, he is an unfailing and irresistible topic of conversation . . . . When two *Spectator* men, past and present, met, the past one always said, 'How is he?' and the present one always knew who 'he' was. The discussion went on inside the office. Often has a door opened to reveal the subject of the conversation, and the fragments of that conversation, as one observer put it, have 'dropped tinkling to the floor' . . . .

It is the subject that has fascinated a succession of *Spectator* men for twenty years — some of them for weeks, some of them for years. Line them up, the colleagues of Wilson Harris. They are a curiously assorted lot, but they have a common factor. John Buchan, Francis Yeats-Brown, Peter Fleming, Derek Verschoyle, R.A. Scott-James, Graham Greene, Frank Pakenham, Frank Singleton, H.E. Bates, Goronwy Rees, W.J. Turner, James Pope-Hennessy, Edward Hodgkin. Some I have never met. Some are dead. But they all worked with him, and I dare swear that none of them could ever forget him.

It was ironic that the article which followed Taplin's, in the issue of 10 April 1953, was by Fleming, recalling his expedition to Brazil in 1932, in the footsteps of Colonel Fawcett, from which he had expected to return as editor designate of *The Spectator*. On the page preceding Taplin's tribute to his predecessor, Fleming took over A Spectator's Notebook, using the pseudonym of Strix.

Wrench used to say of Taplin that he was the wrong build for an editor. Short and stocky, he was educated at Southampton and Oxford, where he read PPE. He had worked at the *Economist* before the war, then at the

Ministry of Food until 1942, and for the rest of the war in the Central Statistical Office, as part of the War Cabinet.

Taplin was an unusual mix: on the one hand, a free-market economist, who after his spell at *The Spectator* joined the Iron and Steel Board, edited *Accountancy* magazine and wrote books on advertising; on the other, he was passionately interested in literature, poetry and the classics. For years he listed his recreation in *Who's Who* as 'reading *Finnegan's Wake*' (later amended to 'reading'). After he left *The Spectator*, Taplin wrote a dramatised version of Hardy's *Two on a Tower* (it was never performed), published a textbook of English verse and taught himself classical Greek. He certainly enjoyed books more than politics (he thought of himself as an old-fashioned Liberal), and possibly more than people. But he got on well with writers: Kingsley Amis and John Wain started writing for *The Spectator* during his time, and he enjoyed the company of Waugh, paying him for his contributions with wine. (Shortly before he left the editorship, Harris had delivered a stern rebuke to Waugh, in A Spectator's Notebook, for having written offensively about Marshal Tito when he paid a visit to Britain.)

Taplin was appointed editor for two years from 1 April 1953, at an annual salary of £2,000. At the age of 42, it was natural that he would want to introduce younger writers and a livelier atmosphere than had his predecessor; but he was, of course, responsible to the same elderly proprietors. At the time of his appointment, Taplin was in correspondence not with Wrench but with the principal shareholder, the 79-year-old Watson, JP, now Sir Angus, who lived in chambers in Newcastle, the interior of which was compared with the lavatories at the National Liberal Club. From there he wrote to remind his new editor that *The Spectator*, while entirely independent politically, 'is opposed to State Socialism, Communism and Nationalisation. It supports social reform in all of its branches and is in sympathy with International Liberalism. It criticises some aspects of our present democratic outlook.'

Under the heading 'Immediate Editorial Policy', Watson decreed that 'no change in the present features of the paper will be made by the new Editor for a month, and then only after careful consultation'. 'When in doubt on questions of policy, follow the *Manchester Guardian*, the *Times* and the *Daily Telegraph*.'

'It would be a useful routine to ring up Sir Angus Watson on the Tuesday morning of each week about 10.30 when any comment arising on the week's policy could be discussed. This method should be adopted as a routine.' Life for a *Spectator* editor could be a bit restricting in those days.

Taplin began by appointing Iain Hamilton as his deputy, and firing the literary editor, Derek Hudson, together with the librarian and other more junior staff. He kept on the Undergraduate Page (Julian Critchley was the contributor, from Pembroke College, Oxford, in July 1953), and the Sporting Aspect (written by the likes of Bernard Darwin, J.P.W. Mallalieu and John Arlott). Sir Compton Mackenzie began a regular column called Sidelight. Taplin also introduced a feature, which he called Spectatrix, written by women only: Jacquetta Hawkes, Jenny Nicholson and Pamela Hansford Johnson were frequent contributors. Nicholas Davenport began his weekly column, Finance and Investment, in October 1953; it continued without interruption until his death in 1979. Early in 1954, John Betjeman joined *The Spectator* to write a City and Suburban column (which one week laid claim to the longest palindrome: Live dirt up a side track carted is a putrid evil).

In his brief spell as editor (less than two years) Taplin was responsible for introducing a number of outstanding young writers to the magazine. Both Brian Inglis and Henry Fairlie, who are more usually associated with Ian Gilmour's period as proprietor/editor, in fact started writing in the books pages under Taplin, while still employed elsewhere. From Washington Robert Towneley (aka Peregrine Worsthorne, but using the surname of his elder brother) wrote several articles in 1953, and in the same year, writing mostly about Egyptian nationalism and the politics of the Middle East, the name of H.A.R. Philby appeared in *The Spectator*'s pages. (This was two years after Burgess and Maclean had escaped to Moscow, and when suspicion was hardening of Philby as the Third Man.) In the 20 November issue there was an article by Nicolson, 'On Not Writing Marginal Comment', in which he described how it felt to be free of the obligation to write a weekly column. He called *The Spectator* 'a dear old thing' and referred to its 'interesting experiment in rejuvenation'. Joyce Grenfell was the week's Spectatrix; Christmas books were reviewed by, for example, Richard Hughes, Peter Fleming, D.W. Brogan, Kingsley Amis, Clough Williams-Ellis, Ludovic Kennedy, Anthony Hartley and J.D. Scott. It was especially the last two names that were to give Taplin, after the pain of his departure had receded, something of significance to remember from his short-lived editorship.

Hartley had been discovered by Hamilton in Paris, where he was studying at the Sorbonne and writing poems about the Muslim philosopher Ibn Khaldun. His first review for *The Spectator*, of two anthologies of recent poetry in July 1953, singled out for praise the contributions of Kingsley Amis and John Wain. He criticised the religiosity of the neo-Romantic poets, calling instead for a new humanism in poetry. In the same year Scott was appointed literary editor, and began regularly to publish the poems of such as Robert Conquest, Elizabeth Jennings, Thom Gunn, Donald Davie, Philip Larkin and D.J. Enright, in addition to Amis and Wain.

Amis had some fun in *The Spectator* at the expense of Edith Sitwell, when Hartley gave her latest volume of poetry, *Gardeners and Astronomers*, an unfriendly review in January 1954. He compared the work of Neo-Symbolists (lots of rich imagery), such as Sitwell and Kathleen Raine, unfavourably with the rigorous young academic poets — Amis and Davie, for example — whom he called University Wits or Metaphysicals. Two weeks later Sitwell replied testily from Hollywood, alluding sarcastically to 'this week's new great poet... little Mr Tomkins (or whatever his name may be)'. The following week, in the Letters pages, Hartley received support from Wain and Jennings, and also, tongue wedged in cheek, from Amis, writing under the pseudonym of Little Mr Tomkins (Name and Address Supplied). In a subsequent letter Sitwell commented that she and Hartley did have one thing in common: their admiration for the work of Amis. She had not read his poetry but was most impressed by his first novel, *Lucky Jim*. Amis replied promptly from Swansea, revealing himself as Little Mr Tomkins and expressing his gratitude for her 'generous praise'. In her last dispatch from Hollywood, Sitwell said she appreciated Amis's candour; not long afterwards they lunched together in London, in the company of others, without any hostile words being exchanged. In June of that year Sitwell was surely delighted not only to be made a Dame but to be described by Compton Mackenzie, in his column in *The Spectator*, as 'the greatest poet that the women of England have yet produced'. (The following year Amis continued the theme of the University Wits by having a go at the 'poetic' prose of Laurie Lee's latest book on Spain, *A Rose for Winter*, which he likened to 'a string of failed poems — failed not-very-good poems too'. He described it as 'vulgar and sensational', suggesting that highbrow travel books would be better written as novels. He also railed in *The Spectator* against a posthumous collection of prose pieces by his fellow Swansean, Dylan Thomas.)

Hartley continued in the books pages to press the claims of those young poets who stood for 'the poetic equivalent of liberal, dissenting England. A liberalism distrustful of too much richness or too much fanaticism, austere and sceptical. A liberalism egalitarian and anti-aristocratic.' What Hartley was trying to do, with his literary editor's encouragement, was to end the domination of the 1930s poets, to gain recognition for a new movement in verse. That these poets, and a few novelists, came to form what was known, for a couple of years, as the Movement, was due to an article — *The Spectator*'s first leading literary article — which appeared in the issue of 1 October 1954. Under the heading, 'In the Movement', J.D. Scott commented that the poetry of the 1950s could be identified by 'its metaphysical wit, its glittering intellectuality, its rich Empsonian ambiguities' (a reference to the guru of the Movement, Sir William Empson, poet, literary critic and sometime professor of English at universities in Tokyo and Peking). More specifically, Scott named the poets Davie and Gunn and three novels (Wain's *Hurry on Down*, Iris Murdoch's *Under the Net* and Amis's *Lucky Jim*) as typifying the character of the Movement. George Orwell and Dr F.R. Leavis were among the literary mentors of the novelists' fictional heroes; neo-Romantics such as Dylan Thomas were definitely 'out'. The Movement's writings were predominantly detached, sardonic, ironic, inclined to be puritanical — or, as Scott put it, 'anti-phoney [and] anti-wet'. The article described the Movement as 'bored by the despair of the Forties, not much interested in suffering, and extremely impatient of poetic sensibility, especially poetic sensibility about "the writer and society"'. The anger of the fictional heroes of Amis and Wain was directed not at the suffering of others but rather at the society which denied them a good life.

The leading article brought letters from Evelyn Waugh, Anthony Thwaite, Denis Donoghue and Malcolm Bradbury. Waugh said the Movement novels reminded him of the work of William Gerhardi, and the new writers were less interesting as a movement than they would be if 'treated to the courtesy of individual attention'. Donoghue compared Davie's poetry with William Cowper's, describing it as of robust intelligence rather than 'glittering intellectuality'.

Two anthologies of Movement poetry were published — Enright's *Poets of the 1950s* in 1955, Robert Conquest's *New Lines* in 1956 — but by 1957 the Movement was being disowned by some of its members, and Wain declared that 'its work is done'. Both Davie and Gunn went to California, breaking free of the provincialism which had characterised some Movement writers. Gunn settled in San Francisco, adopting elements of American Beat poetry in his work.

Though the Movement may have been only a short-lived affair, it owes its genesis to that leading literary article by Scott, which in turn came about because Taplin was anxious to improve the circulation of *The Spectator*. As Scott has recorded, 'Taplin gave the staff a pep-talk. What could we do to liven things up, get ourselves talked about, be more influential, more sensational, and so more circulation-building, more money-making?... I had an idea for a box of fireworks.'

The article certainly went off with a bang, and the explosions continued. It was the first *Spectator* 'campaign', said Hartley, since Harris had declaimed against the sale of contraceptives in slot machines. The circulation graph began to take an upward turn again in mid-October, arresting a decline which had persisted since 1947. Taplin was optimistic about the future. But in early autumn Wrench and Watson, who seldom agreed on anything, had one of their rare meetings, at the Station Hotel in York, at which they resolved to sell their shareholdings in *The Spectator* to a 28-year-old barrister and baronet's son, Ian Gilmour.

2

AHEAD OF ITS TIME

There had been a number (around 30) of suitors for *The Spectator* in the early 1950s. Difficulties would arise, however, when it came to securing the agreement of the shareholders. The situation was likened to a Restoration comedy, in which the girl has to obtain the consent of her trustees, one of whom is a lawyer, another a rake and the third a clergyman. The problem was usually Sir Angus Watson, who would say he wanted to sell, while asserting it was not in Sir Evelyn Wrench's or the Strachey family's interests to do so. Wrench had told his bankers, Coutts & Co., that he wished to dispose of his shares; and it was one of the bank's directors, John Smith (later to become a Conservative MP and founder of the Manifold and Landmark Trusts), who brought Wrench and Ian Gilmour together.

Gilmour, who was well over six feet tall, had been a Grenadier Guardsman at the end of the war and was now in his second year at the Bar, practising in Viscount Hailsham's chambers. There was no denying that, socially speaking, he was well connected: his mother was a daughter of Viscount Chelsea, his stepmother was a daughter of the Duke of Abercorn, his grandmothers were Lady Susan Lygon (daughter of Earl Beauchamp) and the Hon. Lady Meux. (Much of the family money came from Meux's brewery.) And he had married the younger daughter of the Duke of Buccleuch. Watson had admired Sir John Gilmour Bt., Home Secretary for three years during the National Government, and presumed Ian Gilmour to be his son. But there were two baronets called Sir John Gilmour, and Watson had got the wrong one. Nobody wished to put him right for fear of jeopardising a deal; and perhaps because this was the sum of Watson's knowledge of Gilmour, the sale of *The Spectator* to him was agreed. John Strachey was willing to sell the family's ordinary shares, but they retained some preference shares for a few years.

In his manner Gilmour was unassuming, easy-going — but he was also restless. He found the Bar congenial, but he was doing only small common law work and not getting anywhere very fast. He was more disposed to be a political thinker than a legal practitioner, and it was on something of an impulse that he decided he wanted to own a political weekly.

The *Manchester Guardian* described him as 'a high-minded, sharp-minded, questioning young man'. When he arrived at Gower Street he was not impressed by Walter Taplin, believing him to be weak and lacking in any political sense; but he was happy enough for Taplin to go on as editor, at least until his contract came to an end in April 1955. However, a degree of obstinacy existed on both sides: Taplin wanted to continue as editor without interference, as he saw it, from his new proprietor, while Gilmour, in his own words, was 'not prepared to be an absentee landlord'. As editorial secretary, Joan Baylis was well placed to observe the differences between Taplin and Gilmour. She found them 'both infinitely likeable, but temperamentally opposed, the younger and the older man clashed in viewpoint, obstinately gave no ground, and there were raised voices behind closed doors'. It was, perhaps, most of all a conflict of mentality: patrician individual versus former civil servant.

After what Taplin called 'an initial period of misunderstanding' with Gilmour, 'for which I think we were both to blame, [we] find that we can get on well personally. But by that time we have had a rather unnecessary argument and Gilmour has made up his mind that I must go.' Taplin, knowing that Gilmour was about to go up to Newcastle to meet Watson, asked the old Skipper king to intercede. Gilmour's principal recollection of their meeting was that his host told him he kept no alcohol in the house because he feared 'what might happen'. (He once picked up two books in the literary editor's office at Gower Street and pronounced them 'filthy'. Fortunately he was not aware that Francis Yeats-Brown, who for a brief period edited Everyman from the top floor of Gower Street under Watson's patronage, was in the habit of standing on his head in the nude while practising yoga.)

Having met Gilmour, Watson wrote to Taplin to tell him: 'I am very sorry about the present difficulties, but am afraid that you are largely responsible for these. He offered you an agreement on what seemed to me to be generous terms, and there does not appear to have been anything in his subsequent suggestions that you could not have easily accepted.' The letter was dated 2 November and Taplin left at the end of that month.

He received many letters of sympathy — from Wilson Harris, still addressing him 'My dear Taplin' (Taplin replied 'My dear W.H.'), and from the editor of the *New Statesman*, Kingsley Martin, 'If there is anything that I can say in the paper which would help you, please let me know'. John Betjeman wrote to express his sadness: 'There's a friend in high places gone, I said to myself, and what is more there's a jolly good editor gone for whom one was pleased and honoured to work, who had made *The Spectator* far less dull and with whom one felt secure.'

Unquestionably Taplin had improved *The Spectator* in a short time, having introduced a lot of vigorous new writing talent to its pages; and the circulation had just begun to respond to his changes when he fell out with the new proprietor. Taplin's 20 months in the editorial chair should be seen not as the fag-end of the old regime, but rather as ushering in the new *Spectator* of the Gilmour era. When Charles Seaton, *The Spectator*'s inveterate librarian (for 42 years until his death in 1995), was asked who was the best of the 12 editors he had worked with, he would invariably reply, 'Walter Taplin'. With his sound business knowledge, Taplin is remembered as an efficient manager as well as editor, always maintaining good relations with other departments at *The Spectator*. He generally kept a light hand on the reins, though it was said that he could be peremptory at times.

In an article in 1978 by Lord Blake, published to mark the 150th anniversary of *The Spectator*, Taplin's editorship was dismissed in a line, prompting his old friend and colleague at the *Economist*, Donald Tyerman, to write in with a more considered opinion of his brief occupation of the editor's chair. (It was regrettable, too, that, due to an oversight, he did not receive an invitation to *The Spectator*'s 150th birthday ball.) An obituary of Taplin referred to him as 'a very decent man' whose *Spectator* years (he had been deputy editor since 1946) 'were for him professionally the happiest'. After 1954 he took up his commercial interests again (while remaining an occasional contributor to *The Spectator*). In addition to the Iron and Steel Board and his work on advertising, he was consultant for Green Shield stamps and the brewing industry. But he never wrote the book on James Joyce which he had so often said he would. He retired from Kent to Dorset in 1975 and died in 1986.

A family trust of Gilmour's had paid £75,000 for *The Spectator* (the equivalent, in 1998, of over £1 million). A few preference shares were retained by the previous principal shareholders, and Wrench stayed on as chairman. The new proprietor had also had to secure the approval of the ad hoc committee established by Wrench in 1928 to ensure that *The Spectator* did not fall into the wrong hands. Gilmour recalls being interviewed by three or four distinguished figures who, he said, gave him the nod because no one knew much about him. He had no political ambitions at this juncture, nor — a matter to which the committee was bound to give due weight in its deliberations — was he motivated by questions of profit. (When Harry Creighton bought the magazine from Gilmour in 1967, he also had to go before the committee, whose chairman had the shooting rights over Creighton's estate in Sussex. Shortly afterwards he sacked the committee and the arrangement came to an end.)

A stranger to the great and good, and to journalism, Gilmour may have been, but he quickly re-established friendly relations at Gower Street. His years as editor, according to Baylis, who had joined the staff in 1940, 'were more happy, more full of fun, and of more interest to those who worked together in the building, than in any other post-war period'. Taplin was soon contributing again to *The Spectator*'s pages, and Harris came back to Gower Street for the 1954 Christmas party. He accepted an invitation to resume his association with *The Spectator* by writing regular book reviews; the scars seemed to have healed, or at any rate he was prepared to give the new regime his blessing. But less than a month later, on 11 January, Harris died, at the age of 71, leaving a widow, a daughter and £37,000.

The Spectator published two obituaries: respectful, generous in their estimation of his editorial career, but not overly affectionate. One anonymous appreciation, under the heading 'Janus', called him 'a tactful but determined innovator [who] never did depart from tradition; the changes he made served to keep tradition alive'. There was a faint-praise reference to his 'serviceable, well-balanced prose' and another, surprisingly, to 'his Parliamentary reputation as a wit'. The other obituary, signed by R.A. Scott-James, was formal and dispassionate, recalling rather more of his time at the *Daily News* — as diplomatic correspondent he had attended the peace conference at Versailles and the League of Nations in Geneva — than his 21 years as editor of *The Spectator*. Little of Harris's character was disclosed: 'his main personal interests were political, religious, ethical and, in general, practical. His views were severely grounded on common sense.' About his election in 1945 as independent MP for Cambridge University, the obituarist wrote: 'Owing no allegiance to a party, free to take any line he chose in debate and in voting, and enjoying the sort of company which was as the breath of life to him, Harris found a new and singularly congenial activity in his four years in the House of Commons.' What was not mentioned was the effect of his absorption in this activity on the discharge of his editorial responsibilities. Circulation had begun to fall during the immediate post-war years.

Sales figures were said to have suffered when Harold Nicolson gave up his Marginal Comment column; Gilmour took him to lunch at White's to try to lure him back, but was unsuccessful. Nicolson did, however, throw some light on Harris's 'practical' nature, to which his obituary had alluded. Nicolson had described his relationship with his editor as the most shining example of amicable co-operation in the history of journalism, yet the fee he was paid for his Marginal Comment was somewhat lower than the amount received by *The Spectator* each week for the syndication of his column.

The immediate problem, in the wake of Taplin's departure, was the editing of the magazine. As the number two, Iain Hamilton was asked by Gilmour to be acting editor *pro tem*. He had been on the staff for two and a half years, and had been writing theatre reviews for *The Spectator* before that. Hamilton was a romantic, sensitive, soft-spoken Scot, an impression not immediately conveyed by the military style of his moustache and his dark suits. With leanings towards Scottish nationalism in his youth, he had worked briefly for the *Daily Record* in Glasgow after the war, before joining the *Manchester Guardian*, where he remained until 1952. He was a good writer, a poet (two volumes of verse were published in the 1970s) and a good talent-spotter. It was he who brought in Henry Fairlie to do the political commentary, and recruited Brian Inglis from the *Daily Sketch* to be assistant editor. (He also proposed that Peter Fleming should be made deputy editor.) Anthony Hartley, now on the staff, combined theatre criticism with responsibility for the arts and for foreign affairs.

Gilmour proposed to be editor-in-chief, with Hamilton as editor. But he was persuaded by Graham Watson, literary agent and son of Sir Angus

Watson, and an occasional contributor to *The Spectator* during the war, that it was too small a publication to have an editor-in-chief; and so Gilmour called himself editor and Hamilton associate editor. In effect, Gilmour edited the front half of the magazine and Hamilton the back half, an arrangement which continued satisfactorily for the next 18 months. There was one other matter to be resolved: the presence at Gower Street of T.E. (Peter) Utley, the High Tory leader-writer from the *Times* who had been hired by Wrench shortly before he sold *The Spectator*. Encouraged by Dermot Morrah, who was then also a *Times* leader writer, Wrench had offered Utley a job, having heard it rumoured that he had been invited to edit a new right-wing weekly which would present *The Spectator* with unwelcome competition. It is unclear whether this arrangement was made behind Taplin's back, but it is reasonable to assume that Wrench promised Utley that the editorship would be his in the near future. He was a bright young star at the *Times* and would not have left without such an inducement. At any rate he had been given authority by Wrench to transform the magazine, and he was in Gower Street towards the end of 1954, wondering what to do next. Gilmour appointed him associate editor and specialist adviser on politics and religious affairs. But he and Hamilton did not get on. There was no real personal animus, but Utley's responsibilities and authority had not been clearly defined. Utley envisaged an editorial partnership, akin to a joint editorship (while Hamilton was still acting editor), and Hamilton did not. It was embarrassing to have to ask such a distinguished journalist and Conservative thinker to leave; but he had been misled by Wrench, and so it was agreed with Gilmour, shortly after the 1955 general election, that he should go.

Gilmour was soon able to recruit other good 'names' to *The Spectator*'s pages. Jo Grimond wrote occasionally, as did Lord Hailsham, Roy Jenkins, William Douglas-Home and David Ormsby Gore. (Sir Winston Churchill sent Gilmour a telegram to say he had started reading the magazine again, which was probably unconnected with the fact that his son Randolph contributed a few articles.) Norman St John-Stevas contributed a piece on obscenity, and the young Anthony Howard wrote from Christ Church, Oxford, on undergraduate Christianity. The week before the general election, articles appeared by the Chancellor of the Exchequer, Rab Butler, and the Foreign Secretary, Harold Macmillan. They had been commissioned by Utley, rather to Hamilton's embarrassment.

The new prime minister, Sir Anthony Eden, decided to go to the country less than two months after Churchill had resigned. Having hung on until he was 80, his departure was announced during a national newspaper strike. But *The Spectator* was still being published. 'The Conservative party exists again' were the first words of its leading article on 8 April. 'This is both the immediate and most far-reaching effect of Sir Winston Churchill's resignation. For fifteen years the normal working of Conservative politics has been prevented by the fact that Sir Winston Churchill has been leader of the party…. The re-emergence of the Conservative party as such, without a national hero sitting astride it, means two things. It means, first, that the Conservative Central Office will again come into its own…. The second result… is that the relations between the three or four most important Parliamentary leaders once again become of crucial importance.' *The Spectator* went on to praise Eden as 'almost ideally cast for the role of the true party Prime Minister', commenting when the election came that he was 'the outstanding diplomat of the West', a view that was to be radically revised even before the debacle of Suez 18 months later.

While the newspapers were on strike, *The Spectator* was also able to introduce to a wider readership the sort of article for which the magazine, at its best, has always found space. In the issue of 1 April 1955, Douglas-Home had a memorable dig at a certain type of gentleman of the daily press, the famous foreign correspondent. His actual target, though unnamed, was Russell Spurr, whom he called 'my hero, star reporter, two-surnamer and all' and imagined to be an expert linguist in every country he visited. The disillusioning moment for Douglas-Home came when Spurr, travelling on the Manchurian Express, failed to make himself understood when asking for cheese and admitted in print that he had had to go through the motions of milking a cow. Douglas-Home had been happily imagining his hero asking for cheese 'in fluent Chinese, spiced no doubt with a soupçon of the native dialect of the province through which the train happened to be travelling at the time'. Now it had suddenly been revealed to him why this foreign correspondent wrote such gloomy reports.

'"The girls in Peking have lost their sense of fun", for example. Who wouldn't lose their sense of fun when confronted by a speechless Englishman with a contorted face, imitating a cow being milked in a Peking park, in his search for cheese?'

Douglas-Home returned to the same theme in June, mocking René MacColl of the *Daily Express* for writing that when he asked in Moscow about the missing diplomats, Guy Burgess and Donald Maclean, 'everybody looked blank'. The simple explanation, said Douglas-Home, was surely that 'Mr René MacColl, in common with most Scottish and almost all Irishmen, cannot speak one single word of Russian'. Having had more fun at Russell Spurr's expense in a subsequent article, Douglas-Home found himself one week the subject of an item by Pharos in the Notebook. Anne Scott-James had nominated the distinguished playwright one of Britain's best-dressed men, prompting Pharos to write that, while reading this in the *Sunday Express*, he was in a position to observe Mr Douglas-Home at breakfast. 'His waistcoat was buttonless, his trousers gave cause for concern. There was soap on his shirt, and his collar was frayed. Indeed, his only sartorial feature to which exception could not be taken were his braces; and they belonged to his father-in-law.'

Events abroad in 1955 were beginning to assume a pattern which at that stage few could discern. The wind of change had not yet started to blow, but the barometer was already falling. Trouble was brewing in Algeria and Cyprus; mass demonstrations against apartheid were broken up in Johannesburg; in Kenya an amnesty was offered to the Mau Mau. Nasser's nationalisation of the Suez Canal was a year away; but in the meantime *The Spectator* became engaged in a number of causes which, in case there was any doubt, not only confirmed its independence but established Gilmour as proprietor/editor of the leading journal of libertarian opinion.

The House of Commons had voted in February, by a majority of 31, to retain the death penalty for murder. On Easter Sunday the manageress of a Knightsbridge drinking club, Ruth Ellis, aged 28, mother of two children and described in the journalese of the time as a platinum blonde, shot dead a racing driver, David Blakely, outside a pub in Hampstead. They had lived together for two years, and Blakely was about to go off with another woman. At her trial in June, which lasted only two days, Mr Justice Havers ruled that a crime of passion was not recognised in English law; jealousy was no defence. The jury took 25 minutes to reach a verdict, and Ellis was sentenced to death. She was hanged three weeks later in Holloway prison.

The Spectator commented editorially on the sentence on 8 July; the case for a reprieve, it said, was 'overwhelming'. 'However irrational it may be, there is something even more distasteful about hanging a woman than there is about hanging a man. The Home Secretaries during this century have acted on this feeling and since 1900 only 13 women have been hanged. The practice has been to reprieve women murderers unless there are exceptional circumstances.... It is greatly to be hoped that the Home Secretary will soon announce that he has recommended a reprieve.' *The Spectator* appeared to think that he would; five days later, however, Ellis was dead, and by the end of that week Gilmour had weighed in with a devastating first leader, under the heading, which was carried in large letters across the cover, 'The Execution of Ruth Ellis'.

> It is no longer a matter for surprise that Englishmen deplore bull-fighting but delight in hanging. Hanging has become the national sport. While a juicy murder trial is on, or in the period before a murderer is executed, provided that he or she has caught the public fancy owing to there being a sexual element in the crime, even Test matches are driven from the place of honour on the front pages of the popular press. Anything to do with the extinction of a fellow human being has a fascination for the people of this country.
>
> The execution of Mrs Ellis has taken place without much disturbance. Mr Lloyd George, the Home Secretary, has now been responsible for the hanging of two women in the past eight months. This compares with the hanging of twelve women in the previous fifty-four years. Is this increase of something like 1250 per cent the result of an outbreak of feminine terrorism? Of course not. It is merely the consequence of a weak Home Secretary. The decision to hang Mrs. Ellis was one of such obvious barbarity that it is difficult to believe that Mr. Lloyd George came to it without considerable pressure from his advisers. (The fact that his chief adviser, Sir Frank Newsam, had to be summoned over the loudspeaker at Ascot Races for a short conference introduced a somewhat nauseating touch of 'civilisation': grey toppers and black caps go ill together.)...
>
> Capital punishment is absolutely indefensible. Abolition has taken place in thirty-odd countries and never has the murder rate increased. This experience has not been confined to agricultural countries. Belgium, more densely populated than England, and Michigan, heavily industrialised and including the city of Detroit, are among the abolitionist states. There is no

evidence whatsoever that capital punishment is more of a deterrent to murder than is imprisonment. Since the only possible justification for hanging would be that it stopped people murdering each other, there is really no more to be said. There is no need to dwell on the danger that an innocent man may be hanged — a probably innocent man was hanged in 1950.

But it is possible to go further. For it is very probable that capital punishment actually leads to more people being murdered. As Christopher Hollis argued in *The Spectator* last week, the publicity that is given to the murderer in the dock, the mystique that surrounds hanging, is likely to push the psychopath just over the border of sanity into murder. But it is enough to point out how infinitely more healthy our society would become if it were no longer able to read about the ordeal of people waiting execution, or to gaze at photographs of the families of condemned men visiting the prison, or photographs of the public hangman having a day at the races...

The execution of Ruth Ellis may do good. Not even the thickest head could have remained unmoved as the monstrous drama moved to its ending in the still summer heat of Wednesday morning. There is not the slightest doubt that Mrs. Ellis should have been reprieved. As we pointed out last week, it is the prerogative of mercy that keeps hanging alive. The failure of Mr. Lloyd George and his advisers to recognise this fact can hardly fail to have produced a revulsion amongst the thinking population. Even Tory MPs will have been affected. Surely the whole practice of hanging will have been brought into disrepute. When Sir Anthony Eden returns from Geneva, he should change his Home Secretary and then introduce legislation. He can be certain that the only sufferers will be the Sunday newspapers.

15 July 1955

It was no surprise that, by the following week, as announced on *The Spectator*'s Letters page, 'a very large number of letters' had been received. Twenty were published, the majority of them critical of the tone of the leading article rather than the argument against the death penalty. From Kensington Iris Capell wrote: 'Many of us share your view that capital punishment is absolutely indefensible, and we hope for its abolition in this country. But that cause cannot possibly be furthered, and is likely to be greatly hindered, by the exhibition of hysterical and vulgar abuse that you have seen fit to give us.' One correspondent took grave exception to the 'wanton and scurrilous attack on the Home Secretary'; another called the article 'so indefensibly foolish that I am ceasing my subscription'; another commented that it 'looks suspiciously like the maudlin stuff which is the outcome of a hangover'. Mr J.W. Kernick of Chiddingfold wrote: 'I could almost wish that we were living (for a few hours at least) under a totalitarian regime, so that the Home Secretary might really be responsible for one hanging. Whose, you will doubtless guess.'

A number of letters in support of *The Spectator*'s leader were expressed no less passionately: 'Your brilliant attack on the death penalty is unanswerable'; 'I cannot sufficiently express my admiration'; 'Seldom have I read in your columns an argument more commandingly stated'.

In the same issue *The Spectator* added further editorial comment, referring to the fact that Ellis had had a miscarriage 13 days before the murder (she had been pregnant by Blakely), and that, as the prosecuting counsel put it at her trial, she was suffering from 'extreme emotional tension'. As one correspondent put it: 'It is ironical to think that had Mrs Ellis been still pregnant — or even had she had a child 13 days before the murder — everyone (or at least everyone human) would have clamoured for her reprieve.'

The Spectator commented that those who approved of capital punishment had just as great a cause for concern in this case, because 'the prerogative of mercy has broken down'. Ludovic Kennedy wrote to offer the rather dubious assertion that if the Home Secretary had resigned rather than allow the hanging to take place, 'he would have gone down to history as one of the great Home Secretaries of this century; and the death penalty would have been abolished within the year'. In fact the House of Commons did vote to end capital punishment the following February; and *The Spectator* may claim some credit for the shift in opinion which had taken place over the previous months. At the end of June 1956 Gilmour reprinted, from a 1935 *Spectator*, an article by Archbishop Temple in which he argued for the removal of the death penalty from the statute book, in order to 'secure an advance in the ethics of civilisation'. (Under Harris, *The Spectator* had always been against capital punishment.) Ten days later, however, the House of Lords voted overwhelmingly against abolition. The 1957

Homicide Act retained the death penalty for a few murders, and it was not until 1965 that hanging was formally ended — for an experimental period — by the Murder (Abolition of the Death Penalty) Act. Capital punishment was consigned permanently to history at the end of 1969. Gwilym Lloyd George, a man of strong Liberal, if not liberal, traditions, continued as Home Secretary until the advent of the Macmillan government in January 1957, when Butler replaced him.

One of the few signed articles to be written by Gilmour in 1955 concerned the Montagu case (in which Lord Montagu of Beaulieu and two others were convicted and imprisoned for homosexual offences with two airmen). The publication of a book by one of the defendants provided Gilmour with the occasion to take a few swings at Sir Theobald Mathew, the Director of Public Prosecutions, and 'the many repellent aspects of this case'. Two years later, when the Wolfenden Committee proposed that homosexual acts between consenting adult males, when performed in private, should no longer constitute a criminal offence, *The Spectator* gave its support. 'Whatever feelings of revulsion homosexual actions may arouse, the law on this point is utterly irrational and illogical,' *The Spectator* stated in its leading article of 6 September 1957. 'It is impossible to argue that homosexual actions between consenting males are more anti-social than adultery, fornication or homosexual actions between consenting females, none of which are crimes. Not only is the law unjust in conception, it is almost inevitably unjust in practice. Save in very exceptional circumstances, a prosecuton can only be brought on the evidence of one of the parties concerned, who is necessarily as guilty as the party who is prosecuted. Indeed it was a particularly unfair prosecution of this sort [the Montagu case] which was largely responsible for the setting up of the Wolfenden Committee, and it is pleasantly ironical that the actions of those concerned in that case should have led to a recommendation that the law should be changed.'

But it would not be changed under a Conservative government, nor while the popular press was stirring up public opinion against reform. The columnist John Gordon of the *Sunday Express* railed against 'The Pansies' Charter', called *The Spectator* 'The Bugger's Bugle' and wrote (incorrectly) that Gilmour had a homosexual relation. Ten more years were to pass before a Private Member's Bill — introduced by Leo Abse and given tacit support by Labour's Home Secretary (and a former *Spectator* contributor),

Roy Jenkins — was translated into law as the Sexual Offences Act. Homosexual behaviour between consenting adults in private was no longer an offence; 'gay liberation' had begun.

In its attitudes to social reform, *The Spectator* under Gilmour was showing itself to be some way ahead of, or at any rate out of step with, most of the national daily press. Michael Foot wrote in 1958 that 'no journal in Britain has established a higher reputation than *The Spectator* for the persistent advocacy of a humane administration of the law or the reform of inhumane laws'. Gilmour was not slow to criticise the judiciary, or to deride the Lord Chamberlain's theatre censorship.

But *The Spectator* did not confine itself to instigating controversy over law reform. In the week before Ellis was hanged, Evelyn Waugh's attention was engaged by quite a different matter. Under the heading, 'Awake my Soul! It is a Lord', he wrote an article protesting at the attempted invasion of his privacy by Lord Noel-Buxton and Miss Nancy Spain, the latter having written an account of the incident in the *Daily Express*. Mr Waugh was about 'to prepare myself for dinner [when] I heard an altercation at the front door. My poor wife, weary from the hayfield, was being kept from her bath by a forbidding pair.'

Noel-Buxton and Spain had been to visit the Poet Laureate, John Masefield, and afterwards decided to call on Waugh. During a brief confrontation on his doorstep, according to Waugh, Noel-Buxton uttered the words, 'I'm not on business. I'm a member of the House of Lords.' This led Waugh to comment in his article: 'In Lord Noel-Buxton we see the lord predatory. He appears to think that his barony gives him the right to a seat at the dinner-table in any private house in the kingdom. Fear of this lord is clearly the beginning of wisdom.'

An argument then ensued in the letters columns as to whether the words, 'I'm not on business. I'm a member of the House of Lords' had in fact been spoken to Waugh when, presumably, he had demanded to know on what business his uninvited visitors were engaged. Noel-Buxton wrote to say that Waugh had shut the front door in his face, without any conversation having taken place between them. The words attributed to him by Waugh had been taken from Spain's article in the *Express*, and were fabricated by her. Spain replied that 'the relevant passage' in her piece had been read out and 'explained' to Noel-Buxton and that he had raised no objection. Waugh wrote to the effect that, if Spain could put words into the mouth of 'an old and valued friend', albeit one who now called her a liar, 'what monstrous infelicities would she have fathered on her reluctant host, if I had let her in to dinner'.

Noel-Buxton wrote back to deny — convincingly — that the passage in the *Express* article containing his disputed words had ever been read over to him. There had been no attempt to seek his approval for 'offending phrases'. He still seemed bewildered by the incident, referring to Waugh's outburst on the doorstep of his house as insulting 'to the House of Lords as an institution'. He admitted respect for Spain's talents, while writing that 'the whole tone of [her] *Express* article was false'. One correspondent thought Waugh's original article 'of a really staggering unpleasantness'; another came strenuously to his friend Noel-Buxton's defence, calling him 'modest, scrupulous to a fault, and so kindly that he is completely abashed by unfriendliness'. Nancy Mitford wrote to explain why writers are liable to become bad-tempered. 'Nobody would believe the extent to which I am teased and tortured by strangers.... It is the unemployed bore who drives me mad. He writes, he telephones, he even surges into my flat, un-announced, through the french windows.' After three weeks the editor pronounced the correspondence closed; no doubt Waugh had derived the most enjoyment from the affair, and Noel-Buxton had had his faith in human nature badly dented. Spain, like many another journalist, did not want to allow the truth to get in the way of a good story. It had all been good, if not quite clean, fun.

When commercial television began in the autumn of 1955, *The Spectator*, having been one of its few early supporters, thundered: 'It is an impostor, facing three charges of appropriating public funds under false pretences.' But when, a month later, it was announced, after much fevered speculation, that Princess Margaret would not marry her father's equerry, Group Captain Peter Townsend (because he was a divorced man), *The Spectator* was uncharacteristically, and unlike most of the national press, without any firm view on the matter. It predicted 'damage' if the marriage had gone ahead, and 'unfortunate results' from the decision not to marry. *The Spectator* might have been expected to adopt a liberal line on divorce more consistent with its attitudes towards homosexuality and capital punishment. One leading article was concerned to state — though without much conviction — that the princess, having examined her conscience as a faithful member of the Church of England, had taken the decision on her own, without pressure from 'the massed ranks of Monarchy, State, Church, the *Times* and hard-hearted Tory peers'. But one may guess that, had *The Spectator* not just emerged from a bruising encounter with some members of those massed ranks — the term 'the Establishment' had been recently coined — Gilmour might well have been more disposed to encourage Princess Margaret to go right ahead and marry the man she loved.

'The Establishment' was first introduced to the public by A.J.P. Taylor, but it was Henry Fairlie, *The Spectator*'s lively new political commentator, who brought it most provocatively to public notice. Fairlie, a Scotsman, had begun writing book reviews for the magazine in the previous year, while still employed at the *Times*; Hamilton recruited him for the political column, which he started, under the pseudonym of Trimmer, in the very first issue of Gilmour's editorship, 3 December 1954, thereafter writing weekly under his own name from February 1955 until he left to join the *Daily Mail* at the end of June 1956. When people still speak wistfully of Fairlie as the finest of *The Spectator*'s political correspondents, it is remarkable to recall that he held the job for little more than 18 months.

After Oxford, where he read modern history, Fairlie's interest in Liberal politics led to a job with the *Manchester Evening News*, of which he became lobby correspondent at the age of 21. He moved to the *Observer* in 1948, and in 1950 to the *Times* as political leader writer. His weekly column for *The Spectator* was always witty and pungent, never pompous, informed by a sense of political history and with an underlying seriousness of purpose, which was to judge political activities by how they matched up to the ideals to which Fairlie thought all Englishmen should aspire.

To *The Spectator*'s staff, Fairlie was a maddening colleague. His copy was frequently late, and his telephone at home was usually left off the hook, or else unanswered. His marriage was frequently interrupted by brief affairs, and girls with whom he had made assignations were for ever ringing the office to ask where he was. But when he finally turned up, his charm seemed to conquer everyone; it was impossible to be angry with him for long, even when he forgot to repay a loan. And, as Peregrine Worsthorne would recall, 'his private vices were essential to his public virtues': it was usually after a night of philandering or a long drinking session at someone else's expense that Fairlie could be relied upon to produce his best, and most high-minded, journalism.

Of the various stories about Fairlie, most have to do with money. Both his personal and his professional affairs were, to put it mildly, somewhat disorganised. He once found himself arrested (for contempt of court, relating to unpaid debts) at the end of an Any Questions programme in which he had been taking part with, among others, Cardinal Heenan. As he was being taken away, the good cardinal expressed sympathy at Fairlie's plight, saying something to the effect, 'If there's anything I can do...' Having been detained overnight at Brixton prison (prompting his long-suffering wife Lisette to say, 'At least tonight I shall know where he is'), Fairlie rang Heenan the next day to ask for a loan. In the days before plastic credit cards, it was said that Fairlie was able to use his considerable charm to buy train tickets from British Rail 'on tick'. He also established a long line of credit at the bar of the Ritz Hotel, and was accustomed to taking friends to dine at the Savoy Hotel, then signing the bill and having it sent to Gilmour. Baylis remembered him coming to the office during the lunch hour with an empty suitcase, which he proceeded to fill with the most expensive books from the literary editor's room. After he had freelanced for several publications in the early 1960s, Inglis commented: 'Henry left many a newspaper a poorer place'. When he finally left the country in 1966, to avoid his creditors and in particular a libel judgment against him at the suit of Lady Antonia Fraser, whose fitness to pronounce on the moral behaviour of young people Fairlie had questioned on a television programme, he was to spend the rest of his life in the United States (though still writing irregularly from Washington for *The Spectator* and the *Sunday Express*).

Encouraged by Worsthorne one evening in El Vino's, Fairlie decided to take on the Establishment in *The Spectator*. The Foreign Office had finally got round to admitting, more than four years after they absconded to Moscow, that Burgess and Maclean were Soviet agents. Commenting on the fact that, since Parliament was not sitting, a debate on this scandal would not be held for another six weeks, Fairlie opined that here was a fine example of the Establishment at work.

> By the 'Establishment' I do not mean only the centres of official power —
> though they are certainly part of it — but rather the whole matrix of offi-

cial and social relations within which power is exercised. The exercise of
power in Britain (more specifically in England) cannot be understood
unless it is recognised that it is exercised socially. Anyone who has at any
point been close to the exercise of power will know what I mean when I say
that the 'Establishment' can be seen at work in the activities of, not only the
Prime Minister, the Archbishop of Canterbury and the Earl Marshal, but
of such lesser mortals as the chairman of the Arts Council, the Director-
General of the BBC, and even the editor of the *Times Literary Supplement*,
not to mention divinities like Lady Violet Bonham Carter.

Somewhere near the heart of the pattern of social relationships which so
powerfully controls the exercise of power in this country is the Foreign
Office.... At the time of the disappearance of Maclean and Burgess, 'the
right people' moved into action. Lady Violet Bonham Carter was the most
active and the most open.... No one whose job it was to be interested in the
Burgess-Maclean affair from the very beginning will forget the subtle but
powerful pressures which were brought to bear by those who belonged to
the same stratum as the two missing men. From those who were expecting
Maclean to dinner on the very night on which he disappeared, to those who
just happened to have been charmed by his very remarkable father, the
representatives of the 'Establishment' moved in, and how effectively they
worked may be traced in the columns of the more respectable newspapers
at the time, especially of the *Times* and of the *Observer*...

23 September 1955

Lady Violet Bonham Carter was not amused; nor was David Astor,
editor of the *Observer* (and Fairlie's former employer). Over the next few
weeks the Letters columns were weighed down by their protestations (three
letters from each of them), principally in defence of Melinda Maclean, wife
of the defecting diplomat. Their interventions in 1951–52, they said, had not
been to defend Burgess and Maclean but to protect Mrs Maclean and her
family from unreasonable press intrusion. She had been hounded by the
press, she had not given the interviews attributed to her, and the persecution of her was no less reprehensible for the fact that she turned out to be a
Communist herself. 'By its defence and condonation of private persecution
without public trial,' Lady Violet wrote, 'and by the mud it has flung at
those who have condemned and will continue to condemn such methods,

The Spectator can claim to be the first weekly journal in this country to offer its readers a few sips of the pure milk of McCarthyism.'

The argument seemed to get bogged down in the nature of the press interviews given by Mrs Maclean. But it was clear, or should have been, that neither Fairlie, nor *The Spectator* in its leading article on the subject, had intended to ridicule those, such as Lady Violet and Astor, who defended Mrs Maclean from what they — albeit mistakenly — thought was persecution of her.

What Fairlie had intended, and in which design he was notably successful, was not only to stir up those members of the Establishment whom he identified, but to get others to identify themselves. From All Souls College, Oxford, the Warden, John Sparrow, rose quickly to the bait. Fairlie's commentary was 'patently vicious... full of low innuendo and false in almost all its assumptions and suggestions.... Such articles, in the columns of a once responsible paper such as *The Spectator*, can do much harm, and they ought not to be allowed to go unchallenged. In the end, however, it is probably the paper in which they appear that suffers most from their publication.'

From the Establishment eyrie of All Souls, it was magnificently pompous stuff. Much of Sparrow's letter had to do with his membership of selection boards for the Foreign Service, seemingly confirming the kind of influence he exercised in the corridors of power. The following week Sir Robert Boothby, MP, produced a pretty devastating response:

> Sir, I am not surprised that Warden Sparrow has weighed in with an offensive letter about Mr Fairlie's article. All Souls was the headquarters of the Establishment during the decade immediately preceding the Second World War; and it would be difficult to overestimate the damage then done to this country at that disastrous dinner table.

Randolph Churchill came in on Lady Violet's side; Malcolm Muggeridge, one of Fairlie's admirers, and Gordon, the *Sunday Express*'s editor-in-chief, who seldom had a good word to say for *The Spectator*, reckoned that Mrs Maclean had made complete fools of Lady Violet and Astor. Colm Brogan wrote to remind readers that when Sir Rufus Isaacs, Attorney-General in the Asquith government, was found not to have behaved improperly in what was known as the Marconi scandal, the prime minister promptly made him Lord Chief Justice. 'That is how the "Establishment" works when it is really feeling its oats. The prime minister was Lady Violet's father.'

Hugh Trevor-Roper wrote to say: 'No doubt you are right in supposing that there is an "Establishment", though it is hardly a novel discovery to observe that there is here and now, as everywhere and at all times, a governing class.' But it was novel to observe that there existed a nexus of influential people, not bound by party allegiance, who could establish a climate of opinion that, in the modern parlance, would set the agenda. It could not be ignored and, as Fairlie wrote, 'I think its existence is the most important fact about the exercise of power in this country.' Apart from Munich and the Burgess-Maclean affair, Fairlie quoted the recent advent of commercial television as an example of Establishment influence. While the Establishment had collectively been opposed to any change in the status quo, and on that score had been defeated, it had nevertheless ensured that commercial television would not enjoy any more freedom than the BBC. The chairman of the Arts Council and a former director of the Central Office of Information, two fine Establishment figures, were appointed to see to that.

As a political historian, Fairlie had the insight also to observe that the tentacles of the Establishment were growing ever longer, 'due partly to the increase in the number of official and semi-official bodies... and partly to the apparent diminution in the formal powers of the "Establishment" which has made people less suspicious of the actual power and influence which its members exercise'. As a moralist, however, Fairlie was prepared to acknowledge that he would rather have the British Establishment than the American 'power elite' (the bosses of big corporations) who were capable of exerting a more potent, and more malign, influence. 'Personally I would rather live under the cloud of the "Establishment" than under the control of General Motors,' Fairlie wrote on 25 May 1956, ten years before he moved to the United States. 'Thank God for Warden Sparrow and Lady Violet Bonham Carter.'

After all that had gone before, it was a suitably conciliatory valediction, four weeks before he ended his regular relationship with *The Spectator*. Few would deny that Fairlie had been the most stimulating of political commentators: he understood both the nature of political power and the workings of the Conservative party, to which he had a romantic attachment. He was a great admirer of Churchill, calling him a Tory Democrat in a two-page encomium on his retirement as prime minister, and also of Hugh Gaitskell, for his integrity and moderate socialism.

After leaving *The Spectator*, Fairlie developed a rapport with Macmillan (though he was also a fan of Butler) while working for the *Daily Mail*. But his prediction that Labour would win the 1959 general election — the Tories had a majority of 100 — led to his departure from that newspaper. He then wrote for the *Express*, *Encounter*, and *Time and Tide*, plus a number of pieces for *The Spectator*, on and off over the next 20 years. One of his editors, Iain Macleod, would tell his staff: 'You've got to know how to handle Henry. I know how to do it.'

When he went to America, he lived happily enough for a year with his family in a rented house in Georgetown, Washington; then they returned to England without him. His later career, for the most part beset by financial problems, revolved round the *New Republic*, which he used not only as an office but sometimes also as a bedroom. His politics moved noticeably to the left, and he became for a time something of a cult figure to young American liberals. He never went back to England, and died in 1990.

It was a pity that Fairlie missed Suez at *The Spectator*; Nasser seized the Suez Canal a month after his last political column. However, he had written a leading article in April 1956 ('The Lost Leader'), in which Eden was excoriated for his failings. 'His irremediable faults appear to be an exceptional lack of vision or originality and an excess of vanity…. Sir Anthony Eden can hardly do worse than he has done so far. Cannot the party which upholds him find someone who could do better? The country needs a leader who can command respect.'

But Eden did, in the estimation of *The Spectator* at any rate, do considerably worse than he had done so far. Its initial response to Nasser's nationalisation of the canal was similar to the Cabinet's: to denounce the action and threaten the use of force in the last resort, if agreement could not be reached to manage the Suez Canal internationally. In its leading article of 3 August *The Spectator* wrote: 'What Sir Anthony Eden seems, in fact, to have in mind is the old 19th-century plan of a consensus of the powers presenting a united front in the face of an extortionate demand and ready to back their rights by military force. The last element is, indeed, essential.' *The Spectator* went on to propose an alliance with Israel, 'the West's one sure ally', which would provide it with arms and, if necessary, a British military base. (It was not until after Gilmour had visited the Middle East in 1958 that *The Spectator* began to adopt an Arabist stance. In his articles he argued that a rapprochement with Nasser should be reached, and that Arab nationalism was the only alternative to Communism in the region.)

Over the next weeks *The Spectator* started to get worried, as did certain members of the Cabinet — Butler, Sir Walter Monckton, Macleod — over the strength of world opinion (in particular American and Commonwealth) that was gathering against Britain. 'It is a matter of some urgency for this country to prevent ourselves and France from becoming isolated over the Suez issue.' According to *The Spectator*, military force was no longer an option: it could only have been used immediately after the seizure of the canal or else with overwhelming international approval, which was not going to be forthcoming. What was needed was negotiation through the UN, a closer association with Israel and a re-examination of British foreign policy in the Middle East.

Until the end of September *The Spectator*'s Suez leaders were written by Hartley who, apart from being effectively the foreign editor, was, or had also been, theatre critic, book reviewer and poetry editor (with the literary editor, J.D. Scott, he had promoted the Movement in 1953–54). Hartley's principal reaction to the events of that summer was to berate the government for diplomatic incompetence, for failing to see that the United States would not go along with the military option. When Britain started bombing Egypt, Hartley was on a cultural cruise in the Mediterranean, visiting Greece and Turkey. Hamilton was on the point of leaving to take a job with Hutchinson, the publishers; in consultation with Gilmour, Inglis expressed *The Spectator*'s view on the Anglo-French decision to invade the Canal Zone. According to Inglis's later account, Gilmour was fearful of the effect on the readership if they condemned the Suez operation too strongly, while Gilmour's clear recollection is that it was Inglis who counselled caution. The first leader published after Eden decided to initiate bombing raids against Egypt ('The Valley of Decision') put the government's case for action before asking: 'Was the action taken appropriate? And, if so, was it timely? The answer to both questions, it is now clear, is — no.' It was a measured editorial judgment, reiterating *The Spectator*'s support for Israel, regretting the disapproval of the United States and the Commonwealth, and regretting the need for Britain to use its veto at the UN. But after

40 years it is easy to forget the depth of the controversy which Suez generated. In terms of its impact on public opinion, there had been nothing like it since Munich. Since *The Spectator* was against the government over Suez, in many Conservative eyes it was damned. Indignant letters poured in, subscriptions were cancelled. One correspondent said that he had to keep glancing at the top of the page to remind himself that he was not reading the *Daily Mirror*. Other Conservative readers simply thought that loyalty to prime minister, party, country and armed forces demanded support for the Suez operation. To disregard these loyalties was tantamount to treachery. Amabel Williams-Ellis wrote to congratulate *The Spectator* on its stance, saying that her late father, and former proprietor/editor, John St Loe Strachey, would have approved.

The collapse of confidence in sterling, with dire threats from the US Treasury, soon persuaded the Chancellor, Macmillan ('first in, first out'), that the show was over; but the rumours of collusion had still to be substantiated. Anxious to avoid charges of anti-government bias founded on false information. *The Spectator* on 9 November made a point of acquitting the government of 'the original unworthy suspicion… the belief, widespread in other countries — and even here — that the ultimatum to Egypt was a product of Anglo-French-Israeli collusion'. Without knowing the full facts, the editorial view was expressed that Israel, in spite of being condemned by an American resolution at the UN, could have been left to complete its victory over Egypt. In the same week *The Spectator* urged Eden to 'ask himself whether, at the earliest practical opportunity, he would not best serve the country's interests by resigning'. Others were asking why Eden had kept them so completely in the dark about his Suez plans. When he and Selwyn Lloyd, the Foreign Secretary, went to see their French counterparts, Guy Mollet and Christian Pineau, the British ambassador in Paris, Gladwyn Jebb, escorted them to the Quai d'Orsay but was excluded from the meeting. An interview with Lord Sherfield (who as Sir Roger Makins was ambassador in Washington in 1956), published in *The Spectator* in 1995, a year before his death, was also revealing. He said that had the four ambassadors, in Washington, Paris, Cairo and at the UN, had any idea what was going on, they would have been on the doorstep of No. 10 within 24 hours, to tell Eden he could not possibly go ahead.

The Spectator would return to the subject of Suez in subsequent months,

In this issue, when the UN had just compelled the Anglo-French forces to bring their Suez operation to a halt, The Spectator *called for Eden's resignation.*

SPECTATOR

No. 6698   FRIDAY, NOVEMBER 9, 1956   *Ninepence*

RETURN TO REALISM?

Hugh Seton-Watson   Hungary and Europe
J. Grimond, MP   American Reactions
A. J. Ayer on Aldous Huxley

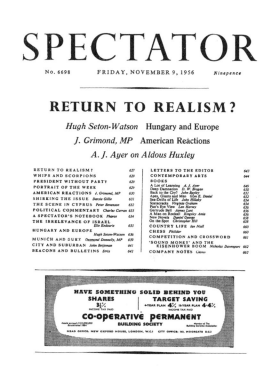

HAVE SOMETHING SOLID BEHIND YOU

SHARES   TARGET SAVING
3½%   4-YEAR PLAN 4% 10-YEAR PLAN 4·4%
INCOME TAX PAID   INCOME TAX PAID

CO-OPERATIVE PERMANENT
BUILDING SOCIETY

HEAD OFFICE: NEW OXFORD HOUSE, LONDON, W.C.1   CITY OFFICE: 163, MOORGATE E.C.2

some would say to the point of obsession. It certainly lost the Conservatives the intellectual vote. Suez constituted one of the major reasons for advising *Spectator* readers to vote against the government in the 1959 general election. 'The continued Conservative pretence that Suez was a good, a noble, a wise venture has been too much to stomach,' was what *The Spectator* had to say. Forgiveness might have been forthcoming had Macmillan ever admitted that an error had been made. Instead he was reminded of his article in *The Spectator* at the time of the 1955 election, when he insisted that 'the primary task [of the free world] must be to forestall aggression'. *The Spectator* continued: 'It is no longer possible to pretend that the government was unaware of Israel's aggressive intentions. Yet Sir Anthony and his colleagues, so far from trying to forestall aggression, deliberately waited until the blow across Sinai was struck, and used it as an excuse to indulge in aggression of their own.'

During the week of the Suez war, it was said that Egyptians behaved with great restraint towards British subjects in their country. Then it was reported in December that a Lieutenant Moorhouse had been murdered by his Egyptian captors. Under the heading 'The Despised', the letters page for the issue of 28 December was led by Mr Czeslaw Jesman, who began a six-week correspondence on the attitudes of the British armed forces, when stationed in Egypt, to the local population. It is probably safe to say that no views were altered or even modified during this debate, but as an exposition of British character and conduct abroad in the last 'imperialist' years (British troops had been in Egypt since 1881), it made wonderful reading.

Having begun his letter by acknowledging that Egyptians had 'some unlovely traits of character', Jesman went on to rebuke the British for the 'racial conceit and zoological xenophobia' which they had exhibited in Egypt, particularly during the second world war, and which was, he said, largely reponsible for the calamitous state of British interests in Egypt today. He cited the frequent singing by British soldiers of obscene versions of the Egyptian national anthem, the insults heaped on King Farouk by drunken officers in the Long Bar of Shepheard's hotel in Cairo and the exclusion of Egyptian officers from the Gezira and Maadi clubs.

The following week two correspondents leapt vigorously to the defence of the British soldier. The Eighth Army had better things to do, said Malcolm Murray-Brown, 'than to pander to the susceptibilities of the Egyptian peasantry'. William Pickard resented the suggestion that Egyptians and Europeans might be considered 'potential equals'. 'The Egyptians, Sir, have at no time during the last hundred years contributed anything of value to the world, and I really do not see why we should flatter them, and prostitute ourselves, by pretending that they have.' Lilian Roff wrote to recall her experience of having 'lived among the Egyptians, travelled in their ghastly derelict trams, witnessed their anti-British acts and listened to their anti-British lies'. The clear inference seemed to be that Johnny Gyppo should consider himself damned lucky that only a thousand of his countrymen had been killed when Britain had recently been obliged to invade their country.

The argument was continued by a Frenchman writing to say that, in view of the Egyptians' equivocal attitude towards Germany in the last war, the British serviceman had been a model of self-restraint and decency in his dealings with the locals. But a Canadian who had served in Egypt for some years had quite a different recollection, which he characterised as 'our studied programme of arrogance towards that race'. Nasser could not have roused the Egyptian people to such fury against us 'if we had displayed in our occupation of Egypt even the most common of courtesies and brotherly behaviour'.

By the time the correspondence petered out in mid-February, quite a lot had been learnt about the British attitude to subject peoples. A correspondent who had worked in various parts of the British empire maintained that there the white man was expected to indulge in behaviour which he would not dream of at home, handing out harsh treatment to the natives, because it was the only thing they respected, and having an obsession with alcohol and sex. He warned that we were now beginning to pay the price for the cruelties and indignities endured by Asians and Africans in the past. It was not an original view, but the point was well made at a time when the colonial era in Africa was coming to an end (the independent state of Ghana was declared the following month, in March 1957). It was all to do with the Briton's innate feelings of superiority when abroad, as Douglas-Home illustrated in his letter:

> Your 'Despised' correspondence reminds me of an occasion before the war when I was staying at our embassy in Rome. A young honorary attaché, asked during dinner how he proposed to amuse us for the remainder of the evening, replied, 'Let's go round the native quarter'. By that he meant the rest of Rome!

In the early weeks of 1957 Gilmour had good reason to feel pleased with the way things were going at *The Spectator*. In his first two years the magazine's radical voice stood out from the national newspaper crowd which, with very few exceptions, tended to be stuffy and unchallenging. *The Spectator* successfully irritated the Establishment and the Macmillan government, while avoiding the charge of priggishness. In bearing its libertarian banner ahead of the crowd, it was anticipating the free-thinking mood of the next decade. In Gower Street Inglis had become deputy editor in place of Hamilton, who was now editorial director of Hutchinson, where he commissioned Hartley to write a book entitled *A State of England* and Gilmour to undertake a scholarly work on the British constitution, *The Body Politic*, which was not published until 1969. Hamilton was also responsible for bringing Edna O'Brien (with whom he was infatuated for a time) and

Brendan Behan to Hutchinson. Though it would be five years before he returned to *The Spectator* as editor, Hamilton continued to write book reviews and to keep in touch with goings-on at Gower Street.

Hamilton's decision to go off to Hutchinson at the end of 1956 may have had something to do with a feeling that, having taught Gilmour to edit *The Spectator*, he was unlikely now to be given the editorship himself. For nearly two years the two Ia(i)ns had worked well together: it was, according to Hamilton, 'arduous and exhilarating, and a good time was had by all'. On press days the two of them would often go together, driven by Gilmour in his Austin Princess, to the printers at Aldershot; Hamilton would then stay the night with Gilmour at Ferry House in Isleworth. Hamilton described his proprietor as 'if anything even more libertarian than Taplin and myself', both in his outlook and his running of the magazine. Gilmour occupied the boardroom, separated from the editor's office (used by Hamilton) by folding doors, which were always open. Gilmour's wife, Caroline, had redecorated the boardroom with strawberry-pink walls, corded silk curtains and a thick Persian carpet which had to be removed each time (usually every three months) *The Spectator* had one of its cocktail parties.

These parties were quite different from the staid affairs presided over by Wrench during the Harris era. (Hamilton recalled Harris once whispering to him in amazement, 'Denis Brogan's on his third sherry!') For a start, Gilmour did not approve of serving drinks in pub measures. Jessie Gage, *The Spectator*'s evergreen housekeeper and telephone operator, was instructed to pour the gin and whisky as if she were offering drinks at home. But she was unfamiliar with this sort of hospitality and, as a result, the drinks were usually so strong that, in Gilmour's words, 'people used to get paralytic'. The Persian carpet in the boardroom would not have lasted long. The guests at *Spectator* parties included not only politicians, businessmen who might steer a little of their advertising budget in the right direction and eminent literary figures, but also a sprinkling of what today would be called the 'glitterati', plus a few disreputable hangers-on. Behan, no doubt well fortified with Gilmour's alcohol, once picked an argument, which developed briefly into an exchange of blows, with Norman Mailer; the pair were separated by Mark Boxer. On another occasion George Gale took a shine to April Ashley until informed that she was a former sailor. Waugh was not amused at one party to have his ear trumpet pinched by Gale's first wife,

Pat. She and her sister had a habit of removing people's shoes whenever the opportunity arose. When Gilmour's wife tried to compliment a well-whiskied William Connor on his Cassandra column in the *Daily Mirror*, the only reply she got was, 'Give ush a kish'.

Ian Fleming was remembered in those days as being always the first to arrive at a *Spectator* party and the first to leave. In more recent years, at the magazine's annual summer party in the garden of its Doughty Street offices, it was Enoch Powell who habitually came first and left after 20 minutes. Gilmour also gave a Christmas party, attended only by staff and regular contributors, at which he was inclined to organise noisy games. Bingo, or housey-housey as he called it, was often played; and one of his favourites involved two people blindfolded and lying on the floor, shouting 'Are you there, Moriarty?' as they tried to hit each other with rolled-up newspapers.

Circulation stood at just under 39,000 at the beginning of 1957. Some subscriptions were cancelled after Suez, but the figures soon picked up again with the introduction, on 25 January, of a new political column. Charles Curran had been covering politics since Fairlie's departure, but as a prospective parliamentary candidate (he became Tory MP for Uxbridge in 1959) he was embarrassed by *The Spectator*'s hostility to the government over Suez, and asked to be replaced. Gilmour tried to get George Gale, who was then abroad and did not receive Gilmour's letter for several weeks. He accepted the offer when he got back to England, but by this time the job, not of political correspondent but rather of parliamentary observer, had been accepted by Bernard Levin.

Levin was taken on, at £1,200 a year, to write a weekly Westminster Commentary under the pseudonym of Taper (taken from Disraeli's novel, *Coningsby*). He had been getting slightly more at his previous place of employment, a journal of current affairs called *Truth*. However, it had backed the government over Suez, and it had neither the circulation nor the influence of *The Spectator*. Inglis had little trouble in persuading Levin where his journalistic future lay. And so began one of the most coruscating, witty and at times withering columns in *The Spectator*'s history. Levin, still in his twenties, was clearly fascinated by, even devoted to, the institution of Parliament, though contemptuous of many of its members. Politicians might be entertained, embarrassed, enraged by his weekly article; but they all read it. Parliamentary sketch-writing was then quite a novel idea. Harry

Boardman was writing a daily piece in the *Guardian* at the time, and Levin has had several distinguished successors over the years in the daily press. But there has never been anyone quite like Taper. The column went on until the October 1959 general election and many of his observations are still a delight to read today.

In his first months he introduced readers to Sir Reginald Bullying-Manner (Manningham-Buller), the then Attorney-General, whom he held in very low regard, and to Sir Shortly Floorcross (Hartley Shawcross), wondering why this wealthy barrister should wish to remain a Labour MP. 'Why should he spend his time wandering about the sixth ugliest building in the British Isles, listening to the futile maunderings of his inferiors, eating vile food, breathing foul air, sitting cheek by jowl with cads?'

Of Butler, for whom he had a respect and affection which he never felt for Macmillan, Levin wrote:

> Mr Butler soft-shoe-shuffled his way in and out of his own inconsistencies. Speakers more naive than Mr Butler sometimes tend to demolish their own arguments with a few indiscreet facts added afterwards. Not Mr B., a boy so wide that I sometimes wonder how he gets through the door.

Levin was perhaps at his scornful best with backbench, backwoods Tory MPs.

> First to rise, by the way, was Lieutenant-Colonel Bromley-Davenport, whom I feel bound to describe, judging by his behaviour in this debate, as a vulgar and clownish fellow. Most members, even the prize fatheads, are content to cheer the good points made by their own side and snort at the bad ones made by the other. Bromley-Davenport yells at both like a Comanche, going puce in the face as he does so, and a great vein sticks out on his neck as though he had swallowed an octopus. Besides, he guffawed at Mr Bevan's stammer; I haven't met anyone who thought a stammer was funny since I was seven years old.

So sharp was his pen that it would be a shame not to reproduce a substantial part of at least one Taper column:

Here, without a word altered, is a series of connected extracts from the proceedings on Tuesday, the Glorious 4th of June, 1957, of Her Majesty's Commons assembled:

Mr Chetwynd asked the Minister of Housing and Local Government whether he will investigate the pollution of the atmosphere at present affecting the Stockton-on-Tees district, and initiate action to detect and remove the cause of the noxious smell which is causing a public nuisance...

MR BROOKE: I understand that there was a bad smell when the Hon. Member was in his constituency...

MR CHETWYND: Is the Minister aware that... the smell was very much worse last weekend when the Prime Minister was there?

Actually it was worse than this, because Hansard in its majesty does not recall the laughter, giggles, chuckles, grimaces and general winsomeness with which the bread was buttered. (Mr Chetwynd, when he got to that dazzling bit about the Prime Minister, was so convulsed with his own wittiness that he could hardly get the words out.) As for me, I had a great desire to go outside and throw up, or even stay inside and do so...

That great statesman, Mr Aneurin Bevan, had a jolly spat with that great statesman, Mr Harold Macmillan, apropos the hydrogen bomb. Mr Bevan was asking the usual question, and the Prime Minister was giving the usual answer, when suddenly some Tories began to barrack. 'Oh, don't be so bloodthirsty, for heaven's sake,' Mr Bevan shouted, and when he sat down it was clear he had lost his temper. Mr Macmillan rose and did his soft-shoe shuffle to the table. Striking an attitude that would have got him thrown out of the Wigan Pier Fol-de-Rols for hamming it up too much, he puffed up his moustache and declared that he deeply resented Mr Bevan's interjection. This was patently nonsense, and many worthy folk showed clearly that they knew it. If Mr Macmillan wants us to accept him as of equal stature with, say, Sir Henry Campbell-Bannerman, he must take good care not to give the game away so often. As for Mr Bevan, if he wants us to accept him as ranking with, say, Miss Margaret Bondfield, he must not ask the Prime Minister silly questions and then shout, yell and bawl in a thoroughly undignified manner when the Prime Minister is giving silly answers. As for Mr Gaitskell, he must take one of those courses advertised on the posters in the Underground and stop blushing when Mr Bevan is making an ass of himself.

The debate on racial policy in Central and East Africa turned, as one might have known, into an elaborate experiment to determine precisely how many clichés can dance on the point of a platitude. Mr Lennox-Boyd, looking very brown (probably from talking to all those Nigerians), set the key with a speech — incidentally, I do wish he wouldn't shout so — which seemed to be composed entirely, and was in fact composed largely, of remarks like 'contrary to the spirit... mutual confidence... harmful to the real interests of the Africans... poisoned atmosphere... greatest possible interest and sympathy... treating human beings as human beings... getting this thing out of proportion... a lead in the right direction... men and women of our stock... carping criticism... loyal service... the ladder ought to be built... interesting leading article in the *Manchester Guardian*... strong action... these regulations which are as distasteful to me as to everybody else... a very great disservice to the cause of orderly progress... in so far as it is proper for a United Kingdom Minister to answer... I must apologise to the Committee for the lengthy speech I have made... '

Mr Callaghan led off for the Opposition with as soapy a speech as I have heard this many a day, and as the evening wore on I became more and more convinced that when Sir Roy Welensky declares that he is not interested in what Westminster has to say on the subject of the Central African Federation, Sir Roy has a point there. A small prize to Mr Nairn (a slightly larger prize for anyone who can tell me who Mr Nairn is) for beginning his speech with the words 'Perhaps I should start by saying that I still travel upon a Southern Rhodesian passport, and that I felt it is a very heavy responsibility to take part in a debate of this sort' — a remark I have not heard equalled since Major-General Spears's splendid announcement, during the 1945 election, that hundreds of millions of Arabs were watching to see how he was faring as Conservative candidate for Carlisle.

7 June 1957

Earlier that year, around the time that Levin began his Westminster Commentary, Gilmour and Inglis also introduced a Consuming Interest column, under the pseudonym of Leslie Adrian. (It was compiled initially by Amy Landreth, later by Jean Robertson.) Much of it was about food and restaurants (rationing had ended less than three years earlier), though it also embraced subjects such as travel, razor blades and launderettes. Apart from Leslie Adrian and Taper, the regulars in a typical issue of February 1957 included Pharos's Notebook (written in-house), Portrait of the Week, Betjeman's City and Suburban column, Strix (Peter Fleming), Country Life by Ian Niall, Randolph Churchill on the press, Nicholas Davenport in the City. Hartley was stylishly running the books pages (though soon to be replaced by Robert Kee, when he went off to the *Manchester Guardian*), and there was a jolly little space-filler, pointing out discrepancies and contradictions in the reporting of stories by the daily papers. Like all lively and provocative journals, it might have been said, *The Spectator* would enhance its reputation with a good libel action. As a result, however, of two sentences in the first issue of March 1957, it got rather more than it bargained for.

Jenny Nicholson, an occasional *Spectator* contributor, married to Reuters correspondent in Rome and daughter of Robert Graves, was in Venice, where the Italian Socialist party was holding its national congress. She filed a piece on Nenni's break with the Communists, published under the heading, 'Death in Venice', which referred in passing to the presence at the congress of three Labour politicians from Britain.

> And there was the occasional appearance of Messrs Bevan, Morgan Phillips and Richard Crossman, who puzzled the Italians by their capacity to fill themselves like tanks with whisky and coffee, while they (because of their livers and also because they are abstemious by nature) were keeping going on mineral water and an occasional coffee. Although the Italians were never sure if the British delegation was sober, they always attributed to them an immense political acumen.

Inglis had sub-edited the article, making minor changes to render the passage less offensive, or less liable to give rise to legal action. (Though judged to be defamatory, one might argue that it commended the politicians for their ability to hold their drink. It did not actually say they were drunk.) It is not clear whether Inglis questioned Nicholson about the piece before publication; apparently she had not seen for herself any of them knocking back large quantities of whisky, but it was common talk among Italian journalists of her acquaintance. The upshot was that all three sued

The Spectator for libel; no form of apology could be agreed (though one was published before the trial); all three plaintiffs. to a greater or lesser degree, perjured themselves in court; the trial judge, Lord Goddard, did not hesitate to show his bias against *The Spectator*; the jury found for the plaintiffs and Gilmour had to pay £2,500 damages to each of them and about £5,000 costs. The story has been told in at least three books*; Crossman's later admissions may have come close to the truth, but it is still hard to judge which of the three politicians behaved most shamefully.

Bevan was the prime mover in the litigation. He admitted in court only to having drunk one glass of whisky, though a few weeks after the trial Crossman told Inglis that Bevan had been drinking heavily. There was no evidence that Bevan had been drunk, since he was known to have a strong head, but several people had seen him consume a great deal of whisky in Venice.

When Iain Adamson was preparing his book (a biography of Gilbert Beyfus, QC, who appeared for the plaintiffs in the action), Crossman told him that both Bevan and Phillips had been the worse for drink and had committed perjury, but that he had been sober. At the time Adamson wrote the relevant chapter, in 1962, Bevan was dead and Phillips was still living. It was hardly surprising, therefore, that he should accuse only Bevan of perjury: 'At no time in Venice was Mr Crossman or Mr Phillips under the influence of alcohol.' However, Crossman stated in his *Diaries*, posthumously published in 1981, that Phillips 'got tiddly by midday and soaked by dinnertime' and 'had been dead drunk for most of the conference'. At a dinner given by the British consul in Venice, his head had fallen into the soup and he had to be escorted back to his hotel.

The question of Crossman's own intake of alcohol is more difficult to establish. At a *Private Eye* lunch in 1972 he admitted, or boasted, that all three of them were drunk in Venice, but on other occasions he denied that he had committed perjury, because he was not drinking whisky. The most likely story is that Crossman put away a lot of wine and Cinzano, but was not as sozzled as Phillips.

---

* *The Old Fox*, Iain Adamson (Frederick Muller, 1963); *Public Scandal, Odium and Contempt*, David Hooper (Secker & Warburg, 1984); *Downstart*, Brian Inglis (Chatto & Windus, 1990).

Why, then, did *The Spectator* not seek to establish the accuracy of its assertion? Not only were the facts not then fully known, but the defendants would have had to rely on the evidence of Italian journalists and barmen, whom a jury, whatever their political views, was less likely to believe than three senior figures in the Labour party (Bevan was Shadow Foreign Secretary and a Privy Councillor, Phillips was General Secretary of the Party and Crossman a member of its National Executive who would become a Cabinet minister in the next Labour government). As a barrister, Gilmour had been taught by his head of chambers, Lord Hailsham, that to plead justification in a libel action was asking for trouble. He knew how inflated the damages might be, were *The Spectator* to fail to prove the truth of its allegations; no doubt he was mindful of the recent award of £20,000 to Jaime Ortiz-Patino for a libel which the *Sunday Graphic* had published and tried to justify. Matters were not assisted by the fact that Randolph Churchill, in the same issue as Nicholson's article, described the £20,000 hand-out as 'a decisive blow for English liberty… it now looks as if British juries are on the warpath against those wealthy malefactors [press barons] and will impose upon them punitive and even prohibitive damages which will affect their balance sheets. And high time too.' (Not long after the Venice article, Churchill became so incensed when Gilmour declined to publish a piece of his which had already been rejected by the *Evening Standard*, that he contacted Crossman to urge him to pursue his case against *The Spectator*.)

Beyfus had acted for Ortiz-Patino, and now he was to appear for the plaintiffs against *The Spectator*. With the possible exception of Gerald Gardiner, Beyfus (the Old Fox was by now in his seventies) was the best advocate of his day. He had no love for Bevan, having once written of him, in an article in *Truth* under the pseudonym of A. Broadside, that he was to be compared with 'some malignant fate, whose politician's life is built on hate'. But he served his clients well. Messrs Bevan, Phillips and Crossman also had another impressive figure on their side, the presiding judge, the Lord Chief Justice, Lord Goddard, whose views on capital punishment, among other matters, did not precisely accord with *The Spectator*'s. His enthusiasm for hanging insane murderers was one which had been deplored in *The Spectator*; he had also been criticised editorially for his handling of two cases of contempt of court. Goddard gave Crossman helpful prompting during his evidence, and there were times when his cross-examination of Gilmour was no less vigorous than Beyfus's. Having failed, over a period of months, to agree the terms of an apology in 'without prejudice' negotiations between the parties, Gilmour was understandably horrified when Beyfus then proceeded to prejudice the defendants' case by disclosing the fact of such negotiations to the jury. It was unquestionably sharp practice, which the Lord Chief Justice showed no inclination to disallow. *The Spectator* was not well served by its leading counsel, William Fearnley-Whittingstall, who was unwell and appeared not to have an adequate command of his brief. Peter Carter-Ruck was solicitor to the defendants, and the plaintiffs employed Lord Goodman who, it was said later, was aware that his clients were being economical with the truth. Bevan had told him, according to one account, that as a future leader of the Labour party he must clear his name of these allegations, even though they were quite true. (When, in 1978, Auberon Waugh wrote in *The Spectator* that Crossman had admitted at a *Private Eye* lunch that they had all been drunk in Venice, Goodman wrote a letter of astonishing naivety, to put it politely, in which he asserted that his distinguished clients would never have lied on oath, because of the risk of being convicted of perjury, that *The Spectator* would have pleaded justification had they not lacked the evidence to do so, and that none of the plaintiffs had ever admitted to him to being drunk. Goodman's points were comprehensively demolished the following week in two letters, from Gilmour and Patrick Marnham.)

Crossman wrote that their pursuit of the action was 'the kind of gamble which no one should responsibly have taken'. It was no financial gamble for them, since Howard Samuel, the Socialist property developer and backer of *Tribune*, had undertaken to meet their costs if they lost. It was rather a joint decision, with the odds stacked in their favour, to lie under oath in order to protect their reputations — the prerogative of politicians, one might say, throughout the ages. Once the plaintiffs knew that *The Spectator* would not try to prove the truth of the article, they had little to worry about. Whether or not Bevan was responsible for initiating the action against *The Spectator*, it was Goodman, according to Crossman in his *Diaries*, who was determined to take the case to court, thinking he 'could win and win kudos'. When it was over, Crossman was 'sure of one thing — that Mr Goodman, who I regard as a pleasant villain, will sleep easier in his bed tonight now that he's got his verdict, despite the disparate and discordant views of his three clients.' Goodman remained very sensitive on the subject: when Crossman's *Diaries* were published in 1981, he threatened libel proceedings against the *Daily Mirror* and the *Times* for their comments on the action taken against *The Spectator*. Levin described it as 'one of the greatest scandals since the war'.

The consequences for *The Spectator* were heavy: the bill for damages and costs was equivalent, in 1998, to well over £150,000. It was said that Gilmour rather lost his nerve for a while; Nicholson certainly lost her taste for journalism. She was so deeply upset by the case that, she told Inglis, she put a curse on Bevan and Phillips. Both they, and the two leading counsel, Beyfus and Fearnley-Whittingstall, were dead within five years of the trial. Poor Jenny Nicholson did not live much longer; she died, aged 46, in 1964.

3

A GOLDEN AGE?

Ian Gilmour was thinking, during the course of 1958, that the time had come to give up the editorship. Joan Baylis assumed that the result of the Venice libel action had some bearing on his decision, though this seems unlikely. More relevantly, he wanted to get on with his book, *The Body Politic*, and Brian Inglis was getting restless. Inglis talked about doing more television (he was already presenting 'What the Papers Say') and writing books. Indeed, had he not been offered the editorship, he would have left.

Gilmour did not want to lose Inglis: he wrote well, he was introducing some bright new contributors (such as Cyril Ray, Alan Brien and Katharine Whitehorn), he was an efficient editorial manager and deputy editor. Years later, Inglis was to write in his autobiography, *Downstart*, that Gilmour was no more than nominal editor — more of an editor-in-chief — during the years 1956–59. Since this is hotly disputed by Gilmour, it would appear that Inglis was indulging in some wishful thinking. Their collaboration, however, was friendly and successful. On the major issues of this period — Suez, the end of empire, racial oppression, homosexual law reform, capital punishment, relationships with America and with Europe — their views almost always coincided. And they were often not dissimilar from those of the *New Statesman*, except that the latter, under John Freeman, supported the Bevanite wing of the Labour party, while *The Spectator* leant more towards Hugh Gaitskell, or at least as far as 'Butskellism'. What might be called New Labour was represented in *The Spectator* by Roy Jenkins and Anthony Crosland, who talked more about economic expansion and social welfare than about nationalisation.

In the back half of the magazine Robert Kee, best remembered for having a bad temper, presided briefly over the books pages, to be succeeded in 1958 by Karl Miller, a slightly dour Presbyterian Scot, of whom Rory

McEwen, *The Spectator*'s artist and resident calypso player, wrote:

> Next we turn to Mr Miller,
> That well-known Highland lady-killer.
> He stays at the office half the night,
> But the books pages never seem to come out right.

Whatever the truth of that, Miller had an impressive line-up of book reviewers, including Simon Raven, Angus Wilson, Christopher Sykes, Frank Kermode, Neal Ascherson, John Coleman, Tosco Fyvel and Denis Mack Smith. The only trouble was that when Miller went to the *New Statesman* as literary editor in 1961, he took most of them with him.

Also in 1958, Brien was hired as arts editor and theatre critic, at the suggestion of his former *Truth* colleague, Bernard Levin. In company with that journal's editor, George Scott, he had once attended a *Spectator* party at which, after Gilmour had left for dinner, 'I insisted on searching the editor's desk and going through all the files, but my heart wasn't really in it'. Brien made this curious admission years later, in a *Spectator* article to mark its 150th anniversary. Perhaps he had been trying to get his own back for the occasion, in 1952, when the first article he submitted to *The Spectator*, on being unemployed, was rejected by Wilson Harris on the ground that no one was on the dole at that time. Brien certainly made his mark on the magazine, through most of the Inglis era and beyond, but he is not remembered with much warmth by some of his colleagues. He was an acquired taste; Inglis took an instant dislike to him at first meeting, though he was soon to change his mind. Evelyn Waugh once wrote of Brien: 'Randolph hired a Jew to insult me in White's'.

Round the corner from 99 Gower Street, the Marlborough Arms became an office extension on most days, for the likes of Inglis, Brien, Whitehorn and Levin. 'We'll have a jar,' Inglis would announce, using the Irish vernacular, around opening time at 12 o'clock. As they walked past the Royal Ear Hospital, one of them was inclined to shout up at the building, 'What about the working classes, then?' Until 1959, Gilmour would often join them at the Marlborough, sometimes taking them on to lunch at the White Tower or L'Etoile, across Tottenham Court Road.

Before he became editor, Inglis took a three-month 'sabbatical' in Italy (though he had been on the staff for less than four years). Now in his forties, Inglis had just married an American divorcee, Ruth Woodeson, in Boston. He took over the editorial chair from 'the young master', as Gilmour was sometimes known in the office, in April 1959.

Inglis had been born into an Anglo-Irish family — his grandfather came from Scotland to Dublin, by way of the North — and spent part of his childhood in Anglo-India. After Shrewsbury and Magdalen College, Oxford, he got a job on the *Irish Times*, then spent most of the war in the RAF, based in West Africa and later in Northern Ireland, on Lough Erne. Another spell at the *Irish Times*, writing a Dail sketch, while flirting with an academic career at Trinity College, Dublin, was followed by an invitation to join the *Daily Sketch* in Fleet Street as leader writer. Here he earned £30 a week, which was more than his previous editor was getting, and was paid a guaranteed sum of expenses higher than the salary of a junior reporter on the *Irish Times*. But having stayed at the *Sketch* for less than a year (and tried to write a novel), he was recruited by Iain Hamilton as *The Spectator*'s assistant editor.

Though his family background was 'West Brit', Inglis did not remain for long in the conventional Protestant Ascendancy mould. Nationalist, anti-English leanings were formed as a student, and fostered in Dublin, where he would wistfully identify himself with other Ascendancy defectors such as Wolfe Tone and Charles Stewart Parnell. Having joined *The Spectator* he tried, unsuccessfully, to get Brendan Behan as a contributor, and was offered by Erskine Childers an account of his father's execution, to be written by Raymond Chandler; but it came to nothing.

Those years in Dublin had made Inglis something of an idealist and, as an old *Spectator* colleague put it, 'a hyper-liberal'. He relished the magazine's tradition of independence — standing 'against the prejudices of all parties', in the words of its founder, Robert Rintoul — and also his own independence of Gilmour. But while his and Gilmour's political positions were both left-centre, the difference between them was that Inglis was not much interested in British politics. (Some would say that his Irishness led him to despise all British politicians.) *The Spectator* became more eclectic under Inglis, and less politically conscious. After Levin gave up Taper following the 1959 general election, when both *The Spectator* and he advised readers not to vote Conservative, he contributed an irregular Westminster commentary under his own name, and wrote about other matters, but there was no weekly political column. Instead, on most of its pages, according to one critic, Inglis would publish 'anything for a laugh'.

There is no doubt that Inglis was a good editor. He was adept at spotting a writer's potential — it was the style of Levin's television criticism for the *Guardian* that led Inglis to think he would make a good commentator on Westminster — and he held the reins of editorship loosely. He established a stimulating atmosphere, an infectious mood both within the magazine's pages and among its staff and contributors. (No editor would do this again until Alexander Chancellor in the mid-1970s.) Inglis himself was a hard worker and a fast typist who would sometimes sweat profusely. When, on Wednesdays, he had put the week's issue to bed at the printers, he would play a game of dominoes. He inspired loyalty, he was a somewhat reclusive, patriarchal figure, 'the still centre of a hurricane', in the words of one regular contributor, and he presided over what is remembered by some as the golden age of *The Spectator*.

It was certainly so for the young team of radicals who ran the magazine. Whitehorn, who had lost her job with *Woman's Own* in 1958, was one of those who found Inglis's *Spectator* both ideologically exciting and enormous fun. She shared an office with the dapperly dressed, 'Bollinger Bolshevik' wine writer, Ray, a former war correspondent who lived in Albany, and was so entertained by him that most of her writing had to be done in the evenings. Miller's working day was also often interrupted by Levin and Brien, whose offices were separated by Miller's and who would arrange to meet halfway, in Miller's room, knowing it would annoy him. In the quartet of Levin, Brien, Ray and Whitehorn there was the bubbly atmosphere of a boisterous clique sharing the same political views and the same presuppositions about what was right and wrong. They were young and brash, they were earning good money (all had writing contracts outside *The Spectator* as well) and they had the satisfaction of being much talked about among the chattering classes. *The Spectator* was journalistically fashionable; and at a time when newspapers such as the *Sunday Dispatch* and the *News Chronicle* were closing down, its circulation rose during Inglis's time by 25 per cent, from 39,000 to 48,000. This was due in some measure to the satirical, and on occasion abusive, tone adopted by some contributors, anticipating *Private Eye*, which began in 1962, and the 1960s vogue for satire in television programmes such as 'That Was The Week That Was'. As deputy editor, Levin, who would later contribute to TWTWTW, was responsible in large part for the satirising of *The Spectator*.

Whitehorn wrote the innovative column, Roundabout, to which she had originally contributed anonymously, and also edited most of the columns at the back of the magazine. She was one of the first female writers to address subjects of concern to women, but without writing a fashion, gardening or cookery column. (She did write a fashion column for the *Observer* at this time, but she brought a new approach to the genre, once famously writing an article on being a slut.) Each week Roundabout used vignettes to make a serious point, whether about hairdressers, schools, train compartments, corsets or fish. On the subject of smoking in cars, she wrote:

> There are ashtrays and windows to pop the cigarettes out of and into the eyes of oncoming cyclists, but the real trouble is lighting cigarettes for the driver. Having first, of course, found the cigarettes in what is laughably known as the glove compartment (in reality the duster, broken sun-glasses, chocolate, Kleenex, gas bill and dead biscuit compartment). The general rule should be that either you look at the mouth you are sticking the cigarette into, or watch the road till it is clear, and then proffer the cigarette; what is commoner is the attempt to do both — which usually results in holding the cigarette just out of reach while the driver's eyes fill with smoke.

And on ladies' lavatories:

> Most men, my colleagues assure me, have, however, very little idea of what a ladies' room is like; so it is perhaps worth saying that although the top end of the trade tries as hard as possible to look like a boudoir in a little love nest in St John's Wood, the other end provides small, bleak, dismally tiled prison cells…. What we need is a Ladies' Directory dealing not with ladies but with Ladies'. There should be warnings about the boiling hot water at the Café Royal and the apt-to-fly-open door of the ladies' premises at the Savage Club.

Such writing was novel for its time; so too was the decision by Inglis and his merry band of radicals not to support the re-election of the Conservative government in 1959, which came as quite a shock to the readership. Although Gilmour had little respect for Macmillan during his first two years as prime minister, in particular because of the government's handling of policy abroad, he would not have advised *Spectator* readers to vote Labour. At the time of the Reform Bill, *The Spectator* announced that it was 'of the Conservative order — even in its rabid radical days'. But when Inglis told Gilmour that he intended to come out against the Conservatives in his pre-election leading article, Gilmour counselled caution but went along with it — and afterwards was glad *The Spectator* had opposed the government. Very little enthusiasm was expressed for Labour and readers were encouraged, where possible, to vote Liberal; but *The Spectator*'s contempt for the government, which 'has lost all sense of responsibility and of shame', was such that, as Levin put it in his Taper column the same week, 'I ardently hope for a Conservative defeat next Thursday'. The magazine took Macmillan's government specifically to task for 'the dishonour of the past four years', over Suez, Cyprus ('total lack of principle'), Kenya (the Hola massacre) and Nyasaland (repudiating the verdict of the Devlin Commission). The government's good home record was acknowledged, but a spell in opposition was recommended, a time 'to recover sanity and self-respect'. Two weeks before the election, articles were published on behalf of the three main parties, by Sir Jocelyn Simon, then Financial Secretary to the Treasury, Roy Jenkins and Mark Bonham Carter; and the following week comments and voting intentions were sought from luminaries such as Lord Beveridge, E.M. Forster, Wolf Mankowitz and Angus Wilson. They were not very instructive, but the contributions from Kingsley Amis and Evelyn Waugh were well worth reading. Amis alluded to his 'natural aversion to the spectacle of any Conservative success', while venturing to guess that, in his constituency of Swansea West at any rate, 'nobody hates the Labour party as much as I do'. Labour was 'sinister as well as fatuous and revolting', but he was going to vote for them. Waugh, whose short piece was headed 'Aspirations of a Mugwump', hoped to see the Conservatives returned with a large majority, but would never vote in a parliamentary election unless a moral or religious issue was involved. 'Great Britain is not a democracy,' he wrote. 'All authority emanates from the Crown.... I do not aspire to advise my Sovereign in her choice of servants.'

In the same week's issue, Taper thought the tide had turned for Gaitskell; it was more than two years since Macmillan had first said, 'Most of our people have never had it so good'. But the Supermac moniker was a powerful one, securing an overall majority of 100 for the government. Margaret Thatcher entered the House of Commons and Edward Heath was made a minister. The Liberal party favoured by *The Spectator* got only 6 per cent of the vote. Taper had had enough: he could not bear, he said, to sit and listen to Macmillan for another five years. The House of Commons was no longer as important a centre of power as the city, the trade unions, the civil service and the mass media. And, 'to tell the truth', Taper concluded, 'politics in this country — even from the sidelines — has ceased to be an occupation for a gentleman. So who goes home? I do.'

In the wake of *The Spectator*'s abandonment of the Conservative party, the lugubrious managing director, H.S. ('Bertie') Janes, who had joined in 1923 and was heartily disliked by most members of the editorial staff, prophesied a gloomy future for advertising revenue. In the event, a few company reports were lost, but not much more. Several letters received from advertisers, however, expressed understandable concern. Lieutenant-Colonel Philip Edgell, managing director of Notley's advertising agency, commented on the irresponsibility of the magazine's editorial line. '*The Spectator* claims to be independent... I would say that for some time now your anti-government obsessions have destroyed your claim to independence as I understand the application of the word in this context.'

He had a point, though within a year the argument against Inglis was not so much that he was anti-government as that he was anti-politics. By 1961 *The Spectator* was losing its reputation, at any rate among politicians, as a serious political weekly. But it was undoubtedly gaining a reputation among a new, more eclectic readership. It was the back half which had the greater appeal, and which a worried *New Statesman* had to acknowledge was superior to its own. The *Statesman* had long boasted about the quality of its books pages, but its rival was now producing an impressive selection of lead reviewers, in addition to Amis and Waugh. F.R. Leavis was writing on D.H. Lawrence one week, Philip Larkin on W.H. Auden another, then Conor Cruise O'Brien on Edmund Wilson. Doris Lessing, Anthony Crosland, Marghanita Laski and Michael Frayn might be contributing shorter reviews. While Waugh's *Tourist in Africa* was being serialised in the maga-

At the 1959 election, the magazine advised its readers not to vote Conservative and Macmillan's government was returned with a 100-seat majority. A week later The Spectator *chose, on its cover, to address less immediate issues. This was Bernard Levin's final column under his Taper pseudonym.*

SPECTATOR

NUMBER 6851   FRIDAY, OCTOBER 16, 1959   PRICE NINEPENCE

Rudolf Peierls   The Scientists and the Bomb
Kenneth Allsop   A Talk on the Wild Side
Taper   After the Ball
Anthony Hartley on Proust

zine in the summer of 1960, John Coleman, in true Spectatorish tradition, wrote an unfriendly review of a new edition of *Brideshead Revisited*, calling it 'still… a basically sapless piece of work'.

In the arts pages Brien was doing the theatre (Bamber Gascoigne took over when he left), Clive Barnes was writing on ballet (before he achieved greater fame as the *New York Times*'s theatre critic), David Cairns on music, Peter Forster on television, Isabel Quigly on cinema (succeeding Virginia Graham, who had been film critic since 1947 and whose correspondence with Joyce Grenfell was published in 1997). At the back there was Whitehorn's Roundabout column, Leslie Adrian's Consuming Interest, Ray's Postscript and wine notes. Later on, Elizabeth David and Raymond Postgate agreed to write alternately on food, Monica Furlong on religious affairs, also on parents and children, Jonathan Miller on medicine and Whitehorn's husband, Gavin Lyall, on motoring. And then there was, as always, Nicholas Davenport In the City. Quentin Blake and Trog provided many of the cartoons and drawings, supported by Maurice Bartlett, Michael Heath and, until his tragically early death, Timothy Birdsall. Many of the vignettes at the top of the regular columns were drawn by the arts editor, Rory McEwen, who was also to die young, at 50, and who became best known for his paintings of fruit and flowers. His elder brother, Sir Robert McEwen, was one of three barristers (the others were Tony Lincoln and Roland Brown) who contributed a legal column under the pseudonym of R.A. Cline. (The trio were known to Gilmour from the days when they had all been together in Quintin Hogg's chambers; the column continued regularly, on something like a fortnightly basis, until 1970, though Brown did not contribute after 1961, when he was made Attorney-General of Tanzania.)

If ever it were true that most people read *The Spectator* from the back, it was so in Inglis's time. When, going backwards, readers had got past the arts (which in those days preceded the books) and the letters, they might find more light entertainment. Patrick Campbell, the Irish writer, contributed an occasional series entitled 'Come here till I tell you'; another, John Bull's Schooldays, was later published as a book. Of the 25 or so who wrote their recollections of school life, most were unfavourable. Brien's experience proved that 'it is not necessary to pay to make your children unhappy'. At Charterhouse Simon Raven was taught it was not dishonourable to 'sneak' on a fellow pupil (the practice of denunciation in order to better one's own position was, of course, also enshrined in the totalitarian ethos). But he did not reveal why he was expelled from the school.

On occasion Inglis would publish a major 'think piece' which, at approximately 12,000 words, would fill most of the front half of the magazine. The first, in September 1959, of which Inglis was very proud, was entitled 'Stalin Merely Smiled' and written by Charles Curran, explaining why, in his opinion, Stalin was so pleased to hear from Truman that America was going to use an atom bomb against Japan. Two months later, Gilmour produced an article of equivalent length on Franco's Spain, anticipating the *caudillo*'s removal by the army and the restoration of the monarchy in the person of Don Juan, father of Juan Carlos. Robert Manning, the Time-Life bureau chief in London, wrote a long piece on Macmillan's tour of Africa (when he made his 'wind of change' speech in South Africa); and the religious correspondent of the defunct *News Chronicle*, Geoffrey Murray, waded into the subject of fringe medicine with a survey of the then relatively new practices of osteopathy, psychotherapy, homeopathy and naturopathy. It was a subject to which Inglis would devote much of his time in the future; curiously,

*In February 1960 Harold
Macmillan famously
announced, while in
South Africa, that 'the
wind of change is
blowing through this
continent'.*

it was the only one of these extended articles that he commissioned. By the end of 1960 they had stopped coming in, and Inglis did not initiate any more.

Some issues of the magazine appear rather unbalanced today, either because a 12,000-word article left little space for anything else in the front half, or because there was sometimes too great an emphasis on what was happening abroad. The issue of 22 April 1960 contained reports from Brazil, Israel, South Africa, West Germany, South Korea, Algeria and a leader on the Defence White Paper; but all was apparently quiet on the domestic political front. Though Levin was writing most weeks, he often veered away from party politics. A Westminster Commentary would sometimes be contributed by an MP, and during 1960 Jenkins was producing an article every fortnight. In June he wrote a masterly critique, 'The Fallacies of Mr Crossman', who believed that only through larger-scale nationalisation could Britain achieve the faster growth rate necessary to avoid defeat for the West in the cold war. Jenkins also took his Labour colleague to task for saying that the party should reconcile itself to a long period out of office and accept that its principal role was to provide an effective opposition.

A leading article in the same issue urged Gaitskell to stiffen his sinews against the unilateralists in his party. Three weeks later Aneurin Bevan died; Desmond Donnelly wrote an appreciation for *The Spectator*. In 1957 (the year of his successful libel action against *The Spectator*) Bevan had made his memorable speech at the Labour conference about sending the Foreign Secretary 'naked into the conference chamber', as a result persuading his party not to renounce the H-bomb. Bevan and Gaitskell had little in common, but the great Welsh parliamentarian would surely have been proud of his leader at the party conference following his death. The conference voted for unilateral nuclear disarmament but not before Gaitskell had made his impassioned promise 'to fight and fight again to save the party we love'.

In the same month Gilmour went to the United States as a guest of Adlai Stevenson and sent back articles for *The Spectator* on the forthcoming presidential election. Almost everyone of the liberal, or libertarian, persuasion would soon be mightily impressed by John Kennedy. But a week before the election, according to Gilmour, he was still 'vastly underrated in England. He is fighting this election on a level far higher than any known in Britain, at least for many years. His concentration on the crucial issue of America's proper role and place in the world has scarcely been equalled in a popular campaign since Gladstone in the 1870s routed the Turks in Midlothian.'

Hamilton was also in America at the same time, on Hutchinson's publishing business. He and Gilmour met for lunch in London on their return, exhilarated by the prospect of a vigorous and self-confident new president who, they hoped, would greatly assist Britain's interests in future, initially by putting pressure on France not to obstruct our application for membership of the European Common Market. According to Hamilton and others, the election of Kennedy was, for Gilmour, what today would be called 'a defining moment': the seed of his political ambition was sown in November 1960. Certainly Gilmour had no ideas of a political career when he acquired *The Spectator* in 1954, nor for several years afterwards did he entertain the notion of going into Parliament. Whether he was inspired by Kennedy to enter British political life is unclear. Gilmour's own recollection is that it was Iain Macleod who sowed the seed in 1961 when he commented to Gilmour that, after years of sniping at politicians in his journal, it was surely time he became one himself. Macleod was very much Gilmour's sort of Conservative; his encouragement would assuredly have had its influence on Gilmour. A few months later, when Gilmour had been turned down by a number of Conservative selection committees, Macleod remarked to one of his Fleet Street acquaintances: 'Of course we all want to help Ian, but what can we do for him while he has that damned albatross of a paper round his neck?' Within two years Macleod was editing the albatross himself.

Gilmour was to lose two editors, however, before the very recently ex-Conservative party chairman and leader of the House of Commons accepted the editorial chair. In Inglis's version of events, it was Gilmour's decision to seek election to Parliament which changed his attitude to *The Spectator* and caused the upset which led to Inglis's resignation in September 1961. But it was in fact only a minor contributory factor. From the time he returned from the United States, Gilmour began to grow more and more disenchanted with Inglis's running of his magazine.

Inglis and his wife were taking an early spring holiday in southern Italy (in Maratea, where they had spent their honeymoon two years before) when he received a letter from Gilmour. It 'baffled and angered me', Inglis wrote later, though what Gilmour had to say should not really have come as a surprise. The gravamen of his complaint was that *The Spectator* had become frivolous and of negligible political significance. It had no recognisable point of view, preferring instead a policy of indiscriminate criticism and employing invective for its own sake. On the last point Gilmour was particularly incensed that Levin had called Hugh Fraser a fathead in print after being warned on several occasions not to be rude about him (Fraser and Gilmour were good friends). He also upbraided Inglis for his intemperate criticism of the Press Council (which had reprimanded *The Spectator* for repeating four-letter words from the Lady Chatterley trial) and for a column of Ray's which was rude about the public relations industry. But Gilmour was most exercised that *The Spectator* was now, as he put it in a subsequent letter, 'completely divorced from the political life of the country'. The long think pieces had dried up, the magazine lacked a political correspondent and the leaders were lightweight, giving a general impression of irrelevance and a lack of involvement in serious issues. To which Inglis replied that *The Spectator*'s influence was still significant but indirect, 'through its insensible jostling of its readers' minds'.

No leader writer had been appointed to replace Gilmour since 1959, so that most leaders came to be written by Inglis himself. He acknowledged that they could be improved, but did not believe 'that the old-style leader has long to live'. Inglis often had trouble writing leaders: his wife Ruth remembered once waking up at night to find him writing one in bed, in the dark.

Inglis was so taken aback by the criticism from his proprietor that he sent him a 21-page reply. Though he did not say so, he felt that part of the reason for Gilmour's irritation was that *The Spectator* was enjoying a success for which its proprietor and recent editor could not claim the credit. Such an interpretation would almost certainly be mistaken: Gilmour may have felt himself somewhat sidelined in the heady atmosphere of radical chic of the magazine under its new editor but, more importantly and even though its finances were looking healthier, he just did not like the Inglis *Spectator*. Inglis argued that they were still politically in harmony, on the centre-left, but whereas Gilmour considered himself on the left of the Conservative party, within the two-party system, Inglis envisaged *The Spectator* representing a new, quasi-anarchic left, associated with neither party.

Their difference of opinion would never have got this far, Inglis insisted, if only Gilmour had come into the office more often and participated more in policy discussion, to which Gilmour retorted that, having given up the editorship, he wanted to let Inglis have a free hand. Inglis agreed to try to find a political correspondent: he approached David Marquand, then a leader writer on the *Guardian*, but no appointment was made. He also said he would find some more serious contributors, while commenting that during Gilmour's five years as editor, ' I do not recollect that you introduced... many contributors of any kind'.

Inglis did bring in a few more new names, such as Julian Critchley on Conservatism and John Cole on trade union affairs. He signed up Graham Greene, A.J. Ayer and one or two others to write a Spectator's Notebook, and commissioned pieces on more serious topics such as science and education. But relations between him and Gilmour would never be the same again. Inglis was quite convinced that it was Gilmour who had changed, not *The Spectator*; and when he learnt in the summer that Gilmour had put himself forward for selection as a Conservative candidate, he thought that explained everything. Of course it did not; Gilmour was much more embarrassed by *The Spectator*'s political irresponsibility than by its perceived hostility to his political interests in having opposed the government at the last election. It was for Inglis a matter of satisfaction that no MP now felt compelled to read *The Spectator*, to which Gilmour responded: 'Whatever one may think of MPs, this seems to me to be a disastrous state of affairs.'

Inglis did want to reach an accommodation with Gilmour. He enjoyed editing *The Spectator* and he was proud that contributors and readers were so enthusiastic about the magazine. It was around the time of his argument with Gilmour about *Spectator* policy that one of the magazine's most laudable campaigns was successfully concluded. This concerned the imprisonment of three Bahrainis on the island of St Helena. They were found guilty in the British-protected state of Bahrain of attempted murder of the ruler, then transported to St Helena to serve their sentences, under the terms of the Colonial Prisoners Removal Act. The bare facts, however, concealed serious irregularities: the verdict against the accused and the Order in Council to the effect that they would serve their sentences in St Helena were announced before the court, which consisted of relatives of the ruler, had even convened. Levin took up the Bahrainis' cause, writing repeatedly on the subject in *The Spectator*, with the vigorous support of a few MPs, in particular Jeremy Thorpe, Woodrow Wyatt and John Stonehouse. Many readers, including a number of clergymen, contributed to an appeal fund. In June 1961, more than four years after their imprisonment, the Bahrainis were released on a writ of habeas corpus, on the grounds that their transfer to St Helena had been illegal. *The Spectator* had played its part in reversing an injustice, and did not hesitate to chastise the government and the Foreign Secretary, Selwyn Lloyd, in particular, for their 'shocking attempts... to mislead the House of Commons and public opinion'.

By now it had been agreed, between Gilmour and Inglis, that the magazine would adopt a more positive, left-wing Conservative line. The proprietor made clear that his attempt to become a Conservative candidate would not alter *Spectator* policy, but Inglis could not accept this. For him the independence, the ideological point of *The Spectator*, had gone. He was also coming to feel that the magazine (or he?) had rather reached a dead end; he was more interested in what was appearing in the back half; and he was thinking about working more in television. The editor's secretary, Joan Baylis, noted 'signs of a slippery slope approaching' in 1961 when the weekly editorial lunch, held every Thursday in the boardroom, would often last until late afternoon, long after any outside guests had departed. This gave offence to the other staff, as did the sight of the diminutive Ray emerging from a taxi before lunch and carrying a large dish with a salmon on it. As a group, said Baylis, *The Spectator*'s editorial stars could be 'arrogant, casual or even insufferable' at these Thursday 'lunches for the boys', which of course included Whitehorn. One lunch guest, Conor Cruise O'Brien, asked Baylis why on earth Gilmour put up with it.

The invitation to Inglis, in early September, to take over the 'All Our Yesterdays' television programme from James Cameron was irresistible. He resigned his editorship, offering to stay until a successor could be found and appointed. His final day as editor was 15 February 1962, when he was presented with a copy of his last issue of *The Spectator*, with its cover head-lines reading, 'Codological — Basic Slag — Leave it for Three Months'. They were Inglis's bugbears: the first referred to worthy but boring articles, 'basic slag' to leaders, which he often longed to dispense with, and the third represented his attitude to tedious correspondence, which would answer itself if left alone for three months. As he left the building that day, Inglis gave Baylis an azalea as a farewell present.

4

THE GATHERING STORM

In 1962 *The Spectator*'s circulation figures were past their peak, advertising revenue was falling off and Ian Gilmour was urged by the managing director, H.S. Janes, to sell the magazine. There was also his own political position to consider. When Brian Inglis wrote to thank Gilmour for having made him editor, he warned him that now, as an official Conservative, he would find it hard 'to take a dispassionate view of what constitutes *The Spectator*'s attitude'. But Gilmour relished the opportunity to make the magazine politically responsible again, and his old friend Iain Hamilton agreed to leave Hutchinson and return to Gower Street as editor. (Had Hamilton declined the offer, Gilmour might well have sold *The Spectator*. In later years he was to say that he should have got rid of *The Spectator* in 1959. One may understand his feelings when, in 1989, Inglis sent him a proof of *The Spectator* chapters in his autobiography, *Downstart*. Gilmour replied, more in sorrow than in anger, that 'I had no idea that I had generated such an enormous resentment, which the passage of thirty years has clearly done nothing to assuage'. Gilmour was upset that their relationship was depicted as an adversarial one, and pointed out that Inglis's account was riddled with errors, only some of which were corrected in the published version.)

Hamilton's brief from Gilmour was to re-establish the magazine as a force in political life, holding a position on the radical, or left, wing of the Conservative party, which, in effect, was what he and Gilmour had set out to do in 1954, following another period of comparative political torpor. Hamilton was not concerned that Gilmour was preparing to enter on a parliamentary career; he had expected it for some time, and they had remained friends while he was at Hutchinson. Their political outlooks were similar, but the possibility had to be faced that, once Gilmour became an MP, *The*

Spectator might wish to take a line on some important issue which was contrary to the declared policy of a Conservative government in which Gilmour might reasonably expect to hold office in the not too distant future. What then? Hamilton suggested that Gilmour would be less embarrassed if the ownership of *The Spectator* were to be tucked away in some trust. But they agreed to deal with such a situation as and when it arose; knowing each other's minds pretty well, neither anticipated any great problem, which was naive of them. However, Gilmour did write down, for the avoidance of any doubt, some of his causes and attitudes. *The Spectator* was pro: Arab nationalism, Common Market, Kennedy, Macleod's colonial policy, the United Nations and Wolfenden (homosexual law reform); and anti: hanging, flogging, nationalisation, Franco. Hamilton was given a five-year contract and a salary of £3,500; and, at his suggestion, Inglis, whom Hamilton had brought to *The Spectator* in the first place, was invited to become a director (and indeed he continued to write fairly frequently for the magazine over the next few months).

Problems arose almost from the start. Now that *The Spectator* was resuming its role as a political weekly with a political stance, sales were expected to fall back. At a time when Conservative support in the country was at a low ebb, this was not the best moment to be espousing the Conservative cause — albeit from a centre-left position. After the Orpington by-election in March (where the Liberals overturned a Tory majority of more than 14,000 to win by nearly 8,000), *The Spectator* alienated a lot of its former Liberal support — it had, after all, advised its readers to vote Liberal less than three years earlier — with a notably patronising and smug leading article, written by Hamilton himself. The Liberals were described as an 'aimless, all-purpose wish-fulfilment machine'. The prospect of a Liberal revival was 'socially and politically pernicious... it could be more than a temporary nuisance in our political life'; it must not be allowed to upset our two-party system. However, the leader concluded, with misplaced confidence, that 'in a few months' time the government's policy at home and abroad [with particular reference to its negotiations for entry into Europe] will in general not only pay off but be seen to pay off... the Tories will have little trouble in rallying all the support they need'. Support for Britain's Common Market entry was at the top of Hamilton's political agenda in 1962.

Whether because he wanted to accommodate Gilmour, whose search for a seat was now general knowledge, or because his own political views were moving rightwards, Hamilton's *Spectator* was now becoming identified as a Conservative organ. Not only readers but contributors, too, began to drift away, disillusioned by what they saw as a Tory rag. Bernard Levin remained as deputy editor for a short while, then departed for the *Daily Mail* and was replaced by Anthony Hartley, who returned to the staff from the *Guardian*. Both Cyril Ray and the cartoonist Trog affected to find *The Spectator*'s politics distasteful and left. The house of cards, the team put together by Inglis, was falling down. But they did not all fall quite as one: Katharine Whitehorn, partly because she was facing a libel action from Willi Frischauer, continued her Roundabout column, though less regularly, until the end of November 1962. Hamilton did his best to persuade her to stay, but there was something for which she could not forgive him. At a farewell party for Levin, after drinks in the office, Hamilton invited a few of Levin's colleagues to lunch at the Garrick Club, from which, as a mere woman, Whitehorn was excluded. It was a slight which she would not forget. Having gone off to the *Sunday Telegraph* in 1961, Alan Brien in fact returned to write for Hamilton, whom he had met at a film festival in Sicily in 1951 and whom he liked and respected.

The circulation figures also took a knock when Janes insisted on abandoning a sales promotion scheme in the United States which had brought in about 4,000 cut-price subscriptions but was not showing any profit for the magazine. Sales were also adversely affected later in the year when *The Spectator*'s cover price was increased from 9d to 1/-. It was not altogether surprising that the sales figure for 1963 fell to 36,597, against 48,018 for 1961 (which included the discounted American subscriptions).

Everyone seemed to accept that circulation losses were inevitable, but Janes soon started talking darkly of the need to reduce editorial costs, the fall in advertising revenue and the likelihood of a deficit in 1963 (during Inglis's time the magazine had made an annual profit of almost £5,000). Hamilton asked for funds to be made available for a promotion campaign, but they were not forthcoming.

On the other side of the coin, however, Hamilton made some useful appointments. The distinguished theatre critic, Ronald Bryden, who had been made literary editor after Karl Miller, was succeeded in mid-1962 by

Robert Conquest, who kept on many of the left-wing reviewers but stayed in the chair for less than a year before moving to America. (During this short period he was said to have made several conquests of young ladies on the very narrow literary editor's desk. A similar story was also told of W.J. Turner, one of his predecessors.) Hamilton was so impressed by David Pryce-Jones's hostile review of Hannah Arendt's book about the Eichmann trial that he at once made him literary editor, but Pryce-Jones also moved to the United States, to take up a teaching post at the University of Iowa in 1964. Hamilton persuaded Henry Fairlie to return to *The Spectator*, brought in some talented new blood fresh from university (Malcolm Rutherford, Alastair Macdonald, Stephen Fay) and, in a notable early success in the first weeks of his editorship, he published the full text of F.R. Leavis's famous attack on C.P. Snow. Snow had given a lecture at Cambridge in 1959, 'The Two Cultures', which was becoming widely used as a sixth-form text. Leavis, also in a Cambridge lecture in February 1962, sought to demolish not only Snow's view of the two 'cultures', which contrasted the response of scientists to man's social condition with the Luddism of literary intellectuals, but also his reputation as a novelist and his prose style. It was Hartley's idea to publish Leavis's lecture in full (it ran to five pages), and it produced a copious response. Most of it was hostile to Leavis, because of the unconcealed malevolence of his attack: 'Snow not only hasn't in him the beginnings of a novelist; he is utterly without a glimmer of what creative literature is, or why it matters.' Many thought that Leavis was diminished by his diatribe; but its more lasting effect was to ruin Snow intellectually. (Pryce-Jones wanted to get Leavis to do some reviewing but, remembering an article of his about his father, 'Mr Pryce-Jones and the Decadence of British Culture', he thought he might have more success if he did not use his own name when writing to him. Pryce-Jones therefore signed his letter 'Joan Baylis' and, when Leavis insisted on calling at Gower Street to meet the literary editor, slipped out of the office and left the editorial secretary with some explaining to do.)

Hamilton published several other long pieces during 1962: by Hartley on English intellectuals, a short story by Kingsley Amis and a seminal article by Conquest on the scale of Stalin's purges of the 1930s. Here, supported by a wealth of detailed evidence, was one of the first, and most impressive, denunciations of the Soviet system and, by extension, of the Western fellow-travellers who supported it. This was six years before the publication of his book, *The Great Terror*, the first of several he was to write on Stalin. (When, after the fall of Communism, an American publisher had the idea of a new edition of the book and a new title, Conquest suggested *I Told You So, You Fucking Fools*.)

Hamilton was pleased when, in the summer of 1962, the newly founded magazine, *Private Eye*, devoted four pages to a spoof of *The Spectator* and commented: 'In the good old days of Kingsley Martin people used to read the *New Statesman* just for a good vomit. Now they read *The Spectator* just for a good vomit instead.' Parodying its attitude to the Liberals since Orpington, *The Spectator*'s diarist, Ballcock, had this to say: 'A friend of mine tells me he knows of a well-known sex maniac, who has spent most of his life on probation for interfering with small girls, who is thinking of voting Liberal at the next election. This puts in perspective, I think, the whole of this so-called Liberal "revival".' In August Gilmour wrote to Hamilton to congratulate him on the way things were going. 'The paper is now very good and respected in opinion-forming circles — which is the only real excuse for its existence.' (Sir Edward Boyle had written recently to Gilmour to tell him that *The Spectator* was much improved.)

There was good stuff at the back of the magazine too. Elizabeth David was contributing some delightful articles on food, and Alan Brien's Afterthought could be memorable. He devoted one column to bores, their characteristics and the various types of bore one might encounter. Indeed, how readily does a certain Tory politician of the 1990s come to mind on reading Brien's concluding paragraph:

> What keeps us chained to the bore who bores for England is that he is a genuine idealist. He honestly believes that without him life would be more boring. By badgering us and buttonholing us, by cornering us and distracting us, he feels he is performing a public service. And, contrary to the great rule of human behaviour that we all recognise in others our own weaknesses, the bore is all the more boring because he is never bored.

In Gower Street Hamilton, though popular, did not impress all his colleagues. Years later Inglis called Hamilton an 'ineffectual' editor; a junior member of the editorial staff said that 'he was not really up to it'. Baylis

SP * CT * T * R

NUMBER 697   FRIDAY, MARCH , 19 2   PRICE NINEPENCE

CHILDRENS
BOOKS
FROM
IRELAND

Private Eye's parody of a Spectator *cover (1 June 1962).*

remembered that he spent a great deal of his time talking, in meetings with the business staff and on the telephone. 'Talk seemed to postpone decisions, to delay dealing with the morning's letters, to put off dealing with trays loaded and overflowing with manuscripts, long overdue to be returned.' She was frustrated at the time it took him to dictate letters, and on occasion she took to providing him with tranquillisers on press day. Gilmour may not have been aware of the atmosphere in the office — Baylis wrote of 'a feeling of malaise in the air' — but he did think that Hamilton had become indecisive and difficult since their days editing *The Spectator* together in 1955–56.

In his efforts to find a seat, Gilmour had his share of rejections by local Conservative selection committees, but his ownership of *The Spectator* did not appear to count against him. He narrowly missed Hexham (a constituency in Northumberland would not really have suited him), then was adopted for Norfolk Central in the autumn of 1962. Ironically, this constituency had declined to re-adopt its MP at the 1959 election because he had opposed the government over Suez. Gilmour had a tricky time explaining his, and *The Spectator*'s, opposition to Suez over lunch at the Royal Hotel in Norwich with the lady chairman of the committee. But the passage of time worked in his favour. At the by-election in November, Gilmour was surprised, and possibly upset, that Hamilton did not go up to the constituency to support him, although it was quite reasonable that the editor should prefer to keep his distance during the campaign. Hamilton had a healthy suspicion of the political establishment, of which he did not consider Gilmour to be a member, but he may have begun to feel uneasy once his proprietor had been elected a member of the House of Commons. A colleague detected a certain coolness developing in their relationship early in 1963.

Neither the editor nor his deputy was very close to Westminster politics. Hamilton was better at writing (he was also doing a monthly theatre column for the *Times Educational Supplement*), and at picking other writers, than he was at the day-to-day business of editing. Hartley was at his best ranging from foreign to literary topics. Both of them also wrote poetry, as did Conquest, who was probably more interested in politics than the other two. The politics were covered by Fairlie, and then by David Watt, appointed political correspondent in May 1963, who came from Brussels where he had been working for the *Daily Herald*. His first piece for *The Spectator*, on being in hospital while at Oxford, paralysed by polio and fitted with an iron lung, appeared in 1955. He wrote drama criticism for the magazine in 1956–57 before moving to the *Scotsman* as diplomatic correspondent. Watt was, in shorthand, both pro-Europe and pro-America (he later spent five years as director of the Royal Institute of International Affairs). Ferdinand Mount, who edited a selection of Watt's writings, *The Inquiring Eye*, commented that his most impressive quality, as a political journalist, was 'his unswerving and sometimes unnerving integrity'. A colleague on *The Spectator* thought him a bit of a prig.

Before Watt's arrival as political correspondent, and almost for the first time in his premiership, Macmillan was starting to get plaudits from *The Spectator*. When he sacked seven of his Cabinet ministers, including the Chancellor of the Exchequer (Selwyn Lloyd) in July 1962, a leading article applauded the decisiveness of his action and the vigour of his leadership, noting with satisfaction that, following the promotion of Reginald Maudling (to Chancellor), Sir Edward Boyle, Henry Brooke and Sir Keith Joseph, 'the liberal wing of the Conservative party is now unmistakably in the ascendant'. Fairlie thought the new Cabinet one of the strongest this century; it could scarcely have been bettered even had Macmillan been able to choose from both front benches of the House of Commons. To mark the beginning of his seventh year as prime minister, in January 1963, Fairlie wrote a long encomium to a man for whom he clearly had both admiration and affection. But the anniversary gave Macmillan no cause for celebration: within days De Gaulle had rejected Britain's application to join the EEC. (The week before, Fairlie had written of 'the emergence of Mr Hugh Gaitskell as the accepted alternative prime minister'; in his article on Macmillan he doubted 'whether the country can afford Mr Gaitskell as prime minister, because of the suspicion which he now arouses in our European allies'; a week later he was dead.)

Macmillan faced his worst crisis in the summer of 1963, when his Secretary of State for War, John Profumo, was obliged to resign for having lied to the House of Commons about the nature of his relationship with a Miss Christine Keeler, who had also had an affair with a Soviet diplomat. The sex-and-security scandal exposed the prime minister to the charge that he had lost control of his government. Watt wrote that Macmillan's exit from the House of Commons after the debate which condemned his handling of the affair was one of the saddest sights in the history of British politics. 'Head more bowed, shuffle even more pronounced than usual, white as a ghost, he seemed to totter with complete finality out of the Chamber.... Was this to be the end of the road for the man who rebuilt his party after Suez, the author of the "wind of change" speech, the great Common Marketeer, the tireless correspondent of Mr Khrushchev and one of the most adroit politicians there has ever been? The cruelty of politics is no respecter of persons.'

Hamilton decided that the prime minister would have to go. It had become clear 'that morale in the Tory party could never be restored under his continuing leadership'. This annoyed Gilmour, even though Hamilton's view was shared by a clear majority of the parliamentary party. Nor did he agree with the headline on *The Spectator*'s leader which, in contrast to the *Times* and other newspapers, declared, of the Profumo affair, 'No Moral

Ian Gilmour was not happy with this portrayal of Lord Beaverbrook by Timothy Birdsall, who died of leukaemia a month later, aged 26.

Eating people is wrong.

Issue'. (The only other occasion that anyone can remember when Gilmour took strong exception to something appearing in *The Spectator* after he had become an MP concerned a cartoon of Lord Beaverbook by Timothy Birdsall. Gilmour thought it in bad taste, though some suggested he was more worried that he might be vilified in the *Daily Express*. Birdsall died of leukaemia in June 1963, aged 26.)

Anthony West wrote a memorable piece, 'McCarthy in Westminster', in which he accused the Labour leadership of employing McCarthyist tactics in 'whoring after the security issue' in order to denigrate Profumo.

> The United States, in its occasional collapses into political squalor, has never exhibited anything so despicable as the spectacle of Mr Harold Wilson leading his entire following away from serious matters to snuffle and jostle round the dirty linen from Miss Keeler's various beds in the hope of finding some easy way to power. To be precise, while America has never had a McCarthyite party ready to clamber to office up a ladder of slander, Britain has now got one.

During the course of the article, George Wigg, 'that industrious garbage-collector', came in for particular criticism, and complained that he was being compared with Senator McCarthy. *The Spectator* offered him an opportunity to reply, which he ignored, and apologised in print, saying that Wigg's interpretation of the article was incorrect. He tried for some time to get damages from the magazine, but eventually gave up.

Articles such as this were not enough to stop Gilmour becoming increasingly disenchanted with his editor. In Gilmour's mind the magazine was ailing and without an ethos. There is no question that the balance sheet was looking sickly and Janes kept urging Hamilton to reduce editorial costs, but *The Spectator* was getting compliments from Fleet Street on the improvement it had shown in recent months. In the office, however, 'the writing on the wall was there and growing more clear every day to those who looked at it,' according to Baylis's account. 'Some of us who went away [on holiday] wondered whether a crisis would be reached during our absence.'

In September, when Hamilton had returned from holiday, he was warned, according to Gilmour, verbally by him and in writing by Janes, that he should, in effect, consider his position. This Hamilton always emphatically denied. He had many conversations with Janes, who would talk gloomily about the future of *The Spectator* and complain of Gilmour's waning interest in it, but was adamant that he received no communication from Janes indicating that his job was at risk. In conversations with Gilmour, he said, the possibility of selling the magazine was sometimes discussed (Roy Thomson and Jocelyn Stevens were mentioned as possible buyers), but Hamilton was never given to understand that he might be jettisoned. In reading the memoranda which Hamilton later wrote when taking legal action against *The Spectator*, one has the impression that he was not in confident command. He seemed to spend so much of his time, during the summer and autumn of 1963, worrying about whether Gilmour would sell the magazine that he may have misread warnings about his own future which were perhaps not made plainly enough, or else were ignored because they came from a man (Janes) whom he mistrusted.

It was the financial situation which most exercised Hamilton at this time. The magazine was going into deficit; at the same time the man responsible for Spectator Publications Ltd had been fired, and a company making advertising commercials, Aspect, which was run by *The Spectator*, was reporting sharply reduced profits. Hamilton blamed Janes for all this, and for declining to retire, having just reached the age of 65. If only *The Spectator* could spend money on promotion, which for many months Janes had refused to sanction, Hamilton thought its troubles would be over. He was probably so obsessed by what he saw as Janes's obstruction and general mismanagement of the business that he quite failed to realise that his own position was in jeopardy. What is clear is that the appointment of an editor to replace him — which he first learnt from the *Evening Standard* — was, as he himself put it, 'a bolt from the blue'.

The events took place over a month (8 October–7 November) that was traumatic for the Conservative party and for *The Spectator*. MPs were assembling in Blackpool on Tuesday, 8 October for their annual conference, on the day that Macmillan was taken ill and told he would have to undergo a prostate operation. On the Thursday his resignation was announced, and Lord Hailsham told the conference he would be disclaiming his peerage. Lord Home decided over the weekend that he would be a contender for the leadership.

In the previous week's issue Hamilton had written a rather woolly leader about Macmillan's intentions, saying that when he had 'dispersed the miasma of the Profumo affair... it may be that he will hand over. But to whom? The choice seems to have narrowed, but there is still no sign of an effective consensus.' No names were given, though Hailsham, whom Gilmour admired, got a friendly mention. For the conference, however, 'absolute solidarity behind the present leader is a prime necessity for the party'.

When Hailsham threw his hat into the ring at Blackpool, Gilmour was among his most vociferous supporters. Having observed his proprietor campaigning ostentatiously for Hailsham, Hamilton decided against publishing an article on him which would have embarrassed Gilmour. He did not, however, endorse Hailsham's candidature in *The Spectator*, nor give editorial support to any of the others, which no doubt caused Gilmour some annoyance. (Gilmour and Julian Amery, who were both Hailsham supporters, made odd political bedfellows. One may wonder how *The Spectator*'s political stance might have changed had Hailsham become prime minister.)

Partly because the Wednesday deadline had to be met, *The Spectator* carried no leading articles on who should succeed Macmillan. The omission from the 18 October issue was understandable, since that was the day Lord Home was invited by the Queen to form a government, but it was somewhat perverse to have a leader on the Labour party in the 11 October issue, and on the Robbins report on higher education in the 25 October issue, yet no editorial comment on the upheavals at the top of the Conservative party. When Home became prime minister, and Iain Macleod and Enoch Powell refused to serve in his government, Fairlie wrote an article, published by *The Spectator* the following week, in which he applauded Macleod's inspired example.

Without it, the left wing of the Conservative party would have suffered not merely a defeat but a rout. 'By his action, it seems to me, he has safeguarded the Conservative party's future, and he has proved once again that he knows how to take hold of events, and create from them quite new possibilities.' Fairlie kept piling on the compliments, leaving his readers in no doubt about his opinion of Macleod. He had resigned 'with great dignity, suggesting great firmness of intent... when it had once again been proved that a Conservative party without Mr Macleod is no Conservative party at all'.

In the same week Hamilton wrote a letter to Macleod, offering *The Spectator*'s columns to him at any time he wished to express his views. Macleod replied at once, on Friday, 25 October: 'Thank you, but not yet. And probably not for a fairly long time. It will then be good to see you again.' That letter would not have been received by Hamilton in the office until after the weekend, by which time Gilmour had offered Hamilton's job to Macleod.

Briefly, the sequence of events that week was that Gilmour telephoned Macleod on the Sunday night to ask if he would like to edit *The Spectator*; they lunched the next day at an Italian restaurant, La Speranza, in Knightsbridge, when Macleod was clearly minded to accept Gilmour's offer, which he confirmed on Wednesday, 30 October. Gilmour had intended to announce the appointment in time for the Sunday papers, having, he hoped, persuaded Hamilton to stay on as Macleod's deputy or as 'executive' editor with Macleod as editor-in-chief. Gilmour was going to put this to Hamilton when they met at White's on Thursday evening (and Hamilton was going to ask him whether he had decided to sell *The Spectator*). But by then the news that *The Spectator* had a new editor was in the pages of the *Evening Standard*.

Macleod had been indiscreet and mentioned his appointment to one or two colleagues. No one can say with any certainty who then passed on the information to the *Standard*. In his biography of Macleod Robert Shepherd names Bill Deedes, then Minister without Portfolio and in charge of press relations; but Deedes denied it in the press at the time, and at a distance of over 30 years he was unsure who had been responsible. Hamilton later suspected Fairlie, who was certainly close to Macleod, and had just declared in *The Spectator* his unbounded admiration for the man whom he now saw as the next Conservative leader. Hamilton was told that Fairlie had dined with Macleod on four occasions in the week following his resignation from the government, and that Fairlie was boasting in Fleet Street that he had got

Macleod *The Spectator* job. Unlikely though this may be, Fairlie's behaviour at this time towards his old friend and mentor Hamilton was eccentric even by his own standards. He had once written to Hamilton: 'You are the first friend I made in journalism. You are in fact one of the five or six friends — not acquaintances — that I regard myself as having.' Yet when Macleod was made editor in Hamilton's place, Fairlie wrote to tell Hamilton what a brilliant appointment it was. The letter is worth quoting in full:

Dear Iain,

You — and everyone else — have obviously realised on what 'side' I would be — and, when anyone has asked me, I have openly stated my position and my views.

I have not the slightest doubt that Macleod's appointment is the best thing that has happened, and ever could have happened, not only to *The Spectator* but to weekly journalism.

The Spectator, as I said all those years ago in *Encounter*, is meant to be a political weekly inside one of the two main streams of politics in this country. Given that, I cannot see how there could be a more imaginative, more promising, or more exciting appointment than that of as trained and acute a political mind as Macleod's.

In view of these feelings (which you must have expected) I cannot with any seemliness say anything to you about other aspects of the whole affair. Nor, if I did, would you think much of anything I said.

I am not sure whether I should have written this letter at all. I cannot, of course, appear to you to justify my attitude — nor is it meant as a justification. It is intended to be only an open statement to you personally of my commitment, to which I think you are entitled.

Yours,
Henry

I expect no reply except 'SHIT' or 'BASTARD'.

Hamilton later came to refer to Fairlie as Felix, after the amoral character, Felix Krull, created by Thomas Mann.

It would always be Hamilton's contention that the idea of replacing him as editor only came to Gilmour, whether or not prompted by Fairlie, after the upheavals over the Conservative leadership. But an agreed statement in court in 1964, which announced the settlement of their differences, confirmed that Gilmour had made up his mind some three months before that a change of editor was necessary. He did not exactly want to get rid of Hamilton: they were friends, after all, and when Macleod accepted his offer, Gilmour thought this might be the ideal solution. Hamilton could surely be persuaded to play second fiddle to a future prime minister; it was not at all the same thing as replacing him with another journalist. Had Hamilton been asked before the news became public, he might have agreed to, as Gilmour put it, 'do an Oliver Poole' (who had just accepted demotion from joint chairman to vice-chairman of the party). True, Hamilton had agreed, in 1955, to be assistant editor to Gilmour, having been acting editor and believing he would be appointed editor. But this was quite different: so shocked was he at being replaced without, as he insisted, any warning that it is doubtful if Gilmour could ever have persuaded him to stay on in a subordinate capacity. Hamilton afterwards quoted Macleod's words from his famous *Spectator* article, 'The Tory Leadership', applying them to himself:

> I am sure that he would have liked me to change my mind... and I like to think that he knew I could not. For myself... it had become a matter of personal moral integrity.

Another line from *The Spectator* (the first sentence of a leader published at the beginning of 1962) would also be quoted wryly by Hamilton: 'The trouble with the Earl of Home is that he is not Mr Butler.'

If only he had been, Hamilton would not have gone to White's on the evening of 31 October to be told by his proprietor that the former Chancellor of the Duchy of Lancaster, Leader of the House of Commons and joint chairman of the Conservative party had taken his job. By this time, 6.30, Hamilton feared that the story in the *Evening Standard* must be true. But when the editor of Londoner's Diary telephoned him that morning, shortly before lunch, to ask when he would be handing over to Macleod, he could not believe what he heard. Having discussed it with his deputy, Hartley, they concluded that the *Standard* must have got the story wrong; Macleod had probably been invited to join the board of *The Spectator*, or he had agreed to purchase an interest in the magazine. But more calls came in from other newspapers during the afternoon, and Brien turned up at Gower Street having been told that Deedes was the source of the information which was now being passed round Fleet Street. Hamilton tried, without success, to speak to Gilmour. He then alerted his solicitor, Michael Rubinstein, to the still uncertain situation.

When he got to White's, Hamilton was met in the hall by Gilmour, carrying two glasses of whisky and offering profuse apologies for the way he had been treated. They sat in a corner of the billiards room and for the next hour Hamilton expressed his amazement at Gilmour's behaviour, and Gilmour his contrition, though it was not his fault that the fact of Macleod's appointment had been disclosed prematurely. Gilmour repeatedly tried to persuade Hamilton to stay on as Macleod's deputy, and Hamilton repeatedly told him it was impossible. He also referred to the financial blow that he would suffer, which prompted Gilmour to offer to help with his son's education fees. When they parted, Hamilton made his way to the Café Royal, where he had arranged to meet his wife Jean and two old friends, Mr and Mrs Timeaus. They remembered his shock and bewilderment, because he had counted Gilmour as a friend, and his increasing anger during the course of the evening. He said he had told Gilmour he intended to sue for breach of contract and damages.

That night Gilmour was interviewed on radio (the BBC's Home Service), saying that Macleod 'will remain entirely independent and will continue to say what he thinks to be right…. He has a platform in which he will put forward the views of progressive Conservatism.' The next day Hamilton gave a press conference at Gower Street, and then adjourned to the Marlborough Arms with his wife and several members of the staff. Levin, who was also there, learnt from Hamilton what had transpired the previous evening at White's and did a piece for 'That Was The Week That Was' the following night which did not please Gilmour at all. 'After 135 years of independence,' Levin said, '*The Spectator* becomes a tool in the political ambitions and intrigues of "the next prime minister but one" and his henchman, who is now also his employer.' Levin also alleged that Gilmour, during the meeting with Hamilton at White's, had referred to himself several times as 'a worm', and that his appointment of Macleod breached the terms of '*The Spectator* Trust'. It must have been particularly galling for Gilmour that his former star political writer was dishing out criticism in this way. He complained to the director-general of the BBC, Hugh Carleton Greene, and got an apology, but only in respect of factual errors about a *Spectator* trust. (An independent committee had approved the transfer to Gilmour of a majority shareholding in *The Spectator* in 1954, but it had no jurisdiction over changes of editor.)

On the same day, Saturday 2 November, *The Times* published a letter from Sir Gerald Barry, a director of the *New Statesman*:

> Newspaper ownership is a public responsibility which… must be seen to be decently discharged. The circumstance in which an editor is sacked, or a paper committed to a certain line of policy, is more than a private affair. It is for this reason that one finds the journalistic ethics currently prevailing in the proprietor's room at *The Spectator* so instructive.

A statement issued on behalf of *The Spectator*'s editorial staff was also carried in Saturday's *Times*. They wished

> to make a vehement protest at the shabby treatment meted out by the proprietor to Mr Iain Hamilton who has enjoyed our full confidence as editor. The fact that he and some of the directors of *The Spectator* were not informed of the change of editorship until it was published in the press speaks for itself. Nor has Mr Gilmour explained his action to the staff. We believe strongly that *The Spectator*, with its long and honourable history of independent opinion, should not be tossed about at the whim of the proprietor or lose its independence by identification with a narrow political faction.

The previous evening Gilmour had spoken in his Norfolk constituency, saying that he still hoped that Hamilton would stay on as deputy editor to Macleod. Speaking in a debate at Keele University on private morality and public responsibility, Inglis, who was on the board of *The Spectator*, said Hamilton had been 'disgracefully treated'.

All the publicity was sympathetic to Hamilton, but on the following Monday the *Daily Express* had a story to the effect that Hamilton should not have been surprised at Macleod's appointment because the meeting at White's had been originally arranged to discuss Gilmour's intention to sell

*This was how Gerald Scarfe saw Ian Gilmour's appointment of Iain Macleod as editor in place of Iain Hamilton (*Private Eye, *15 November 1963).*

The Spectator, due to falling circulation and revenue. It was only when Macleod agreed to take over that Gilmour decided he would keep the magazine after all. Hamilton denied this version in a press statement. When, however, on the same day, the Free Press Society offered to discuss buying *The Spectator* from Gilmour, he was quoted as saying, 'I am no longer interested in parting with *The Spectator*. I now have no thought whatever of selling.' From which it is clear that he had, at the very least, thought about selling before Macleod came along.

Amis had meanwhile been busy gathering names for a letter of protest, which duly appeared in the *Daily Telegraph* of 8 November, above 23 signatures, among them Sir Denis Brogan, Clive Barnes, Isabel Quigly, Simon Raven, Olivia Manning, Angus Wilson, J.H. Plumb, Robert Conquest and John Vaizey.

Sir — As regular contributors to *The Spectator*, we feel that the paper's honourable tradition of independence has been seriously compromised by the recent action of its proprietor. By appointing an active contender for the leadership of the Conservative party as editor in place of a non-partisan journalist of high standing, Mr Ian Gilmour has gravely damaged one of the few remaining journals of free opinion.

Many other contributors, friends and admirers — well over a hundred in all — sent letters to Hamilton, expressing sympathy, shock, outrage, etc. He must have been particularly touched to hear from Peter Fleming that he liked Hamilton's *Spectator* 'better than any of its recent predecessors', and from Nicholas Davenport that 'of all the *Spectator* editors I have known you have been outstanding in the encouragement you have given to independent writers like myself'. Elizabeth David wrote to thank him for the enormous help he had given her, and Murray Kempton in Washington told Hamilton that *The Spectator* had been 'the pleasantest professional association of my life, and that is something I owe to you'.

In Gower Street that first week of November Baylis had been put in mind of 'a tidal wave crashing through the door of number 99'. Journalists from Fleet Street besieged the office — one was found wandering about on the top floor of the building — and several contributors hung about, hoping to pick up titbits of information for *Private Eye*. Peter Usborne, the business manager of *Private Eye*, said the magazine was offering a £5,000 post to Enoch Powell, who had just resigned his job as Minister of Health, because it 'did not want him to feel left out'. Many of the large number of telephone calls and letters from people anxious to take sides fell to be answered by Baylis, 'until my head reeled and my nerves quivered'. (One of the calls, as reported by Strix in A Spectator's Notebook, under the heading 'Ace Newshawk Probes Drama', came from a journalist asking how the new editor spelt his surname.) At a board meeting held on the Thursday a policeman patrolled the pavement in Gower Street as journalists waited impatiently outside the locked front door.

During the week it emerged that the two executive directors, Janes and F.G. Elliot (company accountant), had been informed by Gilmour of the change of editor the day before Hamilton, who was also a director, learnt the news. Sir Evelyn Wrench, still chairman of the board at the age of 81, said it was 'an unfortunate experience' when he first heard, on the television news, that Macleod had been made editor. He thought it might be time for him to retire. Inglis resigned at the end of the board meeting, reiterating his support for Hamilton and belief in his version of events, but Wrench agreed to continue as chairman. 'I have every confidence in Gilmour; and I voted for Macleod,' he said afterwards.

It was Wrench's idea, in 1928 while he was proprietor and editor, to provide in *The Spectator*'s articles of association that no one should become the holder of more than 49 per cent of the voting shares unless he was approved as 'a proper person' by an independent committee. When the committee met in November 1954 and gave its approval to Gilmour, it was presided over by Victor Mishcon, lawyer and then chairman of the London County Council. Mishcon now took it upon himself to write to the *Times* to point out that he gave his blessing to Gilmour on the understanding that he had no intention of entering the House of Commons. 'I feel that it is only right for me to record that I for my part would not have voted as I did had I for one moment thought that he would become an MP as a contestant for one of the national political parties and that he would thereafter seek to appoint the recent chairman of that national political party as editor.' It was a letter of Goodmanesque gravitas; but when, two days later, Wrench, who had appointed the committee, said that he had written to congratulate Gilmour on his decision to seek election to Parliament, it seemed to lose some of its importance. As chairman of *The Spectator*, Wrench also stated that 'since Mr Gilmour acquired a controlling interest in 1954 the independence of *The Spectator* has been plain for all to see. Mr Iain Macleod has recently demonstrated his independence in the most convincing manner.'

Hamilton read out a personal statement to the board at the Thursday meeting, in anticipation of what he had gathered during the week: that Gilmour and Janes were saying that he was aware well before the end of October that he was likely to be dismissed on grounds of incompetence. This was indeed spelt out in a statement made by the board and released to the press, which was of course immediately refuted by Hamilton. (It was published in full in *The Spectator* on 15 November.) The relevant paragraph read:

> The decision to appoint a new editor was not made in haste but after careful consultation between Mr Gilmour and the other two executive directors

which had been going on for several months. Deliberations on the future of the paper took place and the possibility of a change of editor was discussed by Mr Gilmour and Mr Hamilton on 17 September and by the managing director and Mr Hamilton on 27 September. The Board wish to emphasise that this decision was taken long before there was any question whatever of Mr Iain Macleod becoming editor of *The Spectator*.

Clearly Gilmour was concerned to show that he did not decide on a change of editor in order to ingratiate himself with Macleod. (He had, however, been acting somewhat impetuously. During the course of ten days he had been campaigning for Hailsham, whose political line was not exactly *The Spectator*'s, to run the country and then for Macleod to run his magazine for him.) He also wanted to correct the impression put about by Hamilton that he had had no warning of what was to come. In so doing, however, he became the recipient of a libel writ from Hamilton, who was, and was to remain, adamant that he had never been given to understand that he would be replaced as editor. It is hard to arrive incontrovertibly at the truth of the matter, and in particular of the nature of the warnings that may have been given to Hamilton in September. Gilmour, with his natural courtesy and a tendency to appear diffident in conversation, may have mentioned to Hamilton the possible alternatives of selling *The Spectator* or changing editors, but in such a way that Hamilton was led to believe that a sale was the only serious possibility because, as he thought, Gilmour had lost interest in *The Spectator* since being elected an MP. Janes was not a transparently honest man — Hartley referred to him as 'an inefficient executive and an efficient intriguer' — and may well not have given Hamilton any clear indication that his job was under threat. Even if he had, Hamilton was so distrustful of Janes that he might not have believed him. If Hamilton did understand the import of what had been said to him in September, the likelihood is that he chose to ignore it, convincing himself that it would not come to pass.

In the course of the legal actions which Hamilton pursued against Gilmour, written statements from Hartley and Brien confirmed, from their own observations on 31 October, that when he learnt from the *Evening Standard* that he had lost the editorship to Macleod, Hamilton was quite incredulous. When Brien asked him whether the story was true, he remembered his exact words: 'No, of course not. How can it be? It's inconceivable.' Hartley said that, as an old friend and confidant, Hamilton would unquestionably have told him if he thought his position was insecure. 'As it was, it was only a change of ownership that was ever discussed between Mr Hamilton and myself with regard to the future of the paper.'

There was little hope of resolving the change of ownership/editorship discussions without going to court; and perhaps not even then. Both sides wanted to settle, after the heat generated in the first week of November had begun to subside; and a figure of £12,500 was accepted in the summer of 1964, to cover both the breach of contract (which had another three years to run) and the alleged libel. An agreed statement was made in the High Court on 29 July by Hamilton's counsel, Lord Gardiner, QC. As is common with such statements, which have to satisfy both parties, there were lawyers' references to unfortunate misunderstandings and complete sincerity on all sides. On the question of the warnings allegedly given to Hamilton by Gilmour and Janes on two separate occasions in September, to the effect that they were looking for an editor to replace him, it was said that, 'Unfortunately Mr Hamilton understood neither conversation in the sense intended'. (But he did understand, according to Gilmour's account of their meeting at White's on 31 October, that he had twice been given some sort of warning.) It was stated, publicly for the first time, that Gilmour and two executive directors (Janes and Elliot) had decided in principle, on 2 August 1963, that a change of editor should be made. As Gilmour commented later, the agreed statement in open court was if anything less favourable to Hamilton than the one made by the board in respect of which he brought the libel action. However, personal animosity between Gilmour and Hamilton was not long-lived; over subsequent years they resumed their friendship and lunched regularly. (Inglis and Gilmour, on the other hand, met again only once or twice over the next 25 years. And it took Gilmour a while to forgive Levin, not only for his hostility on television but for doing his utmost to persuade several *Spectator* contributors not to write for the magazine again.)

Hamilton freelanced from 1964 onwards; in the 1970s he ran the Forum World Features agency for a time with Brian Crozier, with whom — an illustration of his move to the political right — he also worked at the Institute for the Study of Conflict. In 1957 he had written a delightful book, *Scotland the Brave*; his last book, a biography of Arthur Koestler published in 1982, caused him many problems, largely because his subject, who committed suicide in 1983, proved unco-operative and litigation was threatened. But before that Hamilton had published two volumes of poetry: *Embarkation for Cythera* and, with Ann Thomas, *The Kerry Kyle*. In a preface to the first volume his friend John Betjeman — the Hamiltons lived at the house in Highgate where Betjeman had spent his childhood — wrote, in Gaelic and English:

> Oh, Iain, my old and faithful friend:
> There is joy in me because of you.
>
> I like your poems: they are Scottish and gritty and Glaswegian. You have an
> eye for landscape and an ear for rhythm and rhyme — and a heart.

Whether in prose or verse, it was writing that Hamilton was best at; and he was passionate about both Scotland's and Ireland's Gaelic traditions. With Inglis and Robert Kee, he was a founder member of the British Irish Association. Not long before he died in 1986, Hamilton converted to the Catholic faith.

5

MINISTERIAL INTERLUDE

Iain Macleod was, of course, too shrewd a politician to make any public comment, during the first week of November 1963, on the upheavals at *The Spectator* for which, by agreeing to take the job, he was unwittingly responsible. But it was inevitable that, among all the press coverage, some criticism would be directed at him. Comparisons were invited between the man who had been so shocked at the intrigues that led to the appointment of Lord Home as prime minister and the same man who, a few days later, was happy to be the beneficiary of dealings which left a similarly bad taste in the mouth. In the *Daily Mirror* Cassandra commented that Macleod had got the job 'in grimy circumstances that many people would refuse to be associated with'. It was said that *The Spectator* might be used for a sinister purpose: to harass the new prime minister, then put Macleod in power with Gilmour at his side. On the question of his journalistic experience, one or two sceptics wondered in print whether the writing of a bridge column (for the *Sunday Times*) had quite prepared him for the burdens of editorship.

On 5 November Macleod joined the board of Lombard Banking, and the following day made an eve-of-poll speech in support of Sir John Fletcher-Cooke at the Luton by-election. He did not in fact spend his first day in the office until 2 December, but before then he met most of the editorial staff individually at his flat in Sloane Court. Joan Baylis had been under considerable strain for the fortnight before Macleod asked her to call on him. She was close to tears as she made her way to Chelsea and swallowed a couple of tranquillisers to prepare for her ordeal, expecting to be told that she was to be replaced by Macleod's own secretary. But as soon as he greeted her on the doorstep, 'in the way I came to know so well — the outstretched hand, the cheery smile, and the clear high voice — tension eased in the calm and welcoming atmosphere'. They dealt quickly with relevant correspondence which had been sent to his flat, and a week later Baylis called again. When Macleod was installed at 99 Gower Street, she described his office, which was the boardroom and not the editor's room, as 'a haven of tranquillity and efficiency in which I could breathe'.

Of the other staff who visited Sloane Court during November, all would remain in their jobs with the exception of Anthony Hartley, the deputy editor, who decided to leave after a few weeks, partly in sympathy with Iain Hamilton and also because he thought that an independent journal should not be edited by a prominent politician. (It was to happen again, in 1970, with much less fuss, when Richard Crossman, who had been a minister in Harold Wilson's government, became editor of the *New Statesman*. Macleod was the better editor.) Hartley stayed to look after the four November issues produced while *The Spectator* was, in effect, editorless, including the Christmas number which, among articles by Richard Ingrams, John Betjeman and Clement Freud, published several poems under the title 'Dreams', by the recently unnobled Quintin Hogg. This issue, with a special cover on glossy paper, showing highly coloured owls flying against a dark blue night sky, had had to go to press early. Following the tragedy of 22 November, there was time only to affix to the cover a black and white sticker which announced, baldly and incongruously across the festive owls' wings: 'DEATH OF PRESIDENT KENNEDY'. Hartley wrote the leader, 'Death of a Modern', paying tribute to a man who represented the future. The following week (6 December), Macleod's first as editor, he wrote another leader on Kennedy; but it was also a statement of his own radical Tory beliefs. Kennedy's death, he wrote, had given us the duty to be 'more urgent in our support for the causes for which Kennedy fought. To be more contemptuous of the bigots of right and left alike... to be more urgent in insisting on the brotherhood of man — in Africa or Asia, Alabama or Britain.' It was for the citizen to show a greater determination to serve, and for the government to establish its priorities: 'Education, especially higher education, housing and slum clearance, aid both at home and to the Commonwealth'. In the same week Macleod wrote the Notebook, at once giving notice to his readers that he much preferred George Brown to Harold Wilson, and that he was a keen sporting fan. (Cricket was his first love, and Gary Sobers and Freddie Trueman his heroes.) In this Notebook he also announced new features by old *Spectator* contributors, such as Randolph S.

Churchill: 'Randolph is Randolph is Randolph' was how he reintroduced him. During Macleod's early weeks his acolyte Henry Fairlie wrote the shorter second and third leaders. On 13 December the editor wrote the first of several leaders he was to contribute on Africa (on Kenya's independence); and in the same issue he adopted the pseudonym of Quoodle for A Spectator's Notebook. (The name was taken from Chesterton: 'And Quoodle here discloses / All things that Quoodle can.')

Towards the end of Macleod's first day at *The Spectator*'s offices, he rang Baylis on the internal telephone to ask, 'Can I go now?' She was at once disarmed by his friendliness and informality, and delighted that — in welcome contrast to his predecessor — all correspondence and other business were dealt with immediately and without any wasting of words. As a rule, Macleod was at Gower Street only in the morning; most afternoons he would be at the House of Commons. With his directorship of Lombard Banking came a chauffeur-driven car, which he used to get to and from *The Spectator*.

Some surprise was expressed initially that he chose to use the board-room, which had been Gilmour's office, rather than the room which was traditionally the editor's office. The relationship between them was slightly odd: here was the neophyte MP paying the annual salary (£5,000, for which Macleod was very grateful) of a senior ex-minister accustomed to having a large office. So it was perhaps only natural that he should install himself in the 'ministerial' office at Gower Street. But he certainly did not shut himself in there: the door was open, and staff and contributors were encouraged to call him by his Christian name. One newspaper wrote of the atmosphere of 'dour industry' now prevailing at *The Spectator*. But this was far from the truth; though the criticism was made in the office that Macleod initially ran *The Spectator* by diktat, with scant consideration for the books and arts pages, the mood was lively and optimistic. True, the jolly editorial lunches came to an end, but this was largely because Macleod was not much of a socialiser. At *The Spectator*'s parties he would put in only a brief appearance. It was not that he was unfriendly or felt himself superior; but he was no good at small talk. He could appear brusque, but anyone talking or listening to him was impressed by the way he would focus his attention powerfully on them. If conversations with the editor tended to be brief and to the point, there could be other reasons for this: he might be anxious to listen to the Test Match on the radio in his office, or he might be in intense pain.

Macleod had been injured in the thigh in 1940, during the retreat to Dunkirk, which left him with a limp. But his greater disability was caused by an inflammatory disease affecting his spine which, together with arthritis, made it impossible for him to turn his head without also moving the upper half of his body. At times the pain was so bad that he would lapse into silence. Alan Watkins, who took over from David Watt as political correspondent in October 1964, was one of many who found it disconcerting 'when his silences came down like a fog'. This might happen when they were lunching together. 'The course to follow, as I discovered by a process of trial, was either to remain silent too, which Macleod did not seem to mind at all, or else to carry on talking as if nothing had happened. The course not to follow was to say something like, "Are you sure you're quite all right?" or to send for a glass of water.' At lunch, perhaps in part to dull the pain, Macleod enjoyed alcohol. Gilmour remembered him drinking the best part of a bottle of port at their regular Tuesday lunches at the White Tower.

Macleod was not what would be called today a hands-on editor. He abolished the editorial conference, made only rare visits to the printers in Aldershot on press day, and did not do much commissioning of articles, though he was responsible for bringing in some good journalists. One newcomer to journalism appointed by Macleod was Hilary Spurling, just down from Oxford, who began by writing one or two pieces on lighter subjects such as ballroom dancing. Macleod asked her to do an article on all-in wrestling, which he much enjoyed watching on television, and find out whether the contests were fixed. Knowing nothing about the sport, she asked him for guidance. Seated at his desk, Macleod proceeded to contort his body, agitate his arms and make grunting noises in what Spurling came later to recognise as a wrestling hold known as the Indian deathlock. After her article ('Does the Kidney Squeeze Hurt?') had been published, she was offered the job of arts editor and joined the staff, remaining until 1970. Hilary Spurling remembers Macleod with great admiration and affection, comparing him to an oak tree, but one that was covered with ivy, as his disabilities sapped his strength. His kindness and charm, she said, made you want to work for him; and he always gave staff and contributors a free rein.

This enabled him to tell friends and parliamentary colleagues, somewhat disingenuously, that he could not be held responsible for what appeared in the magazine. During his time as editor Macleod published contributions from Canon Collins, Clement Attlee and George Brown. The idea of appointing a socialist (Watkins) as his political correspondent clearly appealed to him. When Macleod died in 1970 Watkins's predecessor, Watt, wrote that Macleod had been 'fantastically generous in allowing me to express views which he regarded as dangerously heterodox'. He got on well, too, with other contributors not of his own political persuasion, in particular the City columnist, Nicholas Davenport. At the time of the general election Macleod felt constrained to state, in a leader, that he did not necessarily share the political views of his political and financial correspondents. And in the Quoodle column he once wrote that, while in his early days as editor it used to worry him if the back of the magazine (Davenport) contradicted the views expressed in the leader, 'now it worries me if it doesn't'.

The writing gave Macleod much pleasure — the Quoodle paragraphs which he often wrote at weekends, either in bed or while watching sport on television, as much as, if not more than, the leaders which ruffled feathers at Westminster. According to Watkins, a noted arbiter of prose style, Macleod did not write as politicians customarily do; he 'was very close to being a real writer. Certainly he was a journalist of considerable technical accomplishment, being able to pen short and easily understandable sentences without producing a jerky or staccato effect.'

An article which he wrote to mark the 20th anniversary of D-Day, describing his own experience of the invasion, was not only a fine piece of writing but also revealing of his own character.

> Perhaps I was helped by my early voyages on the Minch, but I slept soundly enough through the rough night, and came on deck somewhere around first light. The waves were still choppy and the landing was going to be a hazardous and in part a haphazard affair. But the day was becoming warm. The coast of Normandy began to take shape through the haze. And then as full light began to come one saw the ships and the planes. It was a sight so paralysing that tears came to my eyes. It was as if every ship that had ever been launched was there, and even as if the sea had yielded up her wrecks. It was as if every plane that had ever been built was there, and, so it seemed

in fantasy, as if the dead crews were there too. There had never been since time began such a rendezvous for fighting men: there never will be again. And I remember reciting, not in scorn, but out of sheer delight at being part of that great company in such a place, 'And gentlemen in England now abed...'

Major Macleod was on the planning staff of the 50th (Northumbrian) Division, to which he was very proud to belong. When he got ashore:

> The beach was alive with the shambles and the order of war. There were dead men and wounded men and men brewing tea. There were men reorganising for a battle advance, and men doing absolutely nothing. There were even some German prisoners waiting patiently for heaven knows what. There was a whole graveyard of wrecked ships and craft and tanks of every size. It was like an absurdly magnificent film by Cecil B. de Mille. It was like war.

In the same issue of *The Spectator*, under his Quoodle pseudonym, Macleod disclosed that, a few days after landing in Normandy, he had made a book on the Derby (which was run that year on 17 June at Newmarket). Since most of his punters knew nothing about horse-racing, they bet by name association. When Ocean Swell won at 28–1, and Happy Landing came third at 22–1, bookie Macleod was obliged to pay out substantially more than he had taken in bets.

When Winston Churchill died in January 1965, Macleod recorded how he was much moved both by the lying-in-state in Westminster Hall and the service held at Harrow, Winston's public school. His admiration for Churchill — was there something Churchillian in the fact that Macleod was inclined to spend much of Sunday in bed, writing speeches and articles? — was given full expression in the leader he wrote just before the great man died:

> No doubt the legend of his life will grow in the telling, but he was in fact often held in disdain by his political party, he was often defeated, he was often wrong. Certainly but generously wrong about the abdication of Edward VIII, probably wrong over India, possibly wrong over the Dard-

anelles. He was a lovable fallible man. If the taxi that injured him so gravely in New York in 1931 had killed him, his life would have been written as one of promise unfilled, one of the many that stopped short of greatness. But he lived to keep his tryst with destiny in 1940. Nothing else weighs in the scale against that one colossal contribution to the cause of freedom everywhere. And again it must be proclaimed. We live as free men, we speak as free men, we walk as free men because a man called Winston Churchill lived. Of no other man since time began can that be said. And, as we waited and prayed, there was no more to be said.

Exactly a year earlier, Macleod was held in such disdain by his own party that his chances of ever becoming its leader seemed to have evaporated. In the issue of *The Spectator* dated 17 January 1964 (the biggest-selling single issue ever published), Macleod wrote an article entitled 'The Tory Leadership'. It was prompted by Randolph Churchill's book, just published, which in effect gave Macmillan's version of events the previous October, when Home had succeeded him as prime minister. This so enraged Macleod that he decided he would have to break ranks and break his silence, to give his account of what really happened, within what he termed the 'magic circle', to deny Rab Butler the leadership.

In early January Macleod was giving lunch at White's to J.W.M. (John) Thompson, a political feature writer on the *Evening Standard*, with a view to offering him the job of deputy editor, which had been vacant since Hartley's departure the previous month. When the conversation turned to Randolph Churchill's book on how Home became prime minister, Thompson commented that Macleod ought to review it in *The Spectator*. 'Oh yes, I'm going to,' he replied with a broad smile; 'Macleod speaks — there'll be a row.' 'IAIN MACLEOD WHAT HAPPENED' were the only words on the cover of that 17 January issue, together with photographs of the principal losing contenders for the leadership above a picture of Home. The row which followed was greater than Macleod had foreseen.

This was the last time that a Conservative leader would be chosen by what Macmillan called the 'customary processes of consultation'. Macleod's article paved the way for Edward Heath's election as leader by his fellow MPs in 1965, but at the time of its publication very few people thanked him for it. His disclosures were truly sensational: that, on the day

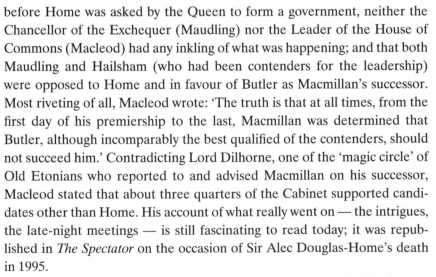

SPECTATOR

NUMBER 7073   FRIDAY, JANUARY 17, 1964   PRICE ONE SHILLING

No single issue of The Spectator *has ever sold more copies than this one.*

IAIN MACLEOD

WHAT HAPPENED

before Home was asked by the Queen to form a government, neither the Chancellor of the Exchequer (Maudling) nor the Leader of the House of Commons (Macleod) had any inkling of what was happening; and that both Maudling and Hailsham (who had been contenders for the leadership) were opposed to Home and in favour of Butler as Macmillan's successor. Most riveting of all, Macleod wrote: 'The truth is that at all times, from the first day of his premiership to the last, Macmillan was determined that Butler, although incomparably the best qualified of the contenders, should not succeed him.' Contradicting Lord Dilhorne, one of the 'magic circle' of Old Etonians who reported to and advised Macmillan on his successor, Macleod stated that about three quarters of the Cabinet supported candidates other than Home. His account of what really went on — the intrigues, the late-night meetings — is still fascinating to read today; it was republished in *The Spectator* on the occasion of Sir Alec Douglas-Home's death in 1995.

The day after the article was published, Macleod went to Twickenham to watch the England v. Wales match. He was besieged by the press, eager for his further thoughts on the Conservative party, but he said only that he was hoping for a draw, which would help Scotland. In the following week's issue (a particularly good one, with articles by George Brown, Ninette de Valois, Goronwy Rees and A.P. Herbert) Watt reported that Macleod's account 'seemed to the party a monstrous treason'. The Letters page carried a number of comments, most of them hostile to the editor. Two telegrams were printed: 'WHAT A NASTY LITTLE BIT OF WORK YOU ARE STOP FIRST NOTICED YOUR EYES AT THE BLACKPOOL CON-FERENCE ON TELEVISION STOP' and one from the film-producing Boulting brothers, who congratulated Macleod on his integrity. Another letter, from the Service Women's Club, referred to the importance of loy-alty — 'Without this a man is a very poor thing' — and a correspondent from Westmorland wrote tellingly: 'By your recent remarks and behaviour we trust that you will always remain a spectator.'

It would not have been in Macleod's character to suppress such criti-cisms, but he was clearly shocked and upset at the strength of the reaction to his article. As Nigel Fisher puts it in his biography of Macleod: 'It was widely thought that he had heaped disloyalty upon disloyalty; that having first cooked his goose, he had now stuffed it with sour grapes.' He was cen-sured by his constituency party, shunned in his Yorkshire home town of Skipton, and a 'brains trust' in Birmingham was boycotted by three Tory MPs due to appear with him. After staying away from the House of Com-mons for about a fortnight, Macleod was taken into the smoking-room by Humphry Berkeley and cut dead by everyone there. He was very depressed: having convinced himself that it was his duty to refute Macmillan's version of events, he expected more support within the party. As he was accus-tomed to bear almost constant physical pain, so he was able to endure the hurt of his rejection with fortitude and self-control. But the emotion which he also unquestionably felt over the manner of appointing the new prime minister may well have caused him momentarily to overlook the Conserva-tives' dictum about loyalty being their secret weapon and the fact that a gen-eral election was only a few months away. (Nigel Lawson, who was then special assistant to the prime minister and would be editing *The Spectator* himself within two years, remembers how much Macleod's article upset Douglas-Home and dampened his otherwise buoyant spirits.) When

Macleod came to survey the aftermath, he saw the prospects of ever succeeding to the leadership of his party disappear out of the window of his *Spectator* office. And yet, as a gambler, there was a part of him that relished the uncertainty of his political future. 'The Conservative party always in time forgives those who were wrong,' he wrote one week. 'Indeed often, in time, they forgive those who were right.' Right or wrong, he came to regret his refusal to serve in Douglas-Home's government. Yet he was back in the Shadow Cabinet before the end of 1964 and was being urged by Gilmour and others to put himself forward for the leadership when Douglas-Home stood down. Had he lived to prove himself a successful Chancellor, he might, in his early sixties, have been favourite to succeed Heath in 1975.

There had been plenty of requests for interviews and photographs when Macleod first arrived at Gower Street; now the journalists were back again in force. Gilmour had said he wanted *The Spectator* to be more talked about; he could not have asked for more. The issue of 17 January was reprinted in order to meet the demand; requests came from numerous newspapers — national, provincial and foreign — to republish the article; others reprinted large chunks of it without permission or payment. Although no record is available, the sale of that week's issue probably exceeded 75,000. The author of the book which prompted Macleod's article did not seem overly concerned that his account had been so directly contradicted. Churchill had a dig at Macleod in the *Evening Standard*, recalling a conversation with him at Blackpool when he (Macleod) apparently said he rather fancied himself as the 'dark horse' in the leadership race, then sent in his press column as usual to his *Spectator* editor, in which he rebuked Cassandra and the *Daily Mirror* for 'a masterpiece of misinformation' in its interpretation of what Macleod had written the week before. In the same issue (24 January) Churchill was taken to task by Conor Cruise O'Brien for his intemperate attacks on the *Times*, and by the editor of the *Daily Worker* for having said that that paper had reviewed his book when it in fact had stated that a review was not possible because no copy of the book had been received.

Macleod would write later that his relationship with Churchill was both stormy and affectionate. It was often carried on, by Churchill, by telegram or on the telephone late at night. On one of his weekend visits to Churchill at East Bergholt in Suffolk, Macleod saw his quarterly telephone bill, which was well over £1,000. In December 1964, in a Quoodle paragraph headed 'Life Without Randolph', Macleod commented that having sent his press columnist 'the gentlest of remonstrances' for failing to produce his copy for two weeks out of the last three, Churchill had announced on American television that he had been sacked.

> Being without Randolph is like being without an aching tooth, a gentleman at arms, a torturer and a trumpeter. Randolph is a bladder of lard, and the stoutest of friends. He talks better (and louder) than anyone I know. I have a wholly irrational affection for him, which has survived everything. With a little bit of luck it should survive this paragraph.

Churchill fired back a letter the following week, making no acknowledgment of Macleod's affection, but instead accusing him of 'Quoodle-faking', because in the course of his gentle remonstrance he had proposed that 'we should call the engagement off'. But their relationship did survive: in September 1965 Churchill was writing again for *The Spectator*. One article began: 'Mr Quintin Hogg is a brilliant advocate: indeed I have retained him for a forthcoming libel action; but he is not a very skilful political controversialist.' When Churchill was about to have a lung operation, Macleod, in the Quoodle column, was moved once again to write of the man he had accused in *The Spectator* of writing a bad book and then 'sacked'. 'It was an unforgettable sight to see him in hospital early this week on the eve of a major operation, dictating his column for *The Spectator*, dispensing Pol Roger 1955 and instructing his surgeons on the conduct of the operation.' When he died in 1968, his former editor and sparring partner described him as 'a great, if somewhat unpredictable journalist', with overwhelming charm. 'No one can take his place, he was irreplaceable.'

Macleod enjoyed the opportunity which the Quoodle column gave him to make a bit of mischief. His dislike of Harold Wilson (who respected Macleod as a potential election winner for the Tories) was, he admitted, irrational; but he could not resist telling stories against him. Macleod was in Edinburgh for the rugby one Saturday in March 1964, while Wilson was there to make a political speech. 'I have often done silly things. I have often realised that I was in the wrong place at the wrong time,' Quoodle wrote. 'But never have I seen anyone look so absurdly out of place as did the leader of the Opposition when, followed by a dour crowd of retainers, he came into the jampacked North British hotel before lunch on Saturday. There was a moment of disbelief as the incredible news was passed round that he was going to make a speech in the Usher Hall on the afternoon of the Calcutta Cup game. "He'll lose every vote in Scotland," said one of Scotland's most capped internationals.' Macleod also took repeatedly against Sir Hugh Carleton Greene, director-general of the BBC, which he would refer to as a left-wing institution. When the issue of commercial radio came up, Macleod gave it his backing in *The Spectator*; he was also in favour of televising Parliament.

The subject to which Macleod devoted most words during his two-year editorship was Africa. During his controversial stint as Colonial Secretary (1959–61), the movement for independence gained momentum. Having negotiated self-governing constitutions for Nyasaland (Malawi) and Northern Rhodesia (Zambia), bitterly opposed by Sir Roy Welensky, prime minister of the Central African Federation, Macleod had much to say about the future of Southern Rhodesia which, under Ian Smith, unilaterally declared its independence a few weeks before he left *The Spectator* at the end of 1965. His views on the pace of advance towards African majority rule — the risk of terrible bloodshed would be much greater, he said, if the process were to be delayed — brought him into conflict with a few ministers, such as Home and Duncan Sandys. But it was a former colleague in Macmillan's Cabinet, Lord Salisbury, who publicly accused Macleod, in the House of Lords, of creating a crisis of confidence in negotiations over Africa, by being 'too clever by half'. Three years later Macleod wrote a signed leader criticising Salisbury's 'paternal philosophy' and explaining his own policy on independence for Africa. This elicited a reply from Hatfield House, denouncing Macleod for abandoning our former colonies to one-party government, Communism and the police state, to avoid the risk of bloodshed. 'Well, it is of course always possible for those who abandon the field on the day of battle to say proudly: "I wasn't hurt, neither were any of the enemy." But the battle will have been lost, all the same.' Macleod weighed in again, a few weeks later, with a withering review of Welensky's book on the 4,000 days of the federation: 'He has learned nothing, he wants to learn nothing of the new Africa.'

Undoubtedly Macleod was at his most radical on Africa; he envisaged the brotherhood of man rather differently from some of his political colleagues. African leaders would come to Gower Street to pay their respects or to consult the former Colonial Secretary. Leo Baron, a liberal lawyer in Salisbury, reported for *The Spectator* from Southern Rhodesia, and Keith Kyle wrote from East and West Africa. On other, domestic issues Macleod was not so predictably progressive as his young proprietor, Ian Gilmour, who years later was categorised by Macleod's widow as 'so wet you could shoot snipe off him'.

While John Thompson, as deputy editor, was putting the magazine together each week, Macleod recruited other foreign correspondents: Drew Middleton, Don Cook, both in Paris, whom he had met when in government, and he continued to make good use of Murray Kempton in Washington and Sarah Gainham in Bonn. He doubled Malcolm Rutherford's salary as foreign editor, and encouraged him to do something else in addition to his *Spectator* job (he started a Latin-American newsletter). Watkins began to write for the magazine during the general election period and, when Watt moved to Washington to work for the *Financial Times*, took over as political correspondent two weeks after the Labour party was returned to power with an overall majority of four.

For four weeks over the election Macleod took to signing his leaders. His first, headed 'Mr H. Dumpty', attacked Mr H. Wilson's plan to nationalise steel against the wishes of Labour voters (Macleod would become Opposition spokesman on steel after the election). In another week he posited the Conservatives as the modernising party; and on election day *The Spectator*'s cover had two logos, one upside down at the bottom of the page, and a caricature drawing of Douglas-Home or, if you turned it round, of Wilson. Macleod's leader was written with true journalistic professionalism, to cover a Tory or a Labour victory, and it ended with words which might have come from one of his rousing conference speeches:

> We, and we alone, belong to the Commonwealth, to the Atlantic Alliance and to the European continent. We cannot keep, much less use, this influence, unless in all things we are up-to-date with our institutions, our methods, our industry, above all our thinking. We are still content with much because it was good enough for our grandfathers.
>
> No man can or should lead this country unless he is prepared to bulldoze

his way through the road blocks to progress: not for the sake of change but because Change is our Ally.

For all that he had been campaigning for the re-election of a Tory government, it was hard to imagine that Macleod was thinking of his patrician leader, Douglas-Home, when he wrote that last sentence. During the campaign Macleod's Quoodle column carried the heading 'A Participant's Notebook' in place of 'A Spectator's Notebook'. The idea for this can be attributed to Robert Conquest who, in the week before Macleod took over the editorial reins in December 1963, signed off his Spectator's Notebook thus: 'I understand that there is no truth in the suggestion that this column will in future be called A Participant's Notebook.' (Conquest had to apologise to Macleod in the *Listener* at the end of January 1964, for having given a Third Programme talk entitled 'Raise the double standard high!', which was 'understood as containing imputations against Mr Macleod's standards of conduct and in particular of insincerity in his attitude to Mr Iain Hamilton'. When Macleod sought to exaggerate the extent of the apology he had received, Conquest threatened to withdraw it.)

In November Macleod commented on the art of making a maiden speech to the House of Commons. He would have enjoyed the irony that, at the beginning of his article, he chose to quote the first words to Parliament uttered by a Mr Robert Maxwell (Lab. Buckingham): 'It is with a great sense of humility that I rise to speak here for the first time.' Macleod recalled his own maiden speech, on priorities in the health service, which had earned him 'loud cheers', according to the report in the *Times*. 'I then repeated this speech at intervals over the next two years, and found myself Minister of Health. Get a good speech, and stick to it. It's the shortest way home.' In a leader on the Queen's Speech, Macleod applauded the government for improving social security benefits, while chastising the new prime minister, under the heading 'Rattle of a Vicious Man', for having called the new member for Smethwick, Peter Griffith, 'a parliamentary leper' before he had made his maiden speech.

In one of his first political commentaries for *The Spectator*, Watkins had also castigated Wilson for making such a major parliamentary blunder. A few weeks later, Watkins wrote about the steel renationalisation debate in terms which suggested to Michael Foot, writing in *Tribune*, that he was pushing Macleod's line in his political commentary. Watkins responded in robust terms, writing that his column 'is not inspired by and does not reflect the views of Mr Macleod or indeed of anyone except myself. I write what I like. This may be difficult for Foot to grasp, but it happens to be so.' It was not only so but, when offered the job of political correspondent by Macleod, Watkins did not feel it necessary to ask for any assurances that he would be free to write what he wanted. He had been acquainted with Macleod, on and off, for several years, and he had wanted to join *The Spectator* ever since the days when, doing his National Service and studying for the Bar exams, he found, through reading Henry Fairlie's *Spectator* column, that his real interest lay in political journalism. When Watt told him he was off to Washington for the *Financial Times*, and that his job was therefore becoming vacant, Watkins wrote initially to Gilmour, while Watt spoke to Macleod on Watkins's behalf. He was invited by Macleod to White's (where they watched the Test match on television) and urged by him to give in his notice immediately to the *Sunday Express*, where he was then writing the Crossbencher column. Watkins remembers that, during his time at *The Spectator*, he and Macleod spoke more about cricket and rugby than about politics. Macleod would never suggest a topic for the political commentary, though when he came to read it on press day he would occasionally affect a mild protest: 'Must you really say that about Ted [Heath]? Well, I suppose if you must, you must.' Their only serious disagreement arose over the matter of dinner jackets which, Watkins wrote, Tories loved putting on at their party conference. For some reason Macleod got very angry at this comment, insisting that it was quite untrue.

Watkins continued to enjoy the same freedom to write as he pleased under Nigel Lawson, but rather less when he had Crossman as his editor at the *New Statesman*. Perhaps in wishing to avoid the charge that, as a senior politician, he would be bound to exert some influence over his political correspondent, Macleod appeared to go out of his way not to give Watkins information or assistance. It was also the case, as Watkins has said, that during his two years as editor, apart from the leaders which he felt obliged to write, Macleod was enjoying a respite from politics.

There was, however, the matter of a new leader of the Conservative party to be settled, when Douglas-Home decided to stand down in the summer of 1965. Having been in part responsible for the new procedure of a ballot of MPs, Macleod remained, as he saw himself in 1963, the next leader but one, and did not stand. Though more of a friend of Maudling, Macleod voted for Heath (who as Shadow Chancellor had written on the Finance Bill in the previous week's *Spectator*) and then wrote a leading article, 'The Quiet Revolution', welcoming his election and the passing of an era characterised by 'the strains of the Eton Boating Song and all that nonsense about grouse moors'. Macleod also repeated his phrase, which he had used at the general election, about the country needing a leader prepared to bulldoze his way through the road blocks to progress. In the same issue Macleod paid tribute to Douglas-Home as 'the best Commonwealth Secretary we have seen, and an excellently good and tough Foreign Minister'. Despite their differences, over policy and over Douglas-Home's succession as prime minister, there was no hostility between them. It was just that Macleod took the view that the Conservative party should not be led by someone like the former Lord Home.

Enoch Powell, who was also a candidate in the leadership election, received 15 votes. Two weeks before the ballot, Macleod had written a friendly article about Powell, admiring of his intellect though criticising his excess of logic. He substantially agreed with Powell on the paramountcy of the market, while expressing his belief in regional planning. A year before, Gilmour had written a piece on Powell's 'pipe-dream' of market capitalism, of which he was rather more critical. (Anticipating disagreement with his editor, Gilmour arranged for it to be published while Macleod was away.)

For the rest of 1965 not very much happened. Roy Hattersley, MP, began his journalistic career with a piece on his native Sheffield, quickly followed by several more, on political topics, which *The Spectator* published. Macleod continued to play chess by telephone with *The Spectator*'s chess columnist, C.H. Alexander, whom he had appointed. But he did not give the magazine a bridge column; as a former tournament bridge player and bridge correspondent, he might have been expected to do the job himself.

Having become Shadow Chancellor, Macleod announced in October that he would have to give up his editorship at the end of the year. The issue then of greatest moment was Smith's threat to make a unilateral declaration of independence for Southern Rhodesia. This he did in November, and Macleod devoted his last, and signed, leader to the subject on the last day of 1965. Having said that he would welcome majority rule in Rhodesia 'at a much earlier date than almost any other member of the House of Commons', he went on, rather surprisingly, to argue against economic sanctions and in favour of talks with the Smith regime, hoping to keep Rhodesia within the Commonwealth. In his valedictory Quoodle column, this senior member of the Shadow Cabinet conceded that his party's solid support for American policy in Vietnam was not reflected in the country (nor would it get *The Spectator*'s backing under Lawson). He referred once more to the prime minister as 'the little man' (he was, in fact, taller than Macleod) and he said goodbye to his pseudonym, the lovable bitch — half-Cairn, half-Aberdeen terrier — created by Chesterton, declining Lawson's invitation to continue the column. Appropriately and approvingly, he quoted Lord Beaverbrook's opinion that politics and journalism were closely allied. *The Spectator*'s Christmas party became also a farewell party for Macleod. To his obvious delight, he was presented with a complete set of Edmund Burke's works in their original leather bindings, with a book-plate, designed by the illustrator Quentin Blake, showing galley proofs lying over the editor's chair. When, on the afternoon of 30 December, Macleod left Gower Street for the last time, there was hardly anyone about. 'A lion had gone out,' his devoted secretary, Baylis, recorded, 'in the way of the proverbial lamb.'

6

TWO MASTERS

Nigel Lawson came to *The Spectator* by way of financial journalism. Having left Oxford with a first in PPE, he did his national service in the Royal Navy, commanding a motor torpedo boat called *Gay Charger*. Before joining the *Financial Times* in 1956, he was interviewed for the secret service, but rather spoilt his chances of acceptance when he nominated Bertrand Russell as the living man he most admired. After a spell as city editor of the *Sunday Telegraph* in the early 1960s, he worked for the prime minister, Sir Alec Douglas-Home, as special assistant. The experience persuaded him that he should thereafter pursue a career in politics. The offer of *The Spectator*'s editorial chair deferred his political ambition for a while, but did not change his resolve. Lawson was not Ian Gilmour's first choice as editor after Iain Macleod. An approach was made initially to William Rees-Mogg, then deputy editor of the *Sunday Times* and a former senior colleague of Lawson at the *Financial Times*. Having declined the offer, Rees-Mogg became editor of the *Times* the following year.

The invitation to Lawson came from *The Spectator*'s managing director, George Hutchinson, who had joined the magazine from Central Office in 1964. A former political correspondent of the *Evening Standard*, he had recommended John Thompson to Macleod as his deputy even before he (Hutchinson) joined *The Spectator*. Hutchinson was respected for his political nous and his journalistic contacts, and liked by everyone. He was the ideal person to bring together two people who were not naturally sympathetic to one another and persuade them that they could work together harmoniously and to their great mutual advantage. So Lawson accepted Gilmour's offer of the editorship, and Gilmour agreed to pay him £7,500 on a five-year contract — but they were never going to get on. (Years later, Gilmour would say that perhaps he should have made Thompson editor rather than Lawson.)

To put it bluntly, as Lawson did, 'we were never soul-mates': they had nothing in common, neither social position nor political outlook, except in so far as they both supported the same party. Because. also, of the marked difference in height between proprietor and editor, Gilmour would sometimes refer to Lawson as 'Napoleon', at other times as 'Niglet'. They had only two political disagreements during the 15 months before Gilmour sold the magazine: one over Lawson's extreme expressions of hostility to Harold Wilson, and the other because of his espousal of devaluation, from early 1966, as the only realistic solution to Britain's economic crisis. At the time this course was opposed not only by the government but by the national press, and it was also contrary to official Conservative thinking. The formal devaluation of sterling, by more than 14 per cent against the dollar, took place in November 1967. Feelings on the subject ran high: after one issue of *The Spectator* in which Lawson, in a leader, had urged devaluation on the government, he received a note from Lord Kennet (as Wayland Young, a committed libertarian thinker and writer) withdrawing an invitation to a party.

Lawson had a reputation among some of his staff and contributors for being brusque and self-important. He put his name on the cover of the first issue he edited, announcing 'NIGEL LAWSON'S NOTEBOOK' (a practice also to be adopted by his son Dominic when he became editor in 1990). He would pace up and down the room during the usually perfunctory editorial conference, holding the lapels of his pastel-coloured suit while giving directions for the following week's issue. It was clear from the beginning that he and the editorial secretary, Joan Baylis, were not going to hit it off. The atmosphere in the office had changed, she said; she no longer felt herself a member of a family. After Macleod, whom she had worshipped, it was almost inevitable that she would take against his successor. She was once said to have exploded, with reference to her new editor, 'I have been used to working for gentlemen!' Lawson said of her, tactfully though somewhat opaquely, 'Her loyalty was to Ian Gilmour'. Baylis lasted less than three months with Lawson, then retired, having been at Gower Street for 26 years. She was replaced by a lively and glamorous girl, Sue Mottram, whom everyone adored. With Lawson's approval, she used to bring her King Charles spaniel to the office. Another secretary working there at this period was Cecilia Hurst, who left in 1968 to marry Alastair Goodlad, subsequently an MP and Chief Whip in John Major's government.

Lawson's great friend, Jock Bruce-Gardyne, with whom he subsequently wrote *The Power Game*, was made foreign editor, a job he combined with being MP for South Angus. (He would turn up at Gower Street on a bicycle, usually wearing tweeds.) Other close colleagues at *The Spectator* — the deputy editor, Thompson, political correspondent, Alan Watkins, and literary editor, Hilary Spurling — enjoyed good relations with Lawson; the picture of discourteous bully was not one that they recognised. On the contrary, he was sympathetic, he attracted loyalty and he was fiercely supportive of contributors who became involved in public controversy over what they had written. When Spurling, who was also theatre critic from 1964 to 1970, had her press facilities withdrawn by Lindsay Anderson, artistic director of the Royal Court, allegedly because of her 'recurrent prejudice' against its productions and because she had walked out of one play, Lawson leapt to her defence, attacking 'Royal Court censorship' and writing two articles on Anderson's 'complaint'. ('The best-known symptom is an acute hypersensitivity to any form of criticism other than that which the patient has deliberately set out to provoke.') He continued to do battle on her behalf — with support from several newspapers and the Arts Council, causing Anderson to speak of tanks rolling into Sloane Square — until the decision to exclude her from the theatre was reversed after six months.

Lawson often complimented Spurling on her theatre reviews, and interfered little with the books pages, except occasionally to ask her to send his old boss, Douglas-Home, a book to review on Scottish history, cricket or country matters. But she was embarrassed to be asked to carry reviews from Enoch Powell, around the time of his inflammatory 'river of blood' speech in 1968. Having taken over the literary editor's job from David Rees — whose only parting piece of advice to her was to throw away all invitations to literary parties — Spurling introduced a number of new names, including Barry Humphries, whose interest at that time was in late 19th-century *belles-lettres*, and Gabriel Garcia Marquez (a short story called 'Tuesday Siesta'). Thinking that the English novel had grown weary since the 1950s, Spurling was one of the first to look towards Latin America. Under her guidance, the books pages offered both more entertainment and more intellectual weight. As arts editor under Macleod, she had recruited Roy Strong and Bryan Robertson as art critics, Stuart Hood to write about television, rather than review individual programmes, Michael Nyman as music critic (who later became a successful composer, particularly of film scores and experimental music) and Henry Tube, aka Hilary Spurling's husband, John, to write on radio. (She took on the theatre herself after trying unsuccessfully to get Germaine Greer to do it.) Isabel Quigly was still cinema critic, Peter Fleming was still writing his Strix column (though rather less frequently), and Consuming Interest remained a regular and popular feature at the back. John Wells was hired to write a press column (succeeding Christopher Booker) and, until Lawson left in 1970, a humorous Afterthought. Lord Egremont (as John Wyndham he had been private secretary to Harold Macmillan) contributed to the Endpapers, writing a charming, occasional column mostly about family life at his grand country house, Petworth.

The Notebook was regularly written by Thompson. He had had more to do in Macleod's time with the task of editing *The Spectator* and getting it to press each week than he did as Lawson's deputy. But press days under Lawson could be a bit fraught: nicknamed by one of his staff the Great Procrastinator, he was inclined to write the leader very late in the day, and then send it by train to the printers at Aldershot after the rest of the issue had been completed. Sometimes it would arrive by different trains, in instalments, and for some reason in green boxes which were used for carrying the typed sheets. Sometimes the guard of the train would forget to drop the leader off at Aldershot station and Lawson would have to transmit it by telephone. Thompson and Watkins would then have to bestir themselves, setting aside the picnic supper thoughtfully provided by Charles Seaton, and get the Lawson leader on to the page in the short time remaining before deadline. (On other occasions Trevor Grove, who joined the staff in September 1967, would supply the picnic, with quantities of taramosalata from a shop in Charlotte Street, and Lawson might arrive at the printers in his Jaguar, which he was noted for driving at alarmingly high speed.)

No sooner had the Shadow Chancellor departed from Gower Street than one of his front-bench colleagues, Angus Maude, wrote an article in *The Spectator*, 'Winter of Tory Discontent', which amounted to a vote of no confidence in their new leader, Edward Heath. Maude said the Conservatives had 'completely lost effective political initiative' and had, in the eyes of the electorate, 'become a meaningless irrelevance'. He accused them of talking like technocrats and being out of touch with what the people wanted. There was too much pussyfooting about the trade unions, tax, crime and the social services. Maude was at the time Opposition spokesman for the colonies, of which post Heath felt obliged to relieve him. The following week Lawson defended Heath in the leading article, saying he would make a far better prime minister than leader of the Opposition. The current Tory malaise, he argued, was due not to Heath but rather to the lack of an *idée force* to drive the party. Europe might provide it in time, but old-fashioned liberalism required too many qualifications today for anyone except Powell (though it would be embraced by Lawson and others a decade or so later).

In his pre-general election leader on 25 March 1966, Lawson described Wilson as 'the outstanding party politician of his generation, the supreme non-statesman for the age of the non-event.... He has increased his stature over the past 17 months at the expense of diminishing everything he has touched.' Praising the Liberals for being the only party in favour of devaluation, *The Spectator* advised tactical voting in order to defeat Labour. In the following week's issue, published on election day, Lawson anticipated the almost inevitable result, heading the leader 'Why Labour Won'. Whenever, in 1966, Wilson or James Callaghan (Chancellor of the Exchequer) announced that the economy was in good shape, *The Spectator* attacked them for deceit, incompetence and duplicity. This was entirely fair comment; but Gilmour thought the bounds of legitimate political criticism had been exceeded when Lawson ended one leader: 'Close observers have long since stopped crediting Mr Wilson with any real political purpose or personal integrity. But at least they believed he possessed technical skill. Now that the country is about to pay the full penalty for his gross economic mismanagement, it is clear that he lacks even this.' Apart from the editor of *The Spectator*, the only other people to advocate devaluation in 1966 were the government's Treasury advisers (one Treasury official, Peter Jay, wrote an article to this effect under a pseudonym). Jay's father-in-law, the Chancellor of the Exchequer, wobbled from time to time, but was always told by the prime minister that it was out of the question. When Wilson delayed taking the decision to devalue until mid-November of the following year. Lawson's leader, 'Mr Wilson Saves Himself', called the delay 'criminally negligent'. For much of the past two years *The Spectator*'s had been a lone voice in insisting that the sterling exchange rate could not be sustained. Now, suspecting once again that Wilson would act in his party's rather than the country's interests, it doubted whether he would allow the additional deflationary measures to be taken to achieve a long-term economic recovery.

A curious little exchange in the House of Commons at the end of May 1966 illustrated Wilson's irritation with Lawson (like Major, he seemed incapable of ignoring, or rising above, press criticism). Gilmour had asked the prime minister what official facilities were given to Gerald Kaufman at 10 Downing Street. Having denied that there were any, Wilson then took it upon himself, in response to a question from a Labour member, to say that official facilities at Downing Street had been granted in the past to a number of Tory speech writers, 'one of whom later, I think, became editor of *The Spectator*'. This was clearly a reference, though rather an odd one, to Lawson, who had worked for Douglas-Home during his brief premiership in 1963–64. The following day, according to the *Times*, Wilson sent letters to Gilmour and to Lawson correcting the 'slip' he had made and explaining that he should have called the facilities granted to Lawson 'unofficial'. A week later, Lawson commented in his Notebook that he had received no letter from the prime minister and wondered whether Mr Benn's postal service was even worse than everyone thought.

Already in 1966 Lawson was having grave doubts about America's increasing involvement in the Vietnam war. In a signed article he commented that 'the risks involved in an American withdrawal from Vietnam are less than the risks in escalating a bloody and brutal war'. The time might soon come when Britain would 'reluctantly feel obliged to join France in publicly deploring the entire South-East Asian adventure of its greatest ally'. Both Lawson and Bruce-Gardyne, his foreign editor, were at one in their opposition to the war, also taking the view, which was subsequently justified, that it would lead to world inflation.

The issue of 3 March 1967 appeared with a new face, a redesign. The most obvious change was a reversion to the traditional layout of a weekly, with the first leader on the front page beneath a deck of cover-lines, the first of which, on 3 March, announced 'Those D Notices — The Full Text: by Alan Watkins'. The *Daily Express* had published a story to the effect that private telegraphic cables were being vetted by the security services. While this was permitted under the wide-ranging terms of the Official Secrets Acts, Wilson took it upon himself to accuse the *Express* of having been specifically in breach of two D (for Defence) notices. The convention is that

Spectator

Number 7236   Friday 3 March 1967   One Shilling and Sixpence

With a newly designed cover, The Spectator *was sold by Ian Gilmour to Harry Creighton during the D notice affair.*

THOSE D NOTICES – **THE FULL TEXT**: BY ALAN WATKINS. ELECTION NOTEBOOK FROM FRANCE INDIA FOR THE INDIANS. **NIGEL LAWSON** ON THE TORIES. BRITISH MUSEUM BLUES. **ANTHONY BURGESS ON TEACHERS**. JOHN WELLS ON DEATH

Defence and the constitution

Every Government has its little local difficulties. But Mr Wilson would be ill-advised to laugh off the abstention by some four dozen Labour members in this week's defence debate, which reduced the Government's majority to thirty-nine. Defence has, of course, always produced some strange responses on the left. There have always been some who believe that one should never bomb a smaller country unless it is Rhodesia, and others who do not believe in defence at all. But this rebellion by MPs of the left, right and centre of the party is a much more serious affair.

The Tories, to be sure, have little to look back to with pride in the conduct of defence policy when they were in office; but nothing has hitherto approached the mass of contradictions that masquerade as a defence policy today. There is, for example, the question of the British troops in Germany. Both the Prime Minister and the Chancellor of the Exchequer, in order to persuade their supporters to accept deflationary measures at home for balance of payments reasons, gave firm pledges that the Germans would meet the full foreign exchange cost of BAOR—or else the troops would be pulled out until they did. Yet it is plain that the Germans will do nothing of the sort—and, indeed, that nothing short of a total withdrawal of BAOR would enable Mr Wilson and Mr Callaghan to keep their word. As for the strategic implications, it is a waste of time looking to the 1967 Defence Review for enlightenment. That document is as certain that the nature of the threat to Europe has changed as it is uncertain about the consequences of this for defence policy.

Worst of all, the Government appears utterly unable to decide what to do if defence requirements and foreign exchange considerations conflict. This basic dilemma was admirably exemplified by Mr Brown during the debate: 'The consequences of any ill-considered withdrawal from the mainland of Europe would be disastrous . . . We are at the moment faced with a serious problem of foreign exchange costs which arise from the stationing of our forces in Germany . . . If they cannot be covered by financial means we shall have to consider proposing a substantial redeployment of forces in order to lighten the burden.'

Unresolved contradiction is equally the keynote of the Government's defence policy East of Suez. Does it still believe that Britain has a military role in the 1970s, or doesn't it? If it does, how does it propose to meet the foreign exchange cost? And how does it justify staying there, at vast cost, merely as an auxiliary of the Americans—and not even one the United States can depend on when she does have a war on her hands, as in Vietnam? Alternatively, if the Government is planning a quiet military withdrawal from East of Suez, what is the justification for spending more than £200 million in foreign exchange in buying from the Americans a further forty F-111s, which have no conceivable role in Europe? These are important questions, and they have not been answered.

Nor have the Prime Minister or Mr Healey ever made clear their conception of the role of Britain's nuclear capability. According to Mr Wilson, this is neither independent nor a deterrent, with the significance of 'a dried

pea on a mountain-top.' Yet the programme goes on, at a cost of over £100 million a year, with periodic Polaris launchings by cabinet ministers' wives. Is it to become part of an Atlantic Nuclear Force? But the ANF idea has been killed. Part of a European Nuclear Force, perhaps? No, the Government is against that. All we know is that the Government is actively promoting a non-proliferation treaty in which Britain's privileged nuclear status would be juridically established.

In the light of these contradictions, it is scarcely surprising that there is unrest on the Government benches. It hardly needed to be further stimulated by a lamentable performance by Mr Healey, during which he evinced the terrifyingly irresponsible belief that 'there is no country on the Continent which does not believe that a prolonged conventional war would inflict damage on it quite as difficult to bear as a strategic nuclear exchange.' But the significance of the Labour back-bench revolt extends far beyond the issue of defence itself.

Helped as it was by the backing of a party conference resolution, and by the relaxation of disciplinary rules by Mr Crossman and Mr Silkin (about which they must by now be having second thoughts), it represents nevertheless the first important symptom of the growing back-bench dissatisfaction with the unconstitutional manner in which this country is now being governed. It is a basic element in the constitution that a government must pay some regard to its election pledges, to the party that supports it, and to parliament as a whole. In propounding the seemingly tautologous proposition that the

---

such notices, having no legal authority, are treated as private requests to newspapers not to publish certain matters which might jeopardise the national security interest. *The Spectator* had never received a D notice from the Services, Press and Broadcasting Committee, which issued them. Watkins, with his editor's support, judged that, since the prime minister had chosen to make an issue of the terms of two particular notices, it was in the public interest that their exact wording should be known. Having performed this signal public service in his political commentary, Watkins went on to doubt whether the notices had been breached in the particular case. His view was subsequently confirmed by a committee composed of Lord Radcliffe, Selwyn Lloyd and Emanuel Shinwell — 'an unlikely and slightly hilarious trio', in Watkins's slightly mischievous words, for which he was rebuked when he appeared to give evidence to the committee. Its report concluded unanimously not only that the *Express* story was accurate but that it did not contravene either of the two D notices cited or the general D notice procedure. Wilson, predictably enough, rejected the findings of the Radcliffe report, prompting *The Spectator* to characterise him as a Walter Mitty figure. 'By riding roughshod over Parliament (as in the decimalisation affair), over his own party (his licensed "dogs"), over public inquiries (Stansted) and now over a committee of Privy Councillors, Mr Wilson is demonstrating that his dream world cannot be confined within constitutional bounds.' *The Spectator* then got some further mileage from the D notice affair by publishing the version of events of Colonel L.G. ('Sammy') Lohan, secretary of the Services, Press and Broadcasting Committee, in the week that he was forced to resign.

During the four months (March–June 1967) that D notices were being debated in the pages of *The Spectator* and elsewhere, control of the magazine changed hands, from a well-known politician to an unknown businessman. Gilmour had owned the magazine for more than 12 years. It had turned a small profit during Brian Inglis's time, but ever since the annual losses had been increasing, and were now around £20,000. Circulation had declined from almost 50,000 in 1961 to little more than 30,000, and the relationship between Gilmour and Lawson, while civil enough, was never warm. It was said he needed money for a business venture, and that his political career would be more rapidly advanced without the embarrassment to him, which he had already suffered on occasion, of owning *The Spectator*. Whatever the reasons, Gilmour resolved that he would sell the magazine but would himself keep clear of negotiations with prospective purchasers. Through his friendship with Peter Walker (later to become a minister in Heath's government), with whom he shared an office and flat in Gayfere Street, Westminster, he entrusted the negotiations to Jim Slater, the 'City whizz-kid' chairman of Slater Walker Securities. But he neglected to inform Lawson, who first learnt of the intended sale from an advertisement in the *Financial Times*.

It was a paragraph in the Londoner's Diary of the *Evening Standard* one Friday which first alerted Harry Creighton, chairman of the Scottish Machine Tool Corporation, to the fact that *The Spectator* was for sale. That evening he went to White's to meet his father-in-law, A.L.P.F. ('Dandy') Wallace, and Lord Boothby. Over dinner at Wilton's, Creighton was urged by Boothby to buy the magazine. He was 39, he had spent some time out east doing his national service and afterwards smelting tin in Penang, and he had made money in business. The idea of being a press baron and perhaps having a seat in Parliament as well clearly appealed to him.

Creighton was known to Slater because Slater Walker had acted for Creighton's company and had a small stake in it; and they got together after the weekend. Within 24 hours a deal with Gilmour had been struck. Of the other interested bidders for *The Spectator*, an American publisher, Conrad Jameson, was the most serious candidate. The brothers Goodhart — Philip (Conservative MP), William (soon to join the SDP) and Professor Charles (economist, appointed to the monetary policy committee of the Bank of England in 1997) — expressed interest but made no offer. One or two other names were mentioned as prospective buyers, but they came to nothing. With Hutchinson's help, Lawson attempted to put together a consortium to acquire the magazine, but it was too late. Apparently Gilmour did receive a higher offer than Creighton's, but Slater was pressing Creighton's suit, Gilmour was anxious to conclude the matter and Creighton was ready to pay him £75,000. Lawson was not consulted; had he been, he said, he could have found a number of much more suitable proprietors. He was not best pleased with Gilmour: the manner of the disposal of the magazine that Gilmour had fashioned so successfully a decade earlier was not entirely satisfactory.

During Gilmour's 12 or so years in charge of *The Spectator*, he had employed four editors and had fallen out with three of them — plus Walter Taplin, whom he inherited. It was understandable that Gilmour should say, with hindsight, that he wished he had sold the magazine in 1959 (before he started appointing editors). *The Spectator* had, of course, enjoyed some entertaining and distinguished periods since 1959, but one may judge that the years of Gilmour's own editorship (1954–59) were the most memorable. Moral campaigns were bravely fought in advance of public opinion, Henry Fairlie and Bernard Levin were at the height of their journalistic powers and, while Iain Hamilton and Brian Inglis worked under Gilmour, a creative harmony prevailed.

Lawson and Creighton did not take to one another. Creighton was in the habit of using an office at the top of 99 Gower Street, but he had little intercourse with his editor, who did his best to steer clear of his proprietor. Lawson's attitude to him, according to Creighton, was one of dumb insolence, saying very little and always finding an excuse not to have lunch with him. The announcement of the change of proprietorship of *The Spectator* (in the issue of 14 April) stated that Creighton 'has already declared his intention to ensure the continuation of the paper in its present character'. But when he tried to reshape aspects of editorial policy, Lawson did not hesitate to point out that his contract guaranteed him editorial independence.

Had Lawson not had a contract with nearly four years still to run, there is little doubt that Creighton would have ended the relationship sooner. Happily for *The Spectator*, however, two new recruits to Lawson's team arrived at Gower Street in September 1967. Like Gilmour, Creighton hoped that Lawson would be able to attract more City advertising to the magazine, and he asked him to expand the financial coverage. Andreas Whittam-Smith, who was already writing in *The Spectator*'s City pages under the pseudonym of John Bull, and was later to become founder editor of the *Independent*, introduced Lawson to Christopher Fildes, then working for the *Times* Business News. Fildes joined the staff, wrote a City Diary and fell in love with Sue Mottram, whom he married in 1969, by which time he was working for the *Daily Mail*. (He would return to *The Spectator* in 1984 to write a weekly City and Suburban column, which continues today.) At the same time Lawson appointed Auberon Waugh to be political commentator. Whether the arrival of these two journalists caused *The Spectator*'s insurers to raise their premiums for defamation cover, or whether Creighton decided he would no longer go on paying any premiums, Lawson felt obliged to issue an office memorandum, headed 'Libel'. 'Mr Auberon Waugh and Mr Christopher Fildes have today joined the staff of *The Spectator*. As from today *The Spectator* ceases to be insured against libel. Gatley on Libel and Slander (6th and 7th editions) may be consulted in my office.'

Lawson and Waugh had first met the previous year at Woodrow Wyatt's house in Wiltshire, where they played croquet on Easter Sunday. It was the day that Evelyn Waugh died; once the obituaries had been published, Lawson invited Waugh to review the various tributes in *The Spectator*. Waugh was later to describe his first article for the magazine as shrill and self-righteous. It was critical of Alan Brien (who had written a piece in *The Spectator*) and Malcolm Muggeridge, in particular, for having portrayed Evelyn Waugh as a social climber and his inner life as a class struggle when, according to his son, his struggle was primarily against boredom which he sought to avoid by being funny. Perhaps the most memorable thing about the article was an oblique reference to Kenneth Allsop's 'warm and compassionate heart', eliciting a letter from him which was published the following week, and a rejoinder from Waugh the week after. Allsop had already been rude in print about Waugh's own novels, which he now described as 'paltry and repellent'. Waugh retorted, in an early example of the talent which he inherited from his father for getting the better of anyone who dared to have a go at him, that he had drawn attention to Allsop's warm and compassionate heart only 'to illustrate the wide disparity of talent which possession of such an article can embrace.... If he does not like people to notice his unfortunate deficiencies, he should not parade them so frequently.'

Waugh was at the time working for the *Daily Mirror*, having been hired by Hugh Cudlipp in 1963 as a 'special writer'. He spent part of his time writing articles about holiday camps and captions to photographs of bathing beauties, though his office hours were more often employed in writing novels. Following the first piece, Lawson encouraged Waugh to contribute other occasional articles. (One, entitled 'Educating Hurricane Emma', on the effects of a recent baby boom among upper middle-class wives who had stopped using the Pill, refreshingly managed to embrace several politically incorrect themes. He applauded the increasing number of babies from the more privileged classes, and defended public-school education, while at the same time commenting that 'all education other than the most rudimentary is nowadays useless'.) It was fortunate that an article written by Waugh for the *Mirror*, in which he attacked Lawson when, as a city journalist, he had obtained peculiarly favourable mortgage terms from London County Council, was never published. For, in the summer of 1967, when Watkins announced his departure to the *New Statesman*, then edited by Paul Johnson, Lawson had the inspired idea of offering the political column to Waugh. (He actually offered it first to Christopher Booker to whom, a couple of years later, Waugh remarked that he was doing the job so much better than Booker would have done. Their relationship was always uneasy, dating perhaps from the time that Booker observed, and photographed, Waugh cheating at croquet. Years later Waugh prevailed upon Max Hastings, then editor of the *Daily Telegraph*, to sack Booker from the 'Way of the World' column so that he could replace him.)

As Waugh freely admitted, he knew nothing about politics at the time.

But Lawson guided him and gave him direction, knowing that he was likely to be a wild card. Waugh was grateful to Lawson and respected him as 'by far the cleverest person I have ever worked with'. Lawson had an instant appreciation of almost any subject and, according to Waugh, was prone only to occasional pomposity. During the nearly two and a half years that he wrote the political commentary for *The Spectator*, Waugh says he learnt one important truth: that practically no one wants to read about politics. (Was this an important reason for the success of *The Spectator* under Inglis?) When Lawson sacked him in February 1970, Waugh became a rather different kind of political correspondent for *Private Eye*, a column he continued to write after he returned to *The Spectator* as a weekly contributor in 1976.

Waugh's period of political writing at *The Spectator* was marked, indeed dominated for a while, by Biafra. The eastern region of Nigeria had proclaimed its independence as the republic of Biafra in May 1967, after tens of thousands of its Ibo population had been massacred and about 2 million put to flight by forces of the federal government. The deliberate starvation and slaughter of the Ibo people continued, significantly helped by the British government, which was supplying arms and ammunition to the Nigerian Federation. No one in Britain appeared much interested, but when a delegation of Biafrans, led by Chief Justice Sir Louis Mbanefo, came to London in 1968 to plead their cause, a very few people (such as Lord Goodman and Lawson) listened and were horrified by what they heard. *The Spectator* took up the Biafran cause first: Lawson wrote a leading article in which he accused the Wilson government of being an accomplice in genocide. Without British support, he said, the federation would not have been able to continue to prosecute its savage war against the Biafran people. Lawson then suggested to Waugh that he should go to Biafra to see for himself what was happening; Waugh thought it 'would be a pleasant diversion from the House of Commons press gallery'.

He had little difficulty in persuading himself that Biafra was a cause that should be espoused. It was a good stick with which to beat the government — the Foreign Secretary, Michael Stewart, came in for particular criticism — but it was also a situation that was bound to affect anyone who went to Biafra. It was Waugh's first visit to Africa; he saw hundreds of Ibos dying of starvation brought about by the policy of a Nigerian government in receipt of material and diplomatic support from Britain; and he became a dedicated campaigner for Biafra. Apart from lengthy articles in *The Spectator*, he wrote a book with Suzanne Cronje, *Biafra, Britain's Shame* (generously reviewed in the magazine by Goodman), and he toured Britain and the United States to promote the cause.

Few on the left supported Biafra, which may have had something to do with the Soviet Union's backing of the federal government, or possibly with *The Spectator*'s impassioned hostility to it. When Waugh adduced evidence in *The Spectator* of a policy of genocide towards Biafra, Michael Foot wrote to declare his support for the Nigerian government, though without saying why he was prepared to overlook the plight of the Biafrans. Another correspondent asserted that the Ibos' behaviour over the years towards other Nigerian tribes merited some sort of reprisal. After a while the *Sunday Telegraph* and the *Times* came out on the side of Biafra, but by the time Lord Carrington agreed to go out there, it was on the point of collapse. Waugh's candidature in a Somerset by-election, on a 'Save Biafra' platform, was too late. But he and *The Spectator* had played an honourable role in campaigning for such a cause, though it was probably always going to be a lost one.

The Lawson *Spectator* was chalking up quite a few 'firsts': in urging devaluation, opposing US policy in Vietnam and now Biafra. Also in 1968, Lawson got Helen Vlachos, the Greek newspaper proprietor and columnist who had escaped to London in the wake of the colonels' coup, to write about the politics of her country. In May 1968 he had the idea of publishing a Revolution Diary by Nancy Mitford during the Paris *évènements*. She was living just outside Versailles; much of her diary, which appeared over two weeks, was concerned with the effects of the general strike.

> The excellent Société d'Assistance aux Bêtes d'Abattoir to which I subscribe has rescued all the livestock out of the immobile trains, so that's a weight off one's mind.

> I've got masses of champagne and no mineral water, so if the tap gives out Marie and I will be permanently drunk.

> I hear that the Embassy Rolls-Royce has been all round Paris delivering cards for the garden party — that's the spirit — up the old land.

> Lucy is yearning over the students again. She says they are out on the streets again this morning, beautiful and polite, collecting money for the old — to give a Molotov cocktail party for them, I expect, said I.

This was also the year of Powell's immigration speech in which he spoke of the River Tiber foaming with much blood. It was described as 'dangerous nonsense' in *The Spectator*, which commended Heath for having acted 'decisively, courageously and correctly' in sacking him. Waugh, in his political commentary, took as his text the words, which he ascribed to 'Enoch: xix 4 68', 'Those whom the Gods wish to destroy they first make mad'. It was an enjoyable irony that three weeks before he was sacked, Powell had an article in *The Spectator* headed 'Power and the Prime Minister'; and he was back again in its pages a month after his dangerous nonsense, reviewing a book on the cult of thuggee in 19th-century British India. When Randolph Churchill died in June (in the same week in which Robert Kennedy was assassinated), one might have expected *The Spectator* to give its cantankerous, erratic but by no means undistinguished press columnist a better send-off. Bill Grundy's press column did little more than republish extracts from the *Times* obituary, while Thompson wrote a short appreciation in his Notebook, pointing out that Churchill's last piece of journalism, a review of Lady Cynthia Asquith's diaries, had appeared in *The Spectator* the previous month. Thompson recalled Macleod saying he would like to write a biography of Churchill one day.

Towards the end of 1968 'Mercurius Oxoniensis' began writing an irregular column, taking the form of a letter, written with dry academic wit, to his 'Friend and Good Brother Londiniensis', which chronicled the goings-on in Oxford academia. Its principal interest lay in the identity of its author, who was the Regius Professor of Modern History at Oriel College, Hugh Trevor-Roper. Fifteen of these letters were published over a period of two years, the last reporting that the author had fled from Oxon to the country, fearing, it was said, a writ from Dr A.L. Rowse. Until 'assur'd that our correspondence has become inviolable, you must expect to hear no more from your distress'd brother to serve you, Mercurius Oxoniensis'. But Maurice Cowling, while doing a stint as literary editor in 1970–71, persuaded Trevor-Roper to resume the letters for a while. The first batch was published as a book and reviewed in *The Spectator* by Trevor-Roper, who speculated on

Mercurius's identity and accused him of name-dropping and occasional inaccuracies. The Cambridge Professor of Political Science, Denis Brogan, was writing a discursive weekly column, Table Talk, at this time, drawing on the impressive range of his knowledge — especially of French history and American politics — combined with a remarkable memory.

Another regular contributor in Lawson's time, with an extraordinary background to qualify him to write on the Soviet bloc, was Tibor Szamuely. He was Hungarian, born in Moscow, and had been educated partly in England. He fought with the Red Army during the war, then taught at the Historical Faculty at Moscow University, where he was overheard one day making a derogatory remark about Georgi Malenkov, the Soviet prime minister, which earned him a sentence of eight years in a labour camp in the early 1950s. Alexander Solzhenitsyn was being held not far away, at the same time, in a similar camp. But Szamuely was released after a comparatively short time and rehabilitated. He was allowed to become vice-chancellor of Budapest University in 1958, and from there he went to Ghana, taking the post of senior lecturer at the Kwame Nkrumah Ideological Institute near Accra, and thence to London, with his family, in 1964. He was an acknowledged authority on modern Russian history, he had had first-hand experience of the iniquities of the Soviet system, and he wrote excellent English. Kingsley Amis, who became a great friend of Szamuely, commented that 'he came to write the language like a master, better than most of those whose native tongue it is'. It was Robert Conquest who introduced Szamuely both to Amis and to *The Spectator*, for which he wrote frequently between 1966 and 1971, while also contributing regularly to other journals and lecturing at Reading University. Though Szamuely's anti-Russian views might sometimes be judged extreme, during these years of fashionable left-wingery his was one of the very few, and most eloquent, voices constantly iterating and returning to the evils and the miseries of Communism.

> The most characteristic feature of a communist state is not so much the political purge or the faked trial as the awful dreariness of everyday life. I am not referring now to the all-pervading drabness and austerity of material existence — shortages, queues, shoddy goods — but to the complete absence of anything resembling what we call 'public life'. These are, quite

simply, countries where nothing happens, where year in and year out one is given no other domestic news except the glorious completion of such-and-such a steel-rolling mill, or the fulfilment by such-and-such a region of its sunflower-seed production plan, or the appointment of Comrade So-and-so as Ambassador to the Upper Volta, or the resolution of a meeting of workers, collective farmers and toiling intelligentsia protesting against some latest outrage by the imperialist aggressors. Or sometimes, as a very special treat, one gets a four-page speech by the Party First Secretary.

Yet once in a while, quite unexpectedly, something does happen: an anti-party group is unmasked, a police chief executed, a prime minister dismissed. Next day, just as suddenly, it is all forgotten, never to be mentioned again, and the turgid waters once more close placidly over the latest unperson.

26 April 1968

This was the period of the so-called 'fascist lunches' held every Tuesday at Bertorelli's Restaurant in Charlotte Street, where like-minded anti-Communists, rather than fascists, would meet. Among the most regular attenders were Szamuely, Amis, Conquest, Anthony Powell and John Braine. Szamuely did much of his writing at night, since he never went to bed until dawn, still fearing that the KGB might come for him in the dark. He became a British citizen shortly before the 1970 general election and his affection for England was as strong as his hatred of Communism. He died of cancer two years later, aged only 47. It would have pleased him greatly that his son George wrote for *The Spectator* during Charles Moore's time as editor.

By 1969 Lawson had established a large number of regular columns in the front half of the magazine; so many that there was often room for no more than one longish article (frequently on a domestic political subject) and three short foreign pieces, including the Foreign Focus written by 'Crabro', usually Jock Bruce-Gardyne. To the political commentary (Waugh) and the Notebook (Thompson), he added Brogan's Table Talk, George Gale's Viewpoint and Grundy's press column, also a Personal Column written by a different person each week (Anthony Burgess, Simon Raven, Christopher Booker, Professor J.H. Plumb, Colin MacInnes were contributors). More often than not, there was Szamuely on some aspect of

Communism, John Rowan Wilson's column on medicine, also on occasion science, television and Leslie Adrian's long-running Consuming Interest. The portrait cover drawing was by Richard Willson, and the only cartoon inside, its subject usually suggested by Lawson, was by Michael Heath. (Heath had done his first drawing for *The Spectator* in 1957, the year that cartoons first appeared in the magazine. Forty-one years and 11 editors later, having become cartoon editor in the mid-1980s, he was doing a weekly strip cartoon, illustrating the Portrait of the Week, providing a gag under the pseudonym of Castro and sometimes the cover drawing as well.)

This roll-call of distinguished writers might seem to have offered an appealing weekly menu for the end of the 1960s — not to mention the books, arts, finance and the rest — but it was attracting fewer and fewer readers. Circulation had stood at around 36,000 when Lawson arrived at the beginning of 1966; four years later it had fallen by almost a third, to less than 25,000. This was due in part to the expansion of the Sunday papers, which were perceived to be better value, and the lack of any promotion for *The Spectator*. A Labour government which looked likely to continue beyond 1970 may have had something to do with it. But, for whatever reason, the decline of both major political weeklies had begun. The *New Statesman*, having reached its highest circulation figure (93,000) under Johnson's editorship in early 1966, had dropped below 80,000 by 1970 (when he left). Over the next six years the sales of both the *New Statesman* and *The Spectator* were almost halved.

By 1969, according to one member of staff, a permanent thundercloud seemed to hang over Gower Street. Relations between Creighton and Lawson deteriorated, and Creighton appeared to be spoiling for a fight. (The best thing to be remembered about Creighton at that time was that he installed a dining-room in the basement. Spurling used it once a week to entertain her contributors.) Some of Lawson's attention was now directed to the task of getting adopted as a Conservative candidate before the next election. He had decided not only to go after a parliamentary seat but, if successful, to give up the editorship. If he was commissioning fewer articles in 1969 than in 1966, he was writing no less: leaders on the worsening situation in Northern Ireland and a number of articles under his own name, one carrying the headline, 'Germany — Too much politics, not enough sex', which one might associate more readily with *The Spectator* edited by his son

Dominic 20 years later. (One of Lawson's most memorable articles impressively demolished the political philosophy of Professor A.J. Ayer who, 15 years later, was to marry Lawson's first wife.)

At the end of a working day it was Lawson's custom to put a bottle of Teachers whisky on his desk; contributors would often drop in for a glass and a chat. It was a good opportunity to discuss future articles with the editor, though not many jokes would be exchanged with him. The appearance of Barry Humphries, therefore, at a *Spectator* party not long before the 1970 general election caused a lot more consternation than it did when, some years later, he attended a *Spectator* lunch disguised as Dame Edna Everage. Humphries was not famous in those days; as an occasional book reviewer, he was invited to the party by Spurling. It was also attended by Heath, not noted for a spontaneous sense of fun, and several leading members of the Opposition, soon to be in government. Without warning and affecting drunkenness, Humphries climbed on to a table during the party and silenced the company by launching into a fruity rendering of 'The One-Eyed Trouser-Snake'. The shock and embarrassment were such that it was a few minutes before someone hauled him off the table and out of the room.

Biafra surrendered in January 1970 — Frederick Forsyth on his return from the region had written a piece which *The Spectator* published in December — leaving Waugh rather disconsolate. He had recently been asked by William Rees-Mogg to write a column for the *Times*, which annoyed Lawson. Waugh felt the urge to annoy Lawson a bit more: he altered one of the leaders on Ulster, but Lawson did not appear to notice. Then, in the second week of February, Gale's column, on celibacy and the Roman Catholic church, made references to the Waugh family which irritated him. So he removed them at the printer's and, on the contents page, instead of the name of George Gale, substituted 'Lunchtime O'Gale' ('Lunchtime O'Booze' was the name coined by *Private Eye* for a drunken hack). Lawson summoned Waugh and promptly sacked him, paying his salary only to the end of the month. Lawson said later that he would have excused Waugh's irresponsible behaviour had he been drunk at the time but, having established that Waugh was quite sober, he could not afford to take the risk that Waugh might do something similar again, or worse — and that next time his victim, unlike Gale, might sue for libel.

Supported by the National Union of Journalists, Waugh sued for wrongful dismissal; by the time the case came before the Marylebone County Court the following year, Lawson had lost his job as editor and been replaced by Gale. The situation, as Waugh wrote, was somewhat confused:

> I, the plaintiff, suing for wrongful dismissal had been rehired [as weekly fiction reviewer] by the person on whose behalf I had been sacked; the man who had sacked me had been sacked himself and had to justify, on behalf of the company which had sacked him, his decision to sack me.

Lawson was the only person to testify for the defence. Gale declined to give evidence for either side, and Watkins and Levin came to give evidence on Waugh's behalf, that, in his words, 'it was perfectly in the tradition of *The Spectator* for the political correspondent to make jocular alterations to the table of contents'. Waugh won the case and was awarded £1,250 (equivalent to the six months' notice to which his agreement entitled him), reduced to take account of tax and other earnings during the period.

Lawson's time at *The Spectator* came to an end only four months after Waugh. He had been adopted as Conservative candidate for Eton and Slough, standing against Joan Lestor, and was away electioneering when his letter of dismissal arrived from Creighton, only a day or two before the general election. (Lestor won, though there was a certain irony in the fact that she lost the seat in the year, 1983, that Lawson became Chancellor of the Exchequer.) Creighton claimed that Lawson's political ambitions were inconsistent with his job as editor (what about Macleod?). But the truth was that he was longing to be rid of Lawson: he fancied playing more of an editorial role himself, or at least having an editor whom he found agreeable. Lawson's contract had less than a year to run, and Creighton agreed, when faced with a writ, to pay it off, while suggesting that Lawson was obliged to mitigate his loss, for instance by applying for the editorship of the *Investors Chronicle*, which had become vacant. The job was in fact offered him by Lord Drogheda, but Lawson said he would take it only if he were guaranteed the editorship of the *Financial Times* when it became available. Such presumption so annoyed Drogheda that he determined Lawson would never get the *FT* job. For the next two or three years Lawson wrote regularly for the *Times* and *Sunday Times*, then was a special political adviser at

Conservative party headquarters before becoming an MP (for Blaby, Leicestershire) at the February 1974 election. His political ambitions took him to the Treasury, as Financial Secretary, following the Conservatives' return to power in 1979. Thereafter he was Energy Secretary until he became Chancellor of the Exchequer, a post he held for six years until his dramatic resignation in 1989.

7

HIGH RISK, LOW REWARD

$\mathbf{H}$arry Creighton may have been longing to appoint his own editor, but having sacked Nigel Lawson he had no very clear idea of who should replace him. He offered the job, rather half-heartedly, to John Thompson, who had an offer from the *Sunday Telegraph* which he was more inclined to accept. Anthony Lejeune and Bernard Levin were also approached by Creighton; Levin urged him to ask George Gale. However, it was not until 19 September that the announcement was made that Gale had been appointed editor.

During this interregnum period, Thompson was acting editor, with assistance from Trevor Grove, who for a time also had to double as literary editor. Hilary Spurling handed in her resignation when Lawson left, but was prepared to stay on until her successor had been appointed. However, when Creighton saw a letter she had written to her reviewers alerting them to the imminent upheavals, he told her abruptly that he did not want to see her in the office again. Grove stayed until Gale made Maurice Cowling literary editor, a job which he was able to do mostly from Peterhouse, Cambridge, only coming to London once or twice a week.

The year 1970 was notable, apart from the general election which returned a Conservative government, for a number of deaths, particularly of world leaders: De Gaulle, Nasser, Salazar. Bertrand Russell and E.M. Forster also died; with his fecund intellect, Sir Denis Brogan was more than adequately equipped to give his personal assessments of them. (But he and *The Spectator* overlooked the deaths in the same year of Kerensky, Daladier and Sukarno.) When Iain Macleod died in July aged 56, a month after he had been made Chancellor of the Exchequer, the acting editor, Thompson, wrote a fine appreciation of his former editor, paying tribute to his 'natural feeling for journalism and... wholly unpompous zest'. Thompson recalled

Macleod's romantic, Disraelian Toryism and his crusading liberal zeal; he had been the only person on the front bench of either party to vote against the 1968 Commonwealth Immigrants Bill, which restricted the entry of Kenyan Asians. Alongside his compassion was his strong libertarian instinct, abhorring what he characterised as the 'nanny state'. In Thompson's view one of the main reasons for Macleod's refusal to serve under Sir Alec Douglas-Home was that 'by his nature he was drawn to the brave, almost solitary stand'. His smouldering, volcanic energy might have made him the strongest reforming Chancellor since Lloyd George. One may also idly wonder whether he would have thought that his fellow Old Fettesian, Tony Blair, had moved somewhat to the right of the sort of Conservative party that Macleod had hoped to lead.

Thompson had had to take over the editing of *The Spectator* some three weeks before Lawson was sacked, while he was contesting Eton and Slough at the general election held on 18 June. The leaders written by Thompson over the election period were not as blatantly hostile to Wilson as Lawson would have been had he written them. But they correctly identified a mood of disillusionment with Labour and contempt for Wilson's complacency. It was an odd election: the polls were forecasting a comfortable Labour victory, the campaign was fought in a heatwave and the national newspapers were on strike. In its leader published on election day, though read by most people after the result was known, *The Spectator* did not make the mistake of assuming Labour would win. When the Conservatives were returned with an overall majority of 30, Heath was praised the following week for his seriousness, his courage and his programme of cautious reform. (He would not get many more plaudits from *The Spectator*.) Kingsley Amis voted Conservative for the first time: he wrote in the election-day issue of 'people with my sort of political record' having to 'grit their teeth, harden their heads and vote Labour out'. But that week's *Spectator* was even more significant for another reason: it contained the last contribution from Strix.

Peter Fleming was by now 63. His health was not obviously declining, but it occupied his mind; at home he appeared taciturn, sometimes depressed. His Strix pieces had become rather less frequent; *The Spectator* did not press him, but was glad to publish one when it came in. His Notebook, which appeared in print on the day of the election, ended with a comment on the 'abominable snowman'. He was definitely pro-yeti, he said, and would like it to be proved that the creature existed. But there was one reason why he was fairly sure this would never happen: for all the alleged sightings of the abominable snowman and its tracks, no one had ever found a specimen of its dung. Fleming's final piece for *The Spectator* was a review, published under his own name on 20 March 1971, of a book propounding the theory that the Russian imperial family had all escaped murder at Ekaterinburg and made their way to Poland by way of Tibet and Chungking. Fleming dismissed the book as worth recommending only 'to connoisseurs of the preposterous'. At the end of April 1971 Fleming was at last given government authorisation to undertake an official history of strategic deception, but in mid-August he collapsed on one of his favourite grouse moors in Argyllshire, having just got a right and left, and died instantly of a heart attack.

Christopher Sykes wrote an appreciation for *The Spectator*; he alluded to Fleming's enigmatic character and to his exceptional manners, mentioned only one of his books, made no reference to his Strix columns and stated incorrectly that he had been president of the Oxford Union. For a man of Fleming's literary stature, who had come to work for the magazine exactly 40 years ago, it was not good enough. (Some years earlier, the *New York Times* had published an obituary of Fleming — 'Noted Writer Reported Slain' — which he had described as 'kindly and even eulogistic, and for that reason dull.... One feels that one has played a trick on Fate, that the Grim Reaper has taken an airshot.' Sykes's obituary was not especially eulogistic, but Fleming would surely have judged it dull.)

Soon after Fleming joined the staff of *The Spectator* in 1931, as assistant literary editor, he took leave of absence to travel to China and Manchuria. Over the next four years he went twice more to the Far East, also to Brazil; from these journeys came his best-known books: *Brazilian Adventure, One's Company* and *News from Tartary*. When he was in England he wrote book and theatre reviews for *The Spectator*, and a column under the pseudonym of Moth. After the war, during which he served briefly under General Carton de Wiart in Norway and later under General Wavell in India and Burma, he began writing 'fourth leaders' for the *Times*. In *The Spectator* he adopted the pseudonym of Strix ('screech-owl' in Latin), which continued for the next 25 years. But Fleming did no screeching in his Strix essays: he was a well-to-do landowner living in South Loamshire and musing, for the most part, on country matters (and, in Ian Gilmour's view, rather too often on shooting). 'Max Beerbohm in tweeds' was the description given by a friendly critic to his weekly column which, although it began in 1946 and finished in 1971 as a notebook, more usually consisted of a single article.

Typically, it might start with an obscure or trivial news item, or an entry in the 'agony' columns of the *Times*, then proceed to amused and ruminative speculation on, for instance, what it might have meant in other circumstances which Strix would then entertainingly conjecture. It was sometimes a little difficult to know whether the eccentricities and the bizarre events of which Strix wrote were derived from experience or from his imagination. Recalling his occasional past appearances as a lecturer, Strix once wrote of a talk, with slides, which he gave, in Hitler's pre-war Berlin, to an audience of mainly SS officers on the subject of China. To the bewilderment of the SS officers, a Chinaman interrupted the lecture to protest that the pictures showed only the backward aspects of his country. When Strix had pacified him and finished the lecture, he learnt that the Chinaman was a student of constitutional law. 'It seemed an odd thing,' Strix commented, 'to be studying in Germany in 1937.'

One of Fleming's more endearing idiosyncrasies was to affect ignorance or stupidity while seeming to delight in relating how impractical and clumsy he was. He was no less modest in his assessment of his literary gifts. In a foreword to one of the anthologies of his Strix columns, *My Aunt's Rhinoceros*, he thanked *Spectator* readers for having 'supported with an extraordinary stoicism this literary equivalent of the Oriental water-torture'. His love of shooting and his talent for self-deprecation were never better combined than in his account of his coat catching fire while he was flighting duck.

The Laughing-Stock of Loamshire

I hardly believe that the thing that happened to me the week before last could have happened to anybody else. One of the reasons for my disbelief is that, unlike most people, I have no sense of smell. Other reasons will suggest themselves as I slice off the *tranche de vie*.

I was shooting with my friend R.W. in the once fashionable county of Loamshire.... In front of R.W.'s house there is a large lake, frequented by mallard, widgeon, teal, pochard, shoveller, tufted duck and other wildfowl. When we returned from shooting the coverts he suggested that we should go down to some hides on the shores of the lake and see whether in the last of the December twilight the duck, which had been disturbed that morning, were flighting in again.

...It was only when I became aware of a sort of haze or miasma emanating from the hide that I relaxed my vigilance and ceased to stare vertically upwards into the slate-coloured void. My first thought was that my dog's wet coat was steaming. I was still trying to square this idiotic notion with my knowledge that he must be as cold as I was when I realised that, whether cold or not, I was on fire.

Haze or miasma my foot! What had tardily caught my attention (and had, I learnt later, for some minutes past been gravely offending the nostrils of the next gun, two hundred yards away downwind) was dense smoke arising from a conflagration in the left-hand pocket of my jacket. The fire had been started by dottle from my pipe; a box of safety matches had provided it with fuel; and the fact that I always have the pockets of shooting-jackets lined with rubber, to keep the cartridges dry, explains why the next gun was feeling the need for a respirator...

When I reached the bank and got the coat off I found that my tweed knickerbockers had also begun to smoulder. I beat out this fresh outbreak with my left hand while with my right hand I lowered the jacket, hissing, into the dark waters of the lake. Though I lost a fountain-pen in the process, the situation was soon restored and I made my way up to the house, shaking with uncontrollable laughter like a character in a novel by Mr Dornford Yates.

Afterwards, thinking it over during a long drive home, it slowly dawned on me that the episode — which, though ridiculous, I saw as a perfectly natural occurrence with more than a touch of inevitability about it — might appear to other people in a different light. The other guns had indeed laughed politely when I showed them my charred and sodden jacket; but what were they saying now?

... However, it was too late now to do anything about it; and I comforted myself with the reflection that, although to be the laughing-stock of Loamshire is not quite on a par with contributing to the gaiety of nations, my life had been enriched by an experience which, however you look at it, is not the sort of thing that happens to people every day.

21 December 1956

Though Fleming's knowledge of, and interest in, politics was practically non-existent, he would probably have found himself out of sympathy with the Creighton/Gale *Spectator*. Gale's appointment came at a time when he was espousing the Toryism of Enoch Powell, which included opposition to Britain joining the European Economic Community. Cowling's role as literary editor was perhaps less significant than the influence he exerted as a leading member of what became known as the Peterhouse mafia.

Cowling was one of the generation at Cambridge during the immediate post-war years. Together at Peterhouse, with Cowling, were Gale, Peregrine Worsthorne and Colin Welch. Denis Mack Smith was Worsthorne's supervisor, Denis Brogan had been made a fellow in 1939, and another Peterhouse fellow, Herbert Butterfield, took up the university chair of modern history in 1944. While Cowling would later influence the political thinking of the journalists Gale, Worsthorne and Welch, their guru was a fellow of another Cambridge college, Michael Oakeshott, whom Worsthorne had met in the Netherlands during the last months of the war, when both were serving in the Phantom unit. Back at Cambridge after 1945, Oakeshott edited the *Cambridge Journal*, expounding his views on the nature of conservatism, which he saw not as 'a creed or a doctrine, but a disposition'. Charles Moore has called him 'the greatest political philosopher writing in English since the 18th century'; but he was not widely recognised and his influence was indirect, exercised through the bright young students who sat at his feet. Although Oakeshott's intellectual resistance to collectivism and state planning foreshadowed the policies of Margaret Thatcher, she found him too much of a theorist. She might also have been put off by his humorously sceptical attitude, which he shared with his co-founder and deputy editor of the *Cambridge Journal*, Desmond Williams, a European historian and a maverick, anarchic figure who was very much part of this Peterhouse group. (As a young man, Williams was an admirer of Hitler, and when he later became professor of history at University College, Dublin, he was a good friend of the future *Spectator* editor, Brian Inglis, whose brand of Irish socialism would have held no appeal for the Peterhouse High Tories.)

A younger recruit to *The Spectator* from Peterhouse in the early 1970s was Patrick Cosgrave (previously at University College, Dublin), whose supervisor was Butterfield and tutor Cowling. The Peterhouse triumvirate of Gale, Cowling and Cosgrave was responsible for changing the tone of the front half of *The Spectator*. It was not so much that their views were objectionable as that there was a stridency about the anti-Market, anti-Heath stance which, repeated week after week, was unappealing. One of those most closely involved described *The Spectator* of the time as 'raw'. This was also due in part to Gale's recent career as a tabloid journalist, for 12 years as reporter and foreign correspondent on the *Daily Express*, and latterly as columnist on the *Daily Mirror*. Until 1955 Gale had been a leader writer and labour correspondent with the *Guardian*; had his journalistic life continued on this path, *The Spectator* under his editorship would have read somewhat differently. (Ian Gilmour had asked him in 1955 to write the political column, before offering the job to Henry Fairlie.)

It was not only Powell's views that Gale respected, but he was also drawn instinctively to a maverick who expressed strong opinions. After all, that was what he was himself. Anyone who listened to Gale's phone-in programmes for the London Broadcasting radio station in the 1970s could have been excused for feeling nervous at the prospect of debating with this gruff, growling bully. He had no time for woolly thinking, no love for government meddling in an individual's affairs. He was, in short, an opinionated man of the libertarian right. But the gruffness, the impatience were only a facade: he was a sensitive, even lovable man who was once well compared with a Toby jug. Beethoven came to another's mind, seeing Gale at Gower Street for the first time, his hair billowing as he strummed furiously away at the keyboard of an ancient typewriter, with paper strewn over the desk and floor around him.

Anyone assuming that Gale was a Conservative would have been mistaken (though he did contribute, under protest, to a volume of Conservative essays published in 1979). While he was, of course, contemptuous of what he might have called wishy-washy Liberals, he did regard himself as a Liberal — rather of the hard-minded, Asquithian sort. Gale intended to publish a work of political philosophy and produced a manuscript draft, which he discussed with Cowling, but nothing more came of it. Perhaps he brooded on it for too long. ('Brooding', together with 'looking, disputing, writing poetry, roasting beef' were listed as Gale's recreations in *Who's Who*.) He sent Kingsley Amis a long poem which he said would end the book, but unfortunately nothing was sent to a publisher before his death, aged 63, in 1990.

When Gale arrived at *The Spectator* in the autumn of 1970, he inherited three people of 'wishy-washy', left-leaning political views: Christopher Hudson, assistant literary editor; Michael Wynn Jones, who had been hired from the short-lived *Mirror* magazine to help get *The Spectator* out each week and who became Gale's associate (effectively deputy) editor; and Peter Paterson, who wrote the political commentary. The point was not relevant in Hudson's case; he looked after the books pages when Cowling was at Peterhouse, dealt with Auberon Waugh's novel reviews, introduced contributors such as Rosamond Lehmann, Sir John Glubb (Glubb Pasha) and Martin Amis, and wrote the cinema column. *The Spectator* was not Wynn Jones's natural habitat and he left after about a year. During that time, however, he was responsible for bringing together a number of columns at the back of the magazine: Country Life, by Peter Quince (a pseudonym adopted by Thompson, who had moved to the *Sunday Telegraph*); City Life, Benny Green; Travelling Life, Carol Wright; The Good Life, Pamela Vandyke Price, and Sporting Life, Clive Gammon. He recruited Tony Palmer to write Notes from the Underground, a controversial column on the counter-culture of youth. (One piece was so controversial that it led to Cowling's resignation.) Wynn Jones was later best-known for having married the cookery author Delia Smith, who once cooked a lunch at *The Spectator*, together with Vandyke Price, at very short notice when the regular cook fell ill.

The socialist outlook of Paterson was not congenial either to Gale or Cowling. A former assistant editor of the *New Statesman*, Paterson had been appointed by Lawson in April 1970 (they had known one another at the *Sunday Telegraph*). In Lawson's absence during the general election, Paterson avoided giving his endorsement to either party, but he plainly thought that Labour would be returned to government. He lasted only two months after Gale's arrival in Gower Street. There was no personal animus between them — they were, and remained, on good terms — but Paterson felt that the Peterhouse mafia was making his position untenable. Their disagreement was, unsurprisingly, over Powell's principles and political future.

A book published in October, *Powell and the 1970 Election*, contained contributions from Gale and Cowling. Worsthorne took the opportunity to write about it in *The Spectator*, and an abridged version of Cowling's essay from the book was also reprinted in the magazine. In the same issue 'A

Conservative' (aka Cowling) reviewed *Right Turn*, a volume on the free-market economy, edited by Rhodes Boyson. ('Another Conservative' also made an appearance at this time.) The following month Paterson, in the course of some animadversions on Powell, commented that his leadership challenge had been 'overtaken, overwhelmed and buried by Mr Heath's election victory'. Within a few days Paterson had met with a similar fate. His only challenge was to the Powell/Peterhouse axis, but he was clearly out of step with the *Spectator* line. On 21 November 'A Conservative' took Paterson to task for suggesting that Powell had no political future and went on to ask how Conservative Paterson claimed to be. He also stated that 'we' — his friends and associates, or those directing policy at *The Spectator*? — 'are sure that entry into Europe combined with a further rebuff to Mr Powell would be deeply resented and we doubt very much, speaking entirely for ourselves, whether we would go on supporting a Heath government if Mr Heath allowed this combination of things to happen'.

In the next issue (28 November) Paterson wrote his valedictory political column, still doing battle with 'A Conservative' — 'Mr Enoch Powell's most passionately woolly supporter', in what Gale described, in an editor's note at the foot of the page, as 'this fine spirited way'. Gale's note went on, confusingly, to say: 'His [Paterson's] disagreement with "A Conservative" has nothing to do with his departure, so far as *The Spectator* is concerned.' But of course it had, certainly as far as Paterson was concerned. The explanation may be that Gale, who was concerned to keep Cowling's influence at bay in the front half of the magazine, did not want to admit that his literary editor, albeit anonymously, had been largely responsible for the demise of his political correspondent. (In a letter Paterson also, quite unfairly, blamed 'that crook Creighton for swindling me out of my salary'. When Creighton heard about it he threatened Paterson with legal action, but Gale persuaded him not to pursue the matter further.)

As if to demonstrate that he had nothing against left-wingers writing *The Spectator*'s political commentary, Gale then appointed a Bevanite socialist and Scotsman, Hugh Macpherson, in place of Paterson. But there were at least two differences between them: Macpherson was an anti-Marketeer and he was Gale's own choice for the job (though neither was in the top rank of *Spectator* political commentators). Gale also made Macpherson opera critic, for a while replacing Rodney Milnes, who wrote about concerts and festivals instead, and invited him to be ballet critic as well (which he turned down). Macpherson had great respect and affection for Gale, he had no dealings with Cowling for the six months that they were colleagues, and he carried on writing the political column for the best part of two years. He was also the first author of the Westminster gossip column, Corridors, written under the pseudonym of Tom Puzzle.

Gale also appointed Sally Vincent, a young feature writer whom he had come across at the *Daily Express*, to write a parliamentary sketch, View from the Gallery. Describing herself as a knee-jerk Marxist, and knowing nothing of the proceedings of Parliament, she cast a fresh, Taper-like eye on the House of Commons which appealed to her editor, though not to the regular, and all male, political commentators. The quite unfounded rumour was even put about, by Macpherson among others, that her column was in fact written by someone else. She was an acute and witty observer, not only of the parliamentary scene: she also wrote several reportorial pieces, under the heading 'As I Saw It', occasionally from the United States, in 1970–71.

Cowling adopted a different approach in the books pages from that which he sought to encourage in the editorial columns of the magazine. Though Powell continued sometimes to write book reviews for *The Spectator*, as he had for some years, Cowling kept Powellism out of the back half. In an attempt to appeal to the expanding pool of undergraduates and graduates from the new universities, he favoured intellectually rigorous reviews penned by academics. The names of Terry Eagleton, Hugh Trevor-Roper and John Casey appear at this period, plus, of course, the Dean of Peterhouse, Edward Norman, and one or two Fellows of the college such as Roger Scruton and Joseph Lee. An occasional review by Brian Griffiths, then lecturer in economics at the LSE, might have led to a more regular arrangement; but after he had been extensively questioned over a long lunch with Gale and Cowling, they decided that he was 'an imperfectly converted Fabian' and therefore not really suitable for *The Spectator*. (Presumably his conversion was completed some time before 1985, when Thatcher made him head of her policy unit. He was ennobled as Lord Griffiths of Fforestfach in 1991.)

One of Cowling's best moves was to appoint Waugh to be weekly novel reviewer less than a year after he had been sacked as political correspondent. Waugh's return had the full support of Gale, whom he had held up to mild ridicule in *The Spectator* when he changed his name to 'Lunchtime O'Gale' on the contents page. Personal criticism of authors and publishers was an innovation of Waugh's in his reviews. He particularly enjoyed baiting Brigid Brophy, and ventured the opinion that it was entirely due to the idleness and incompetence of publishers that so few people bought novels. They seldom sent out works of fiction for review, and 'in addition to gorging themselves with food and drink all the week, [they] generally tell lies when cornered'. Waugh called Margaret Drabble 'a moral and political imbecile', though he was prepared to acknowledge that she was a first-class writer. He once reviewed one of his own novels, conceding that some passages could usefully have been cut.

The *enfant terrible* Palmer's Underground column was meant to provoke angry readers' letters. His targets, for the most part, were the fairly obvious ones — Esther Rantzen, Kenneth Tynan — who might get upset when criticised but had a habit of cropping up in letters pages from time to time. When, however, Palmer wrote an article which began, 'Has Princess Anne had sex?', there was no doubt that this was breaking new, and to the overwhelming majority of readers unacceptable, ground. It was not that the article was critical of the princess — Palmer was in fact quite complimentary about her — but that it was inexcusably vulgar. It was published in August 1971 while Gale was on holiday. Wynn Jones was editing, but Gale had asked Cowling to keep an eye on things. Cowling saw Palmer's article before it was set in type and insisted it should not be used. When Wynn Jones said he was going to use it, Cowling wrote a letter, which he demanded should be published, dissociating himself from the article; but Wynn Jones declined to publish his letter. Creighton, who had been in favour of using the article, instructed Gale, on his return from holiday, to get rid of Cowling; and so Cowling resigned. (Creighton was glad to see the back of him: he wanted a literary editor who wore a bow tie and attended all the literary London parties, not one who spent the great majority of his time in Cambridge.) Wynn Jones was upset by the controversy, and for this and other reasons he left *The Spectator* a week afterwards, though not before he had attempted, in the Notebook, to justify publication. In the week that he departed, Gale used the Notebook tacitly to express his support for Cowling: 'To my mind, *The Spectator* was wrong to publish the article on Princess Anne.' Gale went on to comment, following a point

Evelyn Wrench,
proprietor from 1925,
and editor until 1932,
was chairman of The
Spectator *for 40 years.*

Angus Watson became
the largest single
shareholder c.1930, but
for most of the time was
an absentee landlord in
Newcastle.

*Wilson Harris, editor
1932–53. He was not
happy to be asked to give
up his editorship at the
age of 69.*

*Walter Taplin, editor
1953–54, made some
excellent appointments
during his brief tenure.*

Ian Gilmour, proprietor 1954–67 and editor 1954–59. His early years as proprietor were arguably the best.

*Brian Inglis, editor
1959–62. Inglis is
standing between Nancy
and Alan Brien.
Circulation rose
impressively during these
years and the magazine
became profitable. But
Gilmour thought it
politically irresponsible.*

*Iain Hamilton, editor
1962–63. He did not
have an easy 18 months
as editor. Many
contributors expressed
themselves strongly when
he was replaced.*

Iain Macleod, editor 1963–65, had a highly enjoyable respite from politics towards the end of his life.

Nigel Lawson, editor 1966–70. He was a good campaigning editor, who had little fellow-feeling with either of his proprietors.

George Gale, editor 1970–73. Heath and Europe seemed to be the only two issues during his time.

Harold Creighton, proprietor 1967–75 and editor 1973–75. He presided over the referendum campaign to take Britain out of Europe, while Patrick Cosgrave did much of the editing.

Alexander Chancellor, editor 1975–84. This photograph was taken on the day that Chancellor's departure from The Spectator *was reported in the press. He was responsible for the renaissance of the magazine.*

*Henry Keswick,
proprietor 1975–81, was
the first proprietor not to
do a stint as editor.*

*Algy Cluff, proprietor
1981–85 and chairman
since 1981. He was the
last of* The Spectator's
individual proprietors.

Charles Moore, editor 1984–90, served three proprietors; the last, Conrad Black, was his own choice.

James Fairfax, chairman of John Fairfax Ltd, proprietors 1985–88. He relinquished control of The Spectator *in October 1987 when the company was bought by his half-brother, Warwick.*

Conrad Black, 1988–. When the Telegraph group bought the magazine, he did not expect it to make a profit.

Dominic Lawson, editor 1990–95, sprang a few surprises during his editorship.

Frank Johnson, editor since 1995. He brought in a number of good columnists.

made by a number of readers, that the neologism 'to have sex' was a peculiarly nasty expression.

The reverberations from Palmer's piece caused no less of an upheaval among the readership. No single article, it was said, had ever been followed by so many cancelled subscriptions and such an immediate fall-off in circulation. (This was almost impossible to check, since sales figures were showing a pretty dramatic decline anyway, and Creighton had stopped having them vetted by the Audit Bureau of Circulation.) The letters columns. under the heading 'Tony Palmer and Princess Anne', were filled for the next three weeks with expressions of outrage and disgust. 'You have sunk, and will find it hard to rise again' and 'Palmer must go or your readers will' were typical reactions (though not everyone was troubled by considerations of bad taste; one correspondent wrote that 'it's only because of Auberon Waugh and Tony Palmer and a few others like them that your newspaper is worth buying'.) As the hostile letters kept coming, and *The Spectator* was required to publish a grovelling apology to *What's On* because Palmer had called it a moribund magazine, Gale decided that the thoughts rising from the Underground should in future remain buried; they had become too much of a liability. The column came to an end in October, and Palmer switched to cinema reviewing for a few months.

Readers were lost, too, on the issue of Europe and *The Spectator*'s growing hostility to the prime minister. *The Spectator* was implacably opposed, as it stated in a leader in February 1971, 'to any attempt to join the European Economic Community. It stands fast on the principle of preserving the national identity…. It rejects the purposes of the present negotiations. It believes that the matter of principle outweighs any advantage to be gained or disadvantage to be avoided by entry.' Just before the 1970 general election, Heath had said that the proposed enlargement of the EEC should not take place without 'the full-hearted consent of the Parliaments and peoples' of the applicant countries. *The Spectator* went on hammering away at this point, maintaining that such consent was lacking, that Macleod during the election campaign had promised a free parliamentary vote on the EEC, and that if he was a man of principle, Heath must define what he meant by 'full-hearted consent'.

In response to Britain's signing of the Treaty of Brussels in January 1972, providing for it to join the EEC 12 months later, *The Spectator* commented, in a leader headed 'Resisting the Treaty':

Nicholas **Davenport** on the Euro-money muddle

Gillian Freeman: Life with Uncle
Colin Wilson on British Folk-lore
Tibor Szamuely: Kremlin in a Coma
Pamela Vandyke Price: Skimped Milk
Ernest Gellner on Freud and Reich
Humphry Berkeley: Case for the UN
THE SPECTATOR IN ULSTER
7455 15 May 1971 10p

Leonard Beaton: Heart of the Atomic Matter

Plus ça change… Terms for Britain to join the EEC were agreed in June 1971.

THE PARIS TRIP

If a policy is thought to be both important and wrong, it ought to be resisted root and branch for as long as it is reversible. The Government's European policy remains reversible. The duty of those who oppose it is therefore to resist it with all vigour and on every occasion.

Yet only three months later the editor, in a signed article, 'Coming to terms with Europe', wrote that, in his view, there was no longer any point in continuing to argue the case against EEC membership. An amendment to the European Communities Bill, to allow for a referendum, had been rejected, and it was now practically certain that Britain would join the Common Market in January 1973. Gale had not changed intellectually his views on Europe, but he had been brooding again and now thought that the only realistic thing was to make the best of a bad job. There was nothing to be gained from sustaining opposition unless, which was certainly not Gale's purpose, the intention was also to get rid of Heath as prime minister.

But Cosgrave, who had replaced Wynn Jones as associate editor, had stronger feelings on the subject of the prime minister's future. Cosgrave had begun writing for *The Spectator* under Nigel Lawson, then joined the Conservative Research Department, where he used to brief Heath on Prime Minister's Questions when he was leader of the Opposition and occasionally to write speeches for him. Cosgrave was still at the CRD when his old Peterhouse tutor, Cowling, invited him to write an article on Heath's European policy. Published in June 1971, by 'A Senior Conservative' — which Cosgrave, of course, was not — it caused quite a stir. He accused the prime minister of putting his European ideal — that Britain should become an integrated West European state — before the interests of his party, and said that the party could well survive without him. When two more articles followed from this 'senior Conservative', Michael Fraser, a vice-chairman of the party, asked Cosgrave, as a diligent research department employee, to find out the identity of this nigger in the Conservative woodpile. His failure to do so made Heath's special adviser, Michael Wolff, rather more suspicious than he already was that Cosgrave was the offender. Shortly afterwards, Gale offered Cosgrave the job of deputy editor and, after Macpherson had left at the end of September 1972, political commentator. He had toyed with the idea of inviting Anthony Hartley back to *The Spectator*, but his pro-European credentials disqualified him.

The editor's coming to terms with Europe was not always reflected in the editorials, written by Cosgrave, which continued to castigate Heath for forcing the European Bill through without the 'full-hearted consent' of Parliament. 'With each day that passes, the European Economic Community looks a more ramshackle and clapped-out organisation, a bureaucratic paradise and a political hell,' *The Spectator* declaimed in June 1972, two months after Gale had resigned himself to Britain becoming part of that organisation.

The Spectator received a stack of letters from dismayed correspondents — 'your faithless surrender to the Marketeers', 'no amount of specious argument justifies the abandonment of principle' — when Gale appeared to drop his opposition to Britain becoming a member of the EEC. But most would continue to buy *The Spectator* in the hope, soon realised, that the magazine would renew its opposition once Britain was in Europe, culminating in the

ELECTION DAY FINAL

The Spectator gave little support to Heath at the two 1974 elections.

No. 7601 Week ending March 2, 1974 15p

"Better the devil I know..."

Ralph Harris: who will save us?

John Vaizey and William Pickles on renegotiation prospects

Clive Jenkins: tomorrow's unions

Philip Kleinman: admen and elections

Peter Ackroyd: the press and the election

Benny Green: Goodbye hustings

A vote for Britain

The Spectator is, as Iain Macleod wrote when he was our editor, a Tory paper, but also a radical one. Since Macleod's death we have also, perforce, and without losing those characteristics, become much more nationalist. Britain has been under such steady and unremitting attack, from within as well as without, that we have felt it necessary to defend as best we can both the identity and the interest of this country, in as sharp and clear and detailed a manner as possible, against all the forces arrayed against her. Thus, because we are a Tory and a radical paper, we have been among the steadiest critics of the continuing, humiliating and tragic abandonment of the policies with which this present Government came to power in 1970; and because we are a nationalist paper, we have fought as best we have been able against the destructive entanglement with Europe into which Mr Heath has led us without any vestige of consent from the people of the country. Indeed, we have more than once made plain our view that, whatever the merits or demerits of the modern Conservative Party, there is very little indeed to be said from the point of view of the national interest for its singular, self-willed and over-powerful leader. There are thus no circumstances in which we would like to see the electorate giving Mr Heath the kind of mandate, involving an increased majority in the House of Commons, which he has sought since the outset of the general election campaign.

This is not, however, the same thing as saying that we do not wish to see a Conservative majority returned. Before returning such a majority, nonetheless, the radical Tory will want to ponder the likely result of a vote to that end. It may be that those who agree with Mr Powell that the supreme and over-riding issue of this campaign is British membership — not only without the will, but against the will, of the British people — of the Common Market, and the form in which that membership is likely to develop under the leadership of Mr Heath, will, possibly in large numbers, vote Labour. Others, however, may well feel that so extreme a course is unnecessary, given developments within the EEC since our membership took effect.

Thus, though the Government has insistently derided the Labour policy of renegotiating the treaty of Brussels Mr John Davies has, during the campaign, used that very word to describe

1975 referendum on continued membership. A lot of Heath's supporters, however, were not prepared to go on putting up with Cosgrave's abuse of the prime minister. When he laid into the government for its mismanagement of the dispute with the National Union of Mineworkers in February 1972, one correspondent accused *The Spectator* of having 'out-Wilsoned Wilson'. Another wrote of being 'nauseated' at the attitude to Heath, wondering whether he was reading Richard Crossman in the *New Statesman*. But Cosgrave's blood was up, and he got even more excited at the findings of a *Spectator* poll, which he organised at the 1972 Conservative party conference. Asked whom they would like to see as Heath's successor, should he resign, the delegates expressed their preference almost equally for Robert Carr and for Cosgrave's hero, Powell, who had just passed his 60th birthday. The following month Heath imposed a statutory prices and wages freeze, and Powell asked him if he had taken leave of his senses. Cosgrave was close

The
Spectar
No. 7633 Week ending October 12, 1974 15p

National union– who gets in, who gets out?

Voting for Britain—tactically

This has been the most dispiriting and boring British general election campaign since the war; and parts of it have been not a little disgraceful as well. The disgraceful parts have been evident mainly in relation to the effort of all three campaigns by the party leaders to imply that the conclusion in their manifestos—that Britain was facing, was in the middle of, an unprecedented economic crisis—was wrong, and that their own return to office would provide peace, quiet, and a modest hope of advancement. The only honest campaign would be one in which political leaders confessed the likelihood of extreme hardship, and simply suggested means by which they would attempt to alleviate it. But such footlingly dishonest tricks as that employed by Mr Healey in presenting his now notoriously unsuccessful inflation graph seemed democratic electioneering; and Mr Heath was not much better in the way in which he followed almost every assertion that he was determined not to indulge in personal attacks on his rivals by just such attacks.

In every general election of recent years, save that of 1959 — when the present Shadow Secretary of State for Northern Ireland, and Chairman of the Conservative Research Department, Mr Ian Gilmour, owned and edited the paper — we have advised our readers to vote Conservative; occasionally, as in February of this year, with reservations, but usually wholeheartedly. In weighing our decision this month it was necessary, however, to consider the recent records in power of the two parties; to consider the immediate difficulties the nation faces; and to analyse the relative strengths of Mr Wilson and Mr Heath. When, in February, we recommended a Tory vote we did so out of loyalty as much as, if not more than, out of judgement: The Spectator had taken Mr Heath severely to task several times since 1970 for the muddle, the inconsistency and the — sometimes — barefaced dishonesty of his policies. We, and his many other critics in the party, had every reason to expect that, once the February defeat had signalled the rejection by the electorate of what he then represented himself as

behind in reiterating his contempt for the prime minister.

It is reasonable to assume that quite a number of Heath's supporters stopped reading the magazine around this time. Many others, though no longer sympathetic towards Heath after he had lost the first general election in 1974, were put off *The Spectator* by the increasing virulence of Cosgrave's language. When the prime minister tried and failed to hold on to power, with Liberal support, in March, Cosgrave's leader, 'Exit the Squatter', described the spectacle as ludicrous, pathetic and contemptible. 'Nothing became his leadership of the nation so ill as the manner of his leaving it.... He has spent nine years trying to ruin the Conservative party, and three and a half trying to ruin the country.' After Heath lost the subsequent election in October, Cosgrave called him 'this morbidly pathetic creature', the party's 'most unsuccessful and unlikeable leader this century'.

For all his vituperation, Cosgrave was remarkably percipient in assessing the public mood and anticipating the 1974 election results. In the issue published on election day (28 February) he forecast 'a minority government (probably Labour) or a Labour government with a small majority.... In either case we can expect another election at an early date.' The article was headed 'Egg on my face?' and the following week *The Spectator* and many readers congratulated Cosgrave on going against the wisdom of the opinion polls which had predicted a Tory victory. In his pre-election leader Cosgrave had planned to advise readers to vote Labour, and indeed had written a draft to that effect. (Powell put his weight behind the Labour party at this election.) It would have been the second time in 15 years that *The Spectator* had deserted a Conservative government at a general election. But Creighton would not agree, foreseeing that the circulation graph would show an even steeper decline if the magazine abandoned its Conservative credentials. The story goes that after prolonged argument, which continued until shortly before the printers' deadline, Cosgrave finally put down his glass of whisky and rewrote the leader, encouraging readers to vote Conservative after all. In fact the leader substantially qualified that advice, saying that abstention could be justified in some circumstances, and that the electorate should certainly deny Heath an increased majority.

The headline on *The Spectator*'s leader was 'A vote for Britain'. When the next election came round in October, Cosgrave's leader, headed 'Voting for Britain — tactically', made little effort to encourage readers to vote Conservative; indeed it advised anti-Marketeers, also the Scots and the Welsh, to vote Labour. The Conservative party, he wrote, had to purge itself of the Heath heritage; this could be achieved by electing a Labour government with a tiny overall majority, which would be the best result. Labour won with an overall majority of three seats, and Cosgrave immediately began to press the claims of Sir Keith Joseph for the Tory leadership. A month before the election, Joseph, then shadow Home Secretary, had annoyed Heath by urging control of the money supply to check inflation.

During the early 1970s, more to provide a corrective to its Powellite stance than to back up its opposition to Heath, *The Spectator* took to publishing occasional pieces by Labour MPs — Eric Heffer, Michael Meacher, Frank Field. This was entirely consistent with *The Spectator*'s tradition of giving space to different viewpoints, provided they were well expressed, and with Gale's own libertarian disposition. Shortly before his departure, Gale also published an article which encapsulated his attitudes to freedom of speech. The author was Robert Conquest, former literary editor of *The Spectator*, great friend of Amis and sometime composer of naughty limericks, who took the then Rector of Dundee, Peter Ustinov, to task for having prevented Powell from fulfilling an invitation to speak at the university. Conquest, who seldom found himself agreeing with Powell, objected to Ustinov's assertion that it was legitimate to restrict Powell's freedom to speak when 'we all know what Powell is going to say in advance, and whatever he says is given broad publicity, [so] it doesn't matter whether he says it on campus or elsewhere'. As Conquest commented witheringly, the Rector's idea of freedom was to permit you only to say what you have not said before, and in a place which was acceptable to him. If what you propose to say is unpalatable to the left, then of course it is not inconsistent with freedom of speech that you should be stopped from saying it.

As an attack on intellectual corruption and anti-libertarian prejudice, Conquest's piece was a suitable swansong for Gale, who was sacked a few months later. Though much of the running and the writing of the magazine would in future be undertaken by Cosgrave, who remembers once filling eight pages of a single issue with pieces written by himself, including a long poetry review, the man who replaced Gale as editor in September 1973, making himself, as he put it, 'editor by purchase', was the proprietor himself, Harold Digby Fitzgerald Creighton. The most plausible reason for Creighton's decision to get rid of Gale was the need to save money. Creighton thought he could make a profit from *The Spectator*, that it could be made to work, as if mechanically, like a machine tool, and it irritated him greatly that he was being proved wrong. In the previous year, 1972, having been mocked by a business friend for failing to cut *The Spectator*'s losses, Creighton demanded that Gale reduce the editorial staff from five to four. Apart from the editor, there were Cosgrave, Kenneth Hurren, arts and features and production editor, Charles Seaton, librarian, sub-editor and much more besides, and the literary editor, Christopher Hudson. Hudson was dropped, and Hurren took over the books for a while (though not for long, since Gale made Peter Ackroyd literary editor in the early part of 1973). Creighton also decided to increase the size of the advertising department, to little noticeable effect (except for a rash of small ads for saunas and massage parlours).

Gale used to say that he was fired because Creighton was determined to get himself into *Who's Who*. As proprietor of *The Spectator* he did not qualify automatically, but as editor he would. It irked him that the comedians Eric Morecambe and Ernie Wise had just been included in the biographical dictionary of 'people of influence and interest in all fields', but he had not. In any event, though Gale's sacking came as quite a shock to him, there was no acrimony between the two, no row about anything in particular; Gale was paid an agreed sum of £5,000, and that was that. He continued to stay with his former boss in London and Sussex, and the following year became a fairly regular contributor again. In 1975 he helped with the referendum campaign. Like almost everyone, Creighton always had great respect and affection for Gale.

Larry Adler, the American mouth-organist, was one of Creighton's few great fans. Having been invited by Creighton to write occasional pieces, Adler enjoyed his editor's company in the Gower Street dining-room, and the atmosphere of a private club which he found in the office. Balding, with a shiny pink face and small blue eyes, Creighton was often charming and cheerful. He was indiscreet, loved gossip and was a good host at parties. He was also impulsive, inclined to come up with odd ideas, and his countenance would quickly become choleric when his temper flared. He was around the office a lot, even before he became editor, and would spend much of his time talking. He enjoyed the company of journalists and always got on well with Gale and Cosgrave, but it has to be said that he did not inspire great respect among most of his staff. One described him as 'a necessary burden that had to be carried'.

Creighton clearly fancied himself not only as a buccaneering business-man in the Slater or Maxwell mould, but as a successful proprietor. By 1973 he had given up his own political ambitions: he had tried, and failed, to get himself selected as a parliamentary candidate during Lawson's editorship, and when he later put his name down for his home constituency of Chichester, *The Spectator*'s anti-Heath reputation was such that he was not even called for interview. So he had to content himself with wielding political influence from the sidelines. Lawson had never had any disagreement with him over Europe; once Gale and Cosgrave came along, however, Creighton's apparent enthusiasm for Britain's membership of an expanding Common Market did a volte-face. He was delighted to play host at Gower

Street lunches to anti-Marketeers and to critics of the prime minister from both parties. Wilson came to lunch in 1972, boasting that he would 'screw' Heath, the Civil Service and Roy Jenkins. Joseph and Thatcher became fairly regular guests after Heath's first 1974 election defeat.

When Creighton realised that he was not going to achieve financial success with *The Spectator*, he started having other publishing ideas, most notably in the area of soft pornography. He joked about launching a magazine to be called *Voyeur*, and he bought the *Lilliput* title, which was never published again. Then he invested £10,000 in a new magazine to be called *Cockade* and edited by Harold Fieldhouse, a former editor of *Penthouse*. It folded after one issue. This interest in soft-porn publishing may not have been unconnected with the reputation which he acquired for trying to seduce young secretaries. Juliette Harrison, who came straight from secretarial college, aged 18, to be Creighton's secretary in 1968, was preceded in the job by a glamorous girl who had left abruptly after only a few days. But young Juliette survived, though she and other female members of staff used to be taken by Creighton to Annabel's night-club, in the company of business friends whom he wrote about, and Glan Williams caricatured, in Skinflint's City diary. Sally Vincent was nonplussed one day to be asked by Creighton if she would like to see the emeralds he had bought his wife for Christmas. Hot-panted girls used sometimes to cook and serve at the Gower Street lunches, which not surprisingly enraged at least one of the guests, Germaine Greer, who had recently published *The Female Eunuch*.

Creighton enjoyed gossipy columns, with tidbits of mischievous and sometimes defamatory information. Hudson wrote one such, Bookend by Bookbuyer, which brought writs from Hamish Hamilton and Weidenfeld & Nicolson. Apart from Creighton's own Skinflint, there was Will Waspe's arts diary, somewhat archly written by Hurren, Tom Puzzle's Westminster Corridors, often the work of John Groser of the *Times*, and during 1974–75 James Hughes-Onslow's Peregrinations. At the end of 1970 Juliette Harrison started a racing column, with tips, called Juliette's Weekly Frolic. Having written the first one at the printers' one evening, to fill a space on the City page, she continued for over three years as Britain's first female racing tipster. Gale gave her a notional stake of £100, threatening to end the column when the money ran out after a year. But she had an enthusiastic readership — 'I had a little bet on her 5 to 1 winner, bless the girl!' wrote

General Sir Nevil Brownjohn one week — and a syndicate comprising Nicholas Davenport, Clive Gammon (who wrote Sporting Life and later married Juliette) and Christopher Fildes (*The Spectator*'s previous racing correspondent, using the pseudonym of Captain Threadneedle) guaranteed an overdraft for a further £100. This lasted until she left *The Spectator* in March 1974, after a final, losing, bet on the Grand National. By this time she had overcome resistance from the racing authorities and been given accreditation as a racing correspondent.

One of the problems with Creighton's *Spectator* was its appearance. It was typographically unattractive and it suffered from numerous misprints and poor-quality paper. It gave the impression, an entirely accurate one, of a publication surviving on a shoestring. The printers, waiting for their bills to be paid, threatened an end to credit arrangements. Contributors to the magazine had to be cajoled into writing for £10 or £15 an article. But there was always hospitality at Gower Street, alcoholic lunches at which the whisky bottle was placed on the table after the main course and the press columnist, Bill Grundy, invariably got drunk. (One evening, having just insulted Creighton, he fell down the stone staircase and was hung by his jacket on the railings outside the front door of No. 99. But he delivered his copy on time the following morning.) During the 1974 election campaigns Creighton would give Sunday lunches at the Connaught hotel to Cosgrave and Hurren (at which Gale would sometimes turn up) in order to discuss the forthcoming issue. At this time, and until Alexander Chancellor became editor, *The Spectator* was published on Tuesday.

The handful of editorial staff had to draw deeply from the well of goodwill still enjoyed by *The Spectator* to persuade people to write not only for derisory fees but at a time when the magazine appeared to be in irreversible decline. When Creighton assumed editorial control in 1973, Christopher Booker wrote in the *Daily Telegraph* that its demise could not be long delayed. 'The portals of 99 Gower Street unmistakably bear that contemporary equivalent of the plague cross, the mysterious initials which are allegedly scribbled by doctors over the terminal patient's temperature chart — NTBR, or "Not to be resuscitated".'

But the harbingers of doom did not stop the flow of good writing in *The Spectator*, particularly in the books pages, where the reviewers included Stephen Spender, A.L. Rowse, Norman Stone, Jan Morris, Kenneth

Minogue, Elizabeth Longford, Sir Iain Moncreiffe of that Ilk, Donald Cameron Watt and Leo Abse. Sir Oswald Mosley was invited to give his opinion of Robert Skidelsky's biography of him (not unfavourable). Children's books were once or twice reviewed by Sandra Paul, later to become Mrs Michael Howard. Peter Ackroyd, aged 23 and fresh from Yale, had been appointed literary editor by Gale in the spring of 1973. Before offering him the job, Gale gave Ackroyd a couple of reviews to write and asked him if there was anything unknown to Gale which might affect his suitability to be literary editor. When Ackroyd confessed to 'a bit of a drinking problem' he was hired on the spot. (In Gale's day, and indeed afterwards, alcohol played a not insignificant role in the life of *The Spectator*. When Minette Marrin was taken on as Hudson's assistant in 1971 — Gale arbitrarily added the 'te' to her first name Minet, which he thought insufficiently feminine — her first commission from the editor was to go to the local off-licence and pick up the whisky order.)

Knowing that Creighton was partial to showbusiness names, Ackroyd engaged Elaine Stritch and George Axelrod as occasional reviewers. In the front half a new section, Society Today, was introduced, with regular columns on science from Bernard Dixon and religion by the Very Revd Martin Sullivan, a New Zealander who became Dean of St Paul's and was given to using strong language at the Gower Street lunch table. (He was applauded by *The Spectator* for refusing to allow the Archbishop of Canterbury to use St Paul's for a service on behalf of the European Development Movement: 'The Dean has struck an important blow for the purity of Christianity'.)

A series of articles on prostitution in London was published early in 1974, no doubt with an eye to the flagging circulation figures, but it made no noticeable difference. On economic matters, *The Spectator* was in monetarist alliance with the Institute of Economic Affairs, one of whose directors, Ralph Harris (Lord Harris of High Cross), would contribute articles as a counterweight to the regular neo-Keynesianism of Davenport and, occasionally, Professor Joan Robinson. To students of the Middle East, *The Spectator*'s attitude towards Israel had executed a sharp turn since the Arabist Gilmour years. So favourably disposed was it now — 'It is necessary for every Western fibre to be strained to encourage [Israel] not just to survive but to prosper' — that the editor and political commentator were both invited to Israel as guests of the government.

By the autumn of 1974, however, the attention of Creighton and Cosgrave was most enthusiastically engaged on two campaigns at home: getting Heath out of the Conservative leadership and Britain out of Europe. Having declared himself as a monetarist, Joseph was their early favourite for leader, but when he ruled himself out of the contest they quickly turned to his protégée, Thatcher. Sir Richard Body, who had supported the liberal economy and drawn attention in *The Spectator* in mid-1972 to Professor Hayek's *The Road to Serfdom*, remembers attending a *Spectator* lunch when Joseph was dithering over his candidacy for the leadership. It was Cosgrave who first gave Body the idea that Thatcher should succeed Heath. When he returned to the House of Commons that afternoon, Body sought out Fergus Montgomery (who was to become Thatcher's PPS) and Sir Marcus Fox, and from then the bandwagon started to roll. Having backed Joseph, *The Spectator* wanted to be sure that their new candidate was not going to pull out. Thatcher assured Creighton and Cosgrave that she was made of sterner stuff, and she got their unequivocal support. Cosgrave called her 'the foremost Tory in the country' and headed one of his leaders, 'Woman of the hour'. By the second week of February 1975 she had been elected leader. (Gale was not so convinced: in a personal column at the end of December he had dismissed Thatcher's chances of being elected and instead made the bizarre suggestion that Edward du Cann, 'potentially the most successful and powerful of those whose records are politically clean', should stand for the leadership.)

The referendum on Europe followed in June. *The Spectator* was virtually the only publication against continued EEC membership, and Creighton virtually the only person who really believed that the referendum vote would go against Europe. He put a room in Gower Street at the disposal of the National Referendum Campaign (NRC, chairman, Neil Marten) and Get Britain Out (chairman, Christopher Frere-Smith), and continued to dispense hospitality in spite of his dwindling funds.

The Spectator's anti-European bedfellows were a rum bunch, many of them Labour MPs, plus a sprinkling of union leaders (including Jack Jones and Arthur Scargill, who was Yorkshire regional chairman of Get Britain Out). Tony Benn's son Hilary, rather to his embarrassment, used an office at Gower Street for a while; and Powell was closely involved. Geoffrey Robinson, chief executive of Jaguar Cars (and a future Labour MP, proprietor of the *New Statesman* and minister in Blair's government), wrote an article in *The Spectator* recommending a 'No' vote, because the terms for our EEC membership were unacceptable. Douglas Jay and Clive Jenkins also contributed articles, and a weekly series, 'Sovereign State', was published over several months.

Gale was often at Gower Street, doing his best to run the publicity for the campaign. But the government propaganda machine was never going to give the anti-EEC movement much of a chance. An allocation of £500,000 from public funds was made to the NRC, but it was not shared with Get Britain Out, which was strongly opposed to the NRC's idea that, as in a general election, the campaign should last only three weeks. At one point Marten proposed handing the conduct of the campaign over to Ian Greer, the political publicist who was to come to grief 20 years later. His reputation as long ago as the mid-1970s, however, was such that Frere-Smith, who was also vice-chairman of the NRC, quickly scuppered the idea.

Although liaison between the two committees was not always good, *The Spectator* gave every assistance, on occasion publishing their publicity material almost verbatim as editorials. But apart from the occasional helpful piece from George Clark in the *Times* and C. Gordon Tether ('Lombard') in the *Financial Times*, no other serious journal took up the cause, which was further frustrated by the refusal of several Labour MPs to put aside their party differences and join anti-EEC Conservatives on the same public platforms. Nor did it help that most of the Labour MPs involved were well into their fifties, and a few — Ian Mikardo, Douglas Jay, Barbara Castle — not far short of 70. *The Spectator*'s final flourish, in the issue published on referendum day, was to illustrate on the cover the statue of the Brussels boy urinating over a Union Jack being held above the heads of politicians such as Heath, Roy Jenkins and Jeremy Thorpe. The result of the referendum was a vote to stay in the EEC by a margin of 2:1.

Some months before, Creighton had let it be known that *The Spectator* was for sale. It had become too much of a drain on his resources. Apart from the regular weekly losses, the libel writs were proving expensive. In the only case that went to court — an action by the Crime Writers' Association, arising from one of Tony Palmer's columns — *The Spectator* agreed to pay £5,000 soon after the trial began, when it emerged that the presiding judge, the egregious Mr Justice Melford Stevenson, had a soft spot for the plaintiffs, having recently been entertained at their table.

Creighton had worked on the principle, perfectly sound for a tabloid newspaper, that gossip and provocative writing would attract readers. But it did not work for *The Spectator*, and it cost him money. The trouble with the magazine early in 1975 was that, in spite of Cosgrave's prescience in backing Thatcher, the EEC referendum, which had become almost its raison d'être, was seen as a lost cause, and the magazine's abusive tone was coming to sound like a death-rattle. In some weeks the number of pages had to be cut due to printing disputes. The cover price was raised in March from 15p to 20p, the first increase in almost four years. There were other signs: notices in the magazine urged readers to place a firm order with their newsagents, or alternatively to take out a subscription, 'as most newsagents are reluctant to carry surplus copies'. The message, that the sale-or-return facility was being withdrawn due to low volume and falling sales, was clear. Not only *The Spectator* but the Gower Street building itself was crumbling and badly in need of attention.

Had it not been for the June referendum, Creighton would probably have accepted an offer in the spring to buy the magazine for £30,000. But it was his good fortune that by the summer Henry Keswick, chairman of Jardine Matheson, the Hong Kong trading empire, and recently returned after 15 years out east, had decided he wanted to buy *The Spectator* and gave Creighton £75,000 for it.

8

RESURRECTION

Ian Gilmour had had no thought of entering politics when he bought *The Spectator*, but became an MP eight years later. Both Harry Creighton and Henry Keswick did entertain such thoughts on becoming proprietor, but neither succeeded in getting into Parliament. It was understandable that Keswick should think about a political career, since both his grandfather and great-grandfather had been MPs, for Epsom, before and during the first world war, and he hoped that owning *The Spectator* might ease his passage to Westminster. (The original idea, that Keswick should buy *The Spectator*, came from his cousin Tessa Reay, whom he married ten years later and who was to become Director of the Centre for Policy Studies in 1995.) Keswick was also drawn to *The Spectator* because one of his father's best friends, Peter Fleming, used to stay with the family, in China and in Scotland, and he had been a regular reader of Fleming's Strix columns. His father's other great friend, from their time together in Shanghai in the 1930s, was Sir Christopher Chancellor, formerly Reuters' general manager in the Far East. As Keswick said on taking over *The Spectator*, the only journalist he knew was Sir Christopher's son Alexander, a family friend with whom he had been at Eton and Cambridge, and so he made him editor. The new arrangements were announced in *The Spectator* in the last week of June, and the transfer took place with effect from 1 August.

The first and most urgent problem was to find new premises for the magazine. The £75,000 that Keswick paid for *The Spectator* did not include its Gower Street offices, which Creighton sold separately to Haslemere Estates and are now occupied by the London School of Hygiene and Tropical Medicine. (An allocation of London Weekend Television shares, which Creighton had taken over from Gilmour in 1967, cost him £70,000 when the licence application was approved. Though he sold the shares at a £50,000 profit, needing the money to support *The Spectator*'s losses, they would be worth £2.75 million today.)

The sale to Keswick was greeted with general relief; it meant, at least, that *The Spectator* had a future, which had been in some doubt during Creighton's last months. The weekly circulation figure, which had not been subjected to the usual audit for the past few years, was said to have averaged around 17,000 for 1974, but it was probably nearer 13,000 (and went on falling until 1977, the year when the *New Statesman* dropped below 40,000 for the first time in living memory). No one would judge the Creighton era to be among the more successful periods in *The Spectator*'s history. But some good fights were fought and some good times had. It was to Creighton's credit that *The Spectator*, almost alone, had upheld the views of one third of the electorate on an issue so important to Britain's future, even if its obsession with that issue was unappealing. The tradition of a resolutely independent journal of the right had not been broken. In writing of *The Spectator*'s departure from Gower Street after 46 years, George Hutchinson described Creighton as 'not without aptitude, albeit of a somewhat slapdash, capricious sort'. So he was; and he should perhaps be best remembered for having resurrected the dining-room in the basement of No. 99. Here lunches were held almost daily, and here information and opinion were exchanged — artistic and literary as well as political — which worked to *The Spectator*'s advantage.

In the second week of August workmen moved into 99 Gower Street and began demolishing the extension at the back. *The Spectator* removed itself on a Friday and reopened for business after the weekend, still in Bloomsbury, at 56 Doughty Street. New premises had had to be found at alarmingly short notice, and *The Spectator* was faced with finding temporary accommodation. But by a piece of great good fortune Chancellor's wife, Susanna, heard from a friend that Anthony Blond was thinking of moving his publishing offices from the 18th-century house which the firm occupied in Doughty Street. Blond was known to Chancellor and Keswick, and in a friendly way agreed to get out of the building rather sooner than he had intended (though for the first week or so *The Spectator* was obliged to operate in two rooms). Situated in a wide, quiet Georgian street near Gray's Inn (Dickens had lived a few doors down), the building was occupied between 1895 and 1953 by Laurence Turner, sculptor and carver, who modelled the decorative plaster ceilings and cornices on the ground and first floors. The house was and is ideal for *The Spectator*. It is on four floors (plus a basement), with a staircase which becomes steeper towards the top, where a dining-room and kitchen were soon established. The editor's office (formerly the drawing-room of the house) is still furnished with sofas, and the paved garden at the back is used for *The Spectator*'s annual summer party.

Chancellor's first move, even before the departure from Gower Street, was to announce in the Notebook his aim 'to improve the paper without fundamentally changing its character. That is why we invite you, our readers, to offer your suggestions.' Of those that were published, Lord Shinwell wanted more controversy, while Sir Arthur Driver thought that *The Spectator* should revert to its original role of 'Looker-On', as established by Addison and Steele in the 18th century. One correspondent criticised the number of weekly columns, another said there were too many diary features. Someone quoted the words of the old song: 'Stay as sweet as you are.... Don't let a soul rearrange you.' Other ideas were to improve the typography, reintroduce the front-page leader and bring back Auberon Waugh. Within a few months the last three suggestions were all followed. Even before that, Hutchinson returned to *The Spectator*, this time as deputy editor. He remained with the magazine until his death from cancer in 1980. For Chancellor, who had no experience of nor any consuming interest in politics, Hutchinson was an obvious choice to add political weight. He had been political correspondent of the *Evening Standard*, he had worked at Central Office during Harold Macmillan's last years as prime minister and he was the author of biographies of Macmillan and Heath. He had also worked for *The Spectator* during Gilmour's time, when Nigel Lawson was editor. Hutchinson's colleagues remember him not so much for his political acumen or for his written contributions (latterly there were not very many of them) as for his engaging company. He had a fund of entertaining political recollections, he gave wise counsel on a number of subjects, not all of them serious ones and, unlike some journalists, he was a good listener. His writing had always had a quality of reflectiveness, of standing back for a few moments' thought from the hurly-burly of political events, and in his daily life, too, he would not be hurried. He liked to quote Randolph Churchill, who had been taught by his father never to walk fast, because you will lose dignity; and he would often be heard to say 'Hang on' or 'Wait a sec' if a crisis arose or a deadline was imminent. Hutchinson pinned a sheet of No. 10 Downing Street writing-paper to the mantelpiece in Chancellor's office, on which Macmillan had written, in his own hand: 'Quiet calm deliberation disentangles every knot.' Hutchinson also had a way with words; it was, at least in part, an Edwardian pose that he had inherited from Macmillan. 'I am about to cross the road to the Duke of York public house, there to purchase a packet of cigarettes,' he would announce five minutes before opening time. 'And if you would care to accompany me,' he might say to a colleague, 'we might take a glass of refreshment together.' On one occasion, having hailed a taxi, Hutchinson addressed the driver: 'Ah, there you are, cabbie; would you be so good as to set us down at the foot of Fetter Lane?' To which the reply came: 'Would I f...ing what, guv?'

For a time Hutchinson advised Keswick in his search for a parliamentary seat, helping to identify suitable constituencies as they became available and briefing him before he was called for interview by local selection committees. But it was to no avail: Keswick got on to a few short-lists, but never quite made it. He missed being chosen for Poole by only two votes; and he was very disappointed not to be selected for the old family constituency of Epsom (now Epsom and Ewell) after Sir Peter Rawlinson retired.

At the time of the first Conservative party conference with Margaret Thatcher as leader, *The Spectator*, in a leading article written by Hutchinson, proposed that she should make Heath her Foreign Secretary. It provoked a witty retort from Creighton the following week in a letter headed 'News from Transylvania':

> Ah, ah. The moment my back is turned on the old schloss I see that you are raising the catch on the window, removing the wolfbane and leaving the Tories' true princess to Dracula's nauseating attentions and putrefying ideas.
>
> Where is the faithful young doctor — Patrick Cosgrave — I left on guard? Drugged — or has he too had the tell-tale bite?

No, he had not: continuing as *The Spectator*'s political commentator for another six months, he knew it would be in his interests to keep off the subjects of Europe and Heath, and so turned his attention instead to his heroine, Thatcher, and to discoursing more generally on aspects of Conservatism. But he must have winced to read a letter from two pupils at a Nottinghamshire grammar school who expressed their dismay and disgust that *The Spectator*, as 'the spokesman for true Toryism... should slide down the path to centre-left politics'. Earlier that year Cosgrave had devoted two articles to attacking the centre-left politics of Gilmour, castigating him in particular for seeking to defend Heath's economic record. One might have expected a sharp political divide within *The Spectator*'s offices, since Hutchinson was sympathetic towards Gilmour, for whom he had previously worked, and had written a friendly biography of Heath. In fact he and Cosgrave always got on well, and never allowed their differences over Heath to spoil the hours which they used to spend in amicable discussion over large whiskies at the Duke of York.

However, Chancellor naturally wanted to appoint his own political commentator, and to this end he approached Alan Watkins, who had last done the job in 1967, and since that time had been political correspondent of the *New Statesman*. He had been poached from *The Spectator* (as had Alan Brien) by Paul Johnson, then editor of the *New Statesman*. In 1975 it was edited by Watkins's brother-in-law, Anthony Howard. Chancellor went for a right and left, so to speak, inviting Auberon Waugh at the same time to leave the *New Statesman*, where he was also writing a weekly column, and return to *The Spectator*. It was an old-fashioned raid on a rival, and both Waugh and Watkins appeared to have accepted Chancellor's financial inducements. But when Howard became aware that he was about to lose two of his best writers to the only other political weekly, something had to be done. He reluctantly accepted the loss of Waugh to *The Spectator*, and he could not match Chancellor's offer to Watkins. So he suggested to Donald Trelford, editor of the *Observer*, that he might like to hire Watkins instead, thus deflecting what Howard saw as an attack on the *New Statesman* to, as he put it, 'a less tiresome quarter'. The upshot was that Watkins agreed, in the first week of December, to go to the *Observer*. Keswick, Chancellor and Hutchinson met him at El Vino's wine bar in Fleet Street where they remonstrated with him and increased their offer, and Watkins left them standing at the bar without a new political correspondent. Cosgrave carried on until the following May, when he became a special adviser to Thatcher and John Grigg took on the political commentary.

In the 1975 Christmas issue Cosgrave was advising Thatcher on her first shadow cabinet reshuffle, while on the previous page, in the Notebook, Hutchinson was again trying to find a job for Heath. Having by now dropped the idea of returning Heath to the front bench, acknowledging that 'he and Mrs Thatcher are not compatible', he was determined that Heath should become Speaker on the retirement of Selwyn Lloyd. As 'a truly national figure of the utmost eminence', Hutchinson wrote, no one was better qualified to speak for the Mother of Parliaments and preside over its daily business.

That Christmas issue contained a good mix of previous regular contributors (Brien, Peter Quince) and names (Philip Hope-Wallace, Quentin Crewe), familiar enough, though not in the pages of *The Spectator*. William Trevor wrote a short story for Christmas (the first in a long line of short stories in *Spectator* Christmas numbers), and Shirley Conran reviewed a book on prostitutes. Chancellor was happy to keep Peter Ackroyd as literary editor. Among his many talents — the outpouring of his novels and biographies was to come later — Ackroyd was weekly fiction reviewer, production editor, occasional foreign correspondent (George Gale had sent him to the 1973 war between Egypt and Israel) and, when he gave up the literary editorship, cinema critic. He was good at matching reviewers and books: Lord Shinwell on Golda Meir, William Sargant, head of the Department of Psychological Medicine at St Thomas's Hospital, on Arthur Koestler, Joyce Grenfell on Nancy Mitford, William Douglas-Home on the memoirs of Lady Astor's maid, Rose.

From Magdalene College, Cambridge, a Young Conservative wrote to complain that *The Spectator* was fast becoming respectable and boring. The letter, published on 24 January 1976, went on to describe the leaders as 'dull and turgid', to ask why *The Spectator* had abandoned its support for the death penalty for terrorists, and to regret the passing of the 'Society Today' section and the Tom Puzzle and Peregrinations columns. 'Without Patrick Cosgrave, one would almost despair.' Young Conservatives had never been much to Chancellor's taste; indeed he had never voted Conservative before he came to *The Spectator*. His political inclinations were Liberal and European, but he did not have strong political convictions. Nor did he have strong feelings yet on the direction in which he would take the magazine. In the last Notebook which he wrote before he left the editorship, Chancellor recalled how, when he arrived at *The Spectator*, he was often asked what his policy was going to be. The question unsettled him to such an extent that 'if there was a lavatory in the vicinity, I would lock myself inside it'.

Had Keswick known this, he might well have been a bit worried; he might even have questioned his own wisdom in appointing as editor a family friend (Keswick's mother was Chancellor's godmother) whose only apparent qualifications to edit *The Spectator* were a few years with Reuters and a brief spell as scriptwriter and reporter for Independent Televison News. But it turned out to be an inspired choice: Chancellor was to become one of the best editors in the history of *The Spectator*.

The idea of a *Spectator* policy may have been alien to his thinking, but he certainly knew what he wanted *The Spectator* to be. His aim was to bring together in the magazine a number of talented writers and, with the minimum of editorial interference, let them write. From the *New Statesman* came not only Waugh (he and Keswick had been at prep school together, both of them members of the Woodpeckers scout patrol) but also, with the help of Geoffrey Wheatcroft (appointed associate editor), Richard West, who had written occasional pieces for *The Spectator* in the past, and Jeffrey Bernard, who began writing a television column in January 1976. These three, together with others who were to become regular contributors — Patrick Marnham, Christopher Booker, Richard Ingrams — were also associated with *Private Eye*, and relished the opportunity to try their hands at something other than mischievous gossip and tasteless jokes. There was, of course, no money to be made by writing for *The Spectator*; what brought this motley bunch to Doughty Street (none of them was on the staff) was the Chancellorial charm and the atmosphere which he established, both in the office and in the magazine. For one of its promotional advertisements, Stephen Glover was quoted as having written of *The Spectator* that 'it is, above all else, fun'. There was not much fun to be had at the *New Statesman* in those days (or since), while *The Spectator*'s fun was perhaps more intellectually stimulating than the knockabout stuff which was the staple fare at *Private Eye*. When Chancellor left *The Spectator*, one of his predecessors, Walter Taplin, wrote to congratulate him on having created and maintained the same sort of atmosphere which he had sought to achieve, 'that of an enjoyable party attended by a lot of able and agreeable people'. Whereas *The Spectator* in the recent past had sometimes been ponderous, pompous, coarse, Chancellor succeeded in setting a tone in the magazine's pages

Spectator

14 February 1976   Price 20p

The Russians in Africa: Richard West

Mrs Thatcher: John Grigg

The brewery scandal: Jack Waterman

Foxhunting with Auberon Waugh

Paul Foot   Patrick Cosgrave   Alan Brien

Call off the Cod War

British confrontation with Iceland over North Sea
there are strategic, economic and legal considera-
that issue; and in each area the burden of the
argument favours the Icelanders. Now that the Communists are no longer members of the Reykjavik
government there is less propensity on the part of
Iceland to threaten NATO's tenancy of the military base
at Keflavik; but the temptation remains, if only
because such a threat is the one way in which pressure
can be brought to bear on a doggedly stubborn and
sensitive British government. From Keflavik—where
there is both a sophisticated underwater detection
system and two squadrons of reconnaissance aircraft—
NATO can supervise the passage of the USSR's largest
fleet from its home bases through the Iceland-Faroes
gap on its way to menace the East coast of the United
States. The base is a vital link in the Western chain of
defence, and to put it at risk is an act of irresponsibility.
Neither economically nor legally does Great Britain
have a strong case. The cod fisheries are considerably
less important to the British than to the Icelandic
economy, and though cod has a very substantial British
market, it is not one of vital significance. This fact has,
it seems, been obscured by the failure of successive
governments either to prepare the British fishing
industry for development of other resources, or to adopt
an enlightened cod conservation policy: since the cod

does not breed for the first five years of its life the danger
that over-fishing will destroy, not just simply reduce, the
stock is greater than in the case of other varieties of fish.
Moreover, since Great Britain, like most of the major
fishing nations, has agreed in principle to the establishment of two hundred mile territorial water limits the establishment of Iceland's claim can only be a matter of time.
    Over and above all this it should be said that the tone
and character of British diplomacy in this affair have
been unseemly. More than once Great Britain, having
taken a strong line in argument with her EEC partners,
has, at the crunch, given way. It seems, however, that in
the case of Iceland Mr Wilson and his ministers feel
they can safely play the degrading role of bully. Mr
Wilson's own part in negotiations with the Icelandic
Prime Minister was marked both by displeasing self-
assertion and inconsistency, as his contradictory
instructions to our trawler fleet showed: he could with
advantage displayed instead some of that timidity and
humility he showed in his last confrontation with France
and Germany in Rome. Unfortunately, the Conservative Opposition is in little better case: if they have a
policy on the matter—which it is doubtful—it seems to be
to support the Government. It would be better by far,
for Britain and Iceland alike, if they advocated both
generosity and concession in our transactions with
Reykjavik.

The magazine's cover reverted to a more dignified layout, and a smaller format, early in 1976.

which was at once welcoming, eclectic, amused, not always detached, civilised yet slightly anarchic. Chancellor got the best out of his regular contributors by giving them the freedom, for the most part, to write what they wanted, although he did not hesitate to 'spike' an article which he thought fell below the standards that they and he should be setting themselves. He also had the ability to persuade a reluctant contributor to drop everything for *The Spectator*. When Earl Mountbatten was murdered, on August bank holiday, 1979, Lord Zuckerman agreed to write an appreciation for *The Spectator*, but was then seduced by the *Sunday Times* with the promise of a much larger fee. He so informed Chancellor on the Tuesday afternoon, leaving him with hardly any time to commission another tribute from a suitable person. At six o'clock that evening he telephoned General Sir John Hackett, who was sitting in his garden in Gloucestershire, enjoying a whisky and soda. 'We need you to write a thousand words on Mountbatten by tomorrow morning,' Chancellor told him. 'Why should I put myself out for you and ruin my evening?' the general inquired. 'In order to save *The Spectator*,' Chancellor replied. After a long pause, Hackett came back: 'All right, f... you, I'll do it.' And he did it very well.

The cover of *The Spectator* was given a much more formal appearance under the Chancellor editorship. The illustration or portrait caricature, usually by Glan Williams or Richard Willson, was abandoned in September 1975 in favour of cover lines only, eight of them, alternately in black and colour, filling the whole front page. Then, on 14 February 1976, *The Spectator* adopted a new format (approximately the size it is today), a new logo and, on its front page, displayed five cover lines above the leading article. Inside, The Week was revived (there had been a Portrait of a Week until the end of the Gilmour era), and the order of a few things was changed. Nicholas Davenport's In the City column was brought forward, to the end of the front half, and Letters were moved to the middle, between Davenport and Books. The average issue size was 32 pages, with disconcertingly few display advertisements — the occasional publisher or a company chairman's statement — and a page of classifieds which, when it included advertisements for facilities for homosexuals, prompted letters of complaint from some readers, one a master at Douai School. A year later the leader was moved back to page 3 and The Week was dropped.

Chancellor's first appointment of a regular contributor was a great friend of his, John McEwen, replacing the former Conservative MP, Ernle Money, as art critic. McEwen, who had been deputy editor of *The Studio*, founded by Aubrey Beardsley, wrote a stylish weekly column for the next nine years. (Two of his brothers, Sir Robert and Rory McEwen, had previously been *Spectator* contributors.) When Kenneth Hurren left in October 1976 to edit *In London* magazine, the theatre was taken on by Ted Whitehead. Clancy Sigal became cinema critic, Rodney Milnes continued as opera critic, and Ingrams, editor of *Private Eye*, reviewed television when Bernard gave it up and began a racing column. For a while Marika Hanbury Tenison wrote articles about the growing and cooking of vegetables. A chess column was introduced in March 1977, contributed by Raymond Keene who, 20 years on, showed no signs of wanting to give it up. (A human chess match once took place in Gray's Inn Fields between two Grand Masters, Tony Miles representing the *New Statesman* and Keene for *The Spectator*. Bernard was an unlikely knight and the game was drawn.)

For much of the time, West was peripatetic foreign correspondent, usually managing to persuade a national newspaper to pay his travel expenses, which *The Spectator* could certainly not afford. (On one occasion West was about to depart for Nicaragua with an air ticket from the *Mail on Sunday* but without any cash. The problem was overcome thanks to a substantial loan from the very good-natured landlord of the Duke of York, David Potton, which came in handy when West, stopping over in Miami for the night, found himself arrested in the Playboy Club.) Chancellor also relied on resident foreign correspondents: the most regular of them was the engagingly cynical Nicholas von Hoffman from Washington (where he was known as 'the liberals' liberal'), while Sam White would file less frequently from Paris, always on French politics. Although he had given up the political column, Cosgrave continued to appear regularly in *The Spectator*, often on the subject of Israel, towards which he was well disposed. His successor, Grigg, did not always confine himself to Westminster politics; one week he devoted his column to the political situation in Spain. In October 1976 an article was published on the Greek political scene by Taki Theodoracopulos, who was the son of a wealthy shipowner, a correspondent for an American magazine, *National Review*, and like its editor, William Buckley, not known for his left-wing views. The following year he published a book, *The Greek Upheaval*, which got a hostile review in *The Spectator* from a fashionable, young *New Statesman* writer, Christopher Hitchens (who would soon make a painless transition to *The Spectator*, but who, 20 years later, was still being called a creep by Theodoracopulos in print). Theodoracopulos wanted to continue writing for *The Spectator*, but was not confident that many of its readers, or indeed its editor, were taking his views on Greece seriously. One day in autumn 1977, Simon Courtauld, who was managing editor at the time, asked him to do a piece about night-clubs in Paris, where he was going to spend the weekend. It was written with tongue in cheek, it was amusing, and it was the first of his columns, now totalling over a thousand, to be known as High Life. Taki's surname was dropped on the grounds that it was too long and too difficult to spell and remember. Bernard's column, then called End Piece, became Low Life in August 1978, which was when the long-running weekly double act began. Coinciding, appropriately enough, with his first Low Life column, Bernard reported that a warrant had just been issued for his arrest for non-payment of rates. On the same page Taki was writing about Christina Onassis's marriage to a Russian KGB man.

In the course of his railing against Communist influence in Greece, Taki had been prosecuted in 1976 for criminal libel by the publisher of *Athens News* and sentenced in his absence to 15 months' imprisonment. One wonders whether his great friend, James Goldsmith, may have had this in mind when he instituted proceedings for criminal libel against the editor of *Private Eye*, Richard Ingrams, in the same year. In addition to that action, Goldsmith issued something like 80 writs for civil libel against the distributors of *Private Eye*, for having sold an issue of the magazine which alleged, incorrectly, that Goldsmith attended a lunch the day after the disappearance of Lord Lucan when those present discussed how best to protect their friend from arrest for having murdered his children's nanny. It was said that Goldsmith was urged on to legal action against *Private Eye* by Marcia Falkender, who would shortly recommend him for a peerage in Harold Wilson's resignation honours list (he was given a knighthood instead). It was around this time that *The Spectator*, in the Notebook, began criticising Goldsmith for his oppressive action, because it was clearly designed to cripple *Private Eye*, put it out of business if he could, rather than compensate him for the injury to his reputation. Goldsmith was not the only bizarre name to feature in that honours list, but he was the only one who had declared himself to be hostile to socialism. It was perhaps the same perverse spirit of the time that led *The Spectator* to heap praise on to Wilson when he announced his resignation in March 1976. Cosgrave called him the nicest prime minister since Baldwin, and *The Spectator*'s leading article, written by Hutchinson, described him as 'a most moderate leader' (ambiguity probably not intended) and 'a genuine force for stability'.

None of these encomiums, however, did anything to soften the attitude towards *The Spectator* of the man on whom Wilson had just conferred a knighthood. 'Scum', one of Goldsmith's favourite words for the journalistic profession, was what he called *The Spectator*'s editor and managing editor one day outside the Law Courts when he was with John Aspinall, who stopped to talk to them and offer them a lift. Goldsmith warned Aspinall not to allow them into his car, as they were infectious and he would be sure to contract eczema. Waugh had been quite rude about Goldsmith in his *Spectator* column, speculating about his member and commenting on his 'disgustingly ugly face', knowing, of course, that vulgar abuse of this kind was about the only criticism he could level at Goldsmith without being sued for libel. (Waugh was one of six journalists against whom Goldsmith sought an injunction to restrain them from making adverse comments about his solicitor, Eric Levine.) *The Spectator* was, in Goldsmith's mind, tarred with the *Private Eye* brush and therefore irredeemable, though this did not stop him from trying to buy the magazine in 1980 when he was proprietor of *Now!*, another weekly publication. (He had also tried, and failed, to buy the *Express* and the *Observer*.) After his actions against *Private Eye* had been settled, Goldsmith offered, through *The Spectator*'s pages, a £50,000 prize for the best piece of reporting on subversion in the media.

It was Patrick Marnham who had written the *Private Eye* article which led to all those libel writs from Goldsmith. When he wrote for *The Spectator* about another recipient of Wilson's patronage in 1976, Sir Eric Miller, a property developer who had committed suicide while under investigation by the Fraud Squad, he headed the piece, a trifle tastelessly though in the circumstances entirely aptly, 'Doing the decent thing'. *The Spectator* was beginning to get a reputation for irreverent but intelligent journalism, for producing a surprise every week which, more often than not, came from the pen of a contributor who also wrote for *Private Eye*. There was a perversity, an anarchic tendency about some of their writings, but a thread of good sense could usually be identified as well. West propounded more than once the thesis that Tony Benn was the heir of Cecil Rhodes, because as Energy Secretary he had been responsible for Rio Tinto Zinc getting the contract to operate a uranium mine in South Africa which would enable the apartheid government to manufacture nuclear weapons. While the *Private Eye* ethos was to be fearlessly independent, it was also to beware of giving praise to anyone or anything because independence might then become compromised. If Ingrams gave a favourable notice to, say, a television presenter in his *Spectator* column, you could be sure that the unfortunate person would then get a hammering in the next issue of *Private Eye*. It may have been thought a good idea to ask Waugh to review a collection, by Kingsley Amis, of *Spectator* and *New Statesman* articles covering the Wilson years, but the book was not helped by Waugh writing that he 'can't think of a single reason why anyone should buy it'.

There was no relationship between the two magazines, other than that they shared a few contributors. But this did provoke some critical comment. There was some correspondence of attitude between *The Spectator* and *Pri-*

vate Eye and there had been a similar attitude in Brian Inglis's day, just before *Private Eye* was started; but there was no doubting (*pace* Goldsmith) *The Spectator*'s independence. The first editor of *Private Eye*, Booker, once went so far, in the pages of *The Spectator*, as to call the satirical magazine for which he still wrote regularly 'on its day a strong candidate for the most unpleasant thing in British journalism'. For four years Booker wrote almost weekly for *The Spectator*, initially on the disasters of town hall planning (these articles were adapted for a television programme, 'City of Towers'), and later series on themes such as the disintegration of Western civilisation, Darwinism and the psychopathology of collectivism. (Psychopathology was being rather overworked in *The Spectator*, from time to time also by an eccentric musicologist and football fan, Hans Keller, who had a hectoring and irritatingly self-opinionated prose style.) At this time Booker became rather bogged down in his obsessions with the nature of human existence and personality (with much attention paid to Jung and the anima) and what he saw as the collapse of Western culture. After a collection of his articles was published as a book, *The Seventies*, to which Watkins gave a less than friendly notice in *The Spectator*, he took umbrage and retired from his regular column for a while. But in 1982, as if determined to demonstrate that he would not be the only regular contributor to have one of his books rubbished in *The Spectator*, he rebuked Marnham, who had recently given up the literary editorship, in strong terms for his history of *Private Eye*. Booker also returned to *The Spectator*'s pages with a trenchant attack on Nikolai Tolstoy's theories about the repatriation of Cossacks and Yugoslavs at the end of the second world war — which had impressed him when the book, *Victims of Yalta*, was published in 1978.

The repatriations issue was also taken up by Marnham, Waugh and West who, in a letter to *The Spectator* following publication of Nicholas Bethell's book, *The Last Secret*, proposed a memorial to the 2 million who were imprisoned and died at the hands of Communist governments after being sent back to their countries by Allied forces in 1945. Bethell approached Thatcher who, to her credit, authorised such a memorial against the advice of the Foreign Office, which was particularly exercised by the idea of using Crown land for a monument implicitly critical of the British government. An impressive statue depicting the heads of victims of the repatriations now stands in a little garden in London, opposite the Victoria and Albert

Museum. In addition to the memorial inscription, it is recorded that a previous sculpture, placed on the site in 1982, was 'destroyed by vandals to whom the truth was intolerable'.

On *The Spectator*'s political front Grigg was not proving an enormous success. Quite apart from the fact that, soon after he began writing the political column in May 1976, he was pressing the claims of 'yesterday's man', Heath, to be Foreign Secretary in the next Conservative government — 'Nothing must be said or done to prejudice his acceptance of the Foreign Office if and when [Thatcher] becomes Prime Minister' — Grigg was perhaps too much of a consensualist, too even-handed, too historical in his approach to be a sharp observer of the political scene. According to another regular contributor, 'The whiff of grapeshot was missing from his column'. By the spring of 1977 Chancellor was discussing things with Gale, who thought the political coverage was weak and proposed himself as regular leader writer, political commentator in place of Grigg and author of a weekly right-wing piece 'by a Conservative'. Not surprisingly, Chancellor rejected the last suggestion, but Gale did take on the task of writing the weekly leader; and in September 1977 Ferdinand Mount took over the political commentary. Grigg devoted his final political column to Paul Johnson's conversion to the Conservatism of Thatcher; the second volume of his biography of Lloyd George was published a year later.

The first person to write about Jeremy Thorpe in *The Spectator* after his arrest in August 1978 was Booker, who dilated on his split personality and the web of fate surrounding him. Waugh was on holiday in the Languedoc at the time, but he soon caught up. He had written on the subject when allegations first surfaced in 1976 (listed in *The Spectator*'s index under 'Thorpe: implied sexual irregularities'). Waugh found them not shocking, but very funny; he became absorbed by the story, attending the committal proceedings at Minehead, standing for the Dog Lovers' Party (in memory of Rinka) in Thorpe's North Devon constituency at the 1979 general election, and then agreeing to write a book about the trial.

It was scarcely surprising that Waugh's enthusiasm for the case should lead to some legal headaches at *The Spectator*. His election address to the voters of North Devon, published in his *Spectator* column, was seized upon by Thorpe, who applied for it to be banned for contempt of court (the general election took place between the committal proceedings and the trial).

David Holmes, deputy treasurer of the Liberal party, was accused, with Jeremy Thorpe, of conspiracy to murder a former male model.

"God! I hope that's nothing to do with the Liberal party."

The Lord Chief Justice found against Thorpe but he was reversed on appeal by Lord Denning who, ironically, had been hailed by Waugh the previous year as 'this beautiful man' for having delivered a judgment against Goldsmith's attempt to stop distributors handling *Private Eye*. The column which Waugh wrote for the following week was headed 'Muzzled', but on legal advice it was not published. His comments during the trial at the Old Bailey were fairly circumspect, but problems arose again when he decided one day to go instead to the Royal Courts of Justice, where Goldsmith was being sued for libel by *Private Eye*'s city editor, and write about those proceedings for a change. The issue of 23 June appeared, once again without Waugh's Another Voice but with a note from Chancellor to say that publication of his skilful and interesting account of the case (which, to general amazement, Goldsmith won) had been judged 'unwise'. Chancellor knew that Goldsmith was looking for a reason to start throwing writs in *The Spectator*'s direction, but in adopting the prudent course he was the recipient instead of a nine-page letter of abuse from Waugh, announcing that he was giving up his column for three months to write a book on the Thorpe trial and that he would resume it only if payment of his retainer was continued on a sabbatical basis. Waugh returned to the magazine in the autumn.

With other contributors, too, the threat of a libel writ was never very far away. In spite of persistently provoking his *bêtes noires*, such as Edward Kennedy and the Aga Khan, Taki was only responsible for one serious libel action in 20 years, which went to court and which he and *The Spectator* lost. (He once settled out of court with the Aga Khan, having accused him of tax evasion.) Close attention had always to be paid to his column, not least when he was being rude about his 'friends', one of whom, Arnaud de Borchgrave, once threatened proceedings when Taki made a supposedly lighthearted reference to his behaviour under fire in Vietnam. Ingrams's television column brought one or two legal problems: one week in 1979, two apologies and two letters were published in connection with his comments about the television writer and presenter Ronald Harwood. More often, however, Ingrams's column gave rise to letters complaining that he was constantly critical of programmes which he sometimes admitted to having watched for no more than a few minutes. According to a letter from Bernard Levin, Ingrams used his column to pursue private vendettas and spites, currently against an Indian guru known as Bhagwan Shre Rajneesh who seemingly had Levin under his spell. 'I have known nine editors of *The Spectator*,' Levin wrote, 'and you are the only one sufficiently lacking in professional self-respect to accept such standards from one of its contributors.' Oddly enough, a former editor, Walter Taplin, had written a few months earlier to compliment Ingrams on being 'our best television critic', precisely because he spent most of his time being disparaging. 'In this he is not alone among successful journalists. Look at Bernard Levin, who as "Taper" in *The Spectator* never had a good word to say for Parliament. Look at Jonathan Swift.' One week, unable to find any television programme worth watching, Ingrams wrote about a device for converting old newspapers into combustible blocks. Since there was unfortunately no way of recycling a television set, 'the best thing you can do is to get rid of it altogether'.

Alastair Forbes, of Bostonian background, a cousin of the Roosevelts and a former political columnist for the Rothermere press, aimed his barbs more often than not at royalty or those past suing. But Dame Rebecca West was still very much alive, at 85, when Forbes wrote that her wartime book on Yugoslavia, *Black Lamb and Grey Falcon*, revised and republished in 1977, was 'utterly bogus... Balkan balderdash... [which] qualifies the whole work for reclassification as fiction'. It was, almost inevitably, a quarrel between two outsiders — one biased towards the Serbs, the other instinctively pro-Croat — who had no more than a superficial knowledge of Yugoslavia's history. Dame Rebecca, having been fed with nationalistic Serb propaganda on her visits to Yugoslavia, regarded Prince Paul as a traitor when he agreed to join the Axis and the Serb officers who overthrew him as heroes. Forbes shared the views of the minority of Croats who remained loyal to the memory of the departed Habsburgs; but as an intimate, which he claimed to be, of European nobility, there was of course one Serb, Prince Paul (who was a friend of Chips Channon and the 'Cliveden set' in the 1930s), to whom he would naturally give his support. Dame Rebecca was not going to take any lessons on Yugoslav history from Forbes, and she threatened legal action.

In delicate and lengthy negotiations with her solicitor, *The Spectator* agreed to retract any suggestion that her account had been written in bad faith but managed to avoid paying her any money. Within two months, however, of the publication of an apology Forbes felt constrained to libel her again, in a review of the memoirs of Prince Clary. It was a thoroughly mean trick to play on an impecunious magazine and its indulgent editor and literary editor. The latter, Wheatcroft, did not immediately associate Forbes's reference to 'such incorrigible would-be historians as that pathetic lady who... misspelt the word Habsburg throughout the thousand taradiddling pages of her two-volume magnum opus' as another swipe at Dame Rebecca. But she, of course, was not slow to react, and *The Spectator* was obliged to apologise yet again, this time with a statement in open court and the payment to her of a four-figure sum, which she donated to the Serbian Orthodox Community in London. Ann Fleming had been proved right in her warning to Chancellor that, sooner or later, Forbes was bound to get *The*

Spectator into trouble. (In 1980, when she called him bitter and vindictive in a letter to *The Spectator*, Forbes replied that 'the best libel lawyer in the land' had advised him that such an allegation would entitle him to huge libel damages but that he would forbear to claim his legal rights because he still wore the clothes of Ann Fleming's late husband Ian, which had been bequeathed to him.)

Dame Rebecca's relations with the magazine were not severed: she had written a Notebook shortly before Forbes's first hostile review, and after the settlement she came to lunch at Doughty Street. Around the time of the West affair, Forbes wrote one of his *tours de mots* (4,000 words in all) on Peter Townsend and Princess Margaret. He found very little good to say about either of them, calling the princess 'ill-educated, ill-informed and sullen', but whether because so few readers were able to struggle through the tangled thickets of his often impenetrable prose, or because the princess's relationship with Roddy Llewellyn was currently receiving much adverse press comment, very few letters of complaint were received and only one, from Hugh Trevor-Roper, was published. It may be that, after a while, no one took Forbes's verbose effusions very seriously, but there was no denying that he had had personal contact with a number of prime ministers, from Churchill onwards, and grand European and American families. His recollections of their behaviour and their peccadillos (and of the many occasions when he had, *naturellement*, been a guest in their houses or at their tables), however partisan, unreliable and long-winded they might be, did provide occasional insights and quite a lot of harmless fun. He continued to review books for *The Spectator* for some years, never missing an opportunity to remind readers of the closeness of his friendship with the Kennedys, Churchills, Mitfords and every European prince and princess alive in the 20th century. A friendly, single-page profile of Forbes published in 1985 produced from the subject a letter correcting a few minor factual errors which, with the usual self-indulgent dropping of names, was more than twice the length of the article.

More serious exception was taken to the anti-Jewish attitudes, or so they were perceived, of several contributors who, coincidentally or not, were all (Ingrams, Booker, Waugh, Marnham) associated with *Private Eye*. Waugh occasionally told Jewish jokes in his column ('Q. Why are pound notes green? A. Because the Jews always pick them before they are ripe.') or referred to having eaten a disgusting kosher breakfast. But it was when Ingrams and Booker were both critical of a television programme on the Holocaust in 1978 that the letters began to pour in. Chancellor also received private letters from MPs accusing *The Spectator* of an anti-semitic tendency, and over the next few years would get complaints at intervals from the Board of Deputies of British Jews. (A delegation from the board once turned up at Doughty Street on the day that the National Front had chosen to daub the office windows.) The magazine had long had a reputation for hostility to Israel — Ian Gilmour was founder chairman of the Council for the Advancement of Arab-British Understanding — which seemed almost impossible to shed, despite Creighton's and Cosgrave's pro-Israel stance and the articles which continued to appear from time to time in vigorous support of Israel, including, in May 1978, a leader of congratulation on Israel's 30th birthday. The lack of understanding between Israel and *The Spectator* was such that the Israeli ambassador once informed Chancellor that he kept a file on Marnham. *The Spectator* was certainly against Menachem Begin at the time — Marnham went on about the activities of the Stern and Irgun gangs in the 1940s — and it was anti-Zionist, but not anti-semitic.

In a typical week it was quite common for there to be four or five articles from abroad, or on a foreign topic. (Some of the analytical pieces were sharper than others: when the Shah was overthrown at the beginning of 1979 Edward Mortimer hailed a glorious revolution, while Roger Cooper, who was to be imprisoned in Teheran during the 1980s, gave more measured appraisals of the country's future.) Except when general elections or the annual party conferences came round, the coverage of domestic politics, apart from the political commentary, was not wide. In Chancellor's time, *The Spectator*, unlike the *New Statesman*, did not have a structured or coherent approach to the subjects it covered, nor was much time spent on debating the magazine's 'line', which had a closer affinity with William Cobbett or G.K. Chesterton than with the Institute of Economic Affairs or the Centre for Policy Studies. The prospect of Thatcher becoming prime minister in 1979 did not excite *The Spectator*, whose readers were advised to set aside their reluctance to vote for her (were they so reluctant?) and 'be brave'. The Labour MP, Eric Heffer, wrote the Notebook in the week before the poll, and no sooner had the Conservatives won than Germaine Greer wrote a very unfriendly piece about Britain's prospects under a new

Mrs Thatcher, drawn by Mark Boxer for The Spectator *at the time she became prime minister.*

prime minister of 'terrifying obtuseness'.

For all its seeming lack of political commitment, however, the new *Spectator* was at last increasing circulation. Its unstructured formula was its strength, because it encouraged writers who were individualists — libertarian in outlook and anti-statist — and who seemed to catch the changing mood (though this did not mean that they would vote for the Conservative party; their conservatism was spelt with a very small 'c'). In a leading article in the *Times*, published on 22 September 1978 to coincide with *The Spectator*'s 150th anniversary, William Rees-Mogg congratulated the magazine on the important part it was playing in the movement away from collectivism, which he called 'the most interesting intellectual movement of our times'. It was only in the last few years, he wrote, that the Left had forfeited its monopoly, which it had enjoyed for decades, of the best and most intellectually stimulating writers. Now almost all the mental energy and originality was coming from writers who, if not of the Conservative Right, were essentially anti-socialist, 'libertarian rather than hierarchical... from the tradition of Locke and Liberty rather than that of Burke and Community'. *The Spectator*, in the estimation of the editor of the *Times*, now had an intellectual vitality that was lacking in the *New Statesman*, whose sales had fallen from 85,000 to below 40,000 in the previous ten years. *The Spectator*'s were little more than a third of that figure, but the gap was beginning to close. There was good reason to celebrate *The Spectator*'s anniversary, which was marked by a 96-page issue and by a ball at the Lyceum Theatre in London, at which most of the usual suspects — political, journalistic and professional party-going — were in evidence. In that week's issue, in addition to articles reminiscing about *The Spectator*, and a history of it by Lord Blake, Nicholas Davenport, instead of interpreting the workings of the City or exposing some economic nonsense being perpetrated by the government, was for once writing about himself.

He was celebrating 25 years of writing a financial column for *The Spectator*, and recalling how he had berated both Tory and Labour governments for their 'stop-go', dear money policies over much of that quarter century. What had exercised Davenport perhaps most of all was the consequent alienation of the working class through unemployment, a theme which he addressed in a book, *The Split Society*, four long extracts from which were published in *The Spectator* in 1963. The situation got worse under Wilson, leading Davenport to start his vigorous advocacy of a mixed capitalist economy shared between managers and workers. He believed not only in establishing employees' shareholdings in individual companies but in forming a public unit trust which would embrace every industry, including the natonalised industries. *Memoirs of a City Radical* was the title of his best-known book; as Christopher Fildes wrote of him, 'He was in fact a City man among radicals and a radical in the City.' In the last column which he wrote before his death, aged 86, in May 1979, Davenport was still pursuing his pet subjects. Awaiting the first Budget following the Conservative election victory, he advised Sir Geoffrey Howe to cut the bank rate at once and to 'rely on getting a better response from labour on productivity through lower taxes and... through participation in profits'. His column ended on a confident note, giving Thatcher a better chance than any man of arresting Britain's economic decline.

It was greatly to the credit of the nine editors for whom Davenport wrote, and also characteristic of *The Spectator*, that he should enjoy complete freedom of criticism during all the years that he contributed to the magazine. Though Iain Macleod must have been embarrassed on occasion by his views on the economy, and George Gale was no doubt profoundly irritated by them, no editor ever tried to influence his column. Perhaps no one quite dared to interfere with, much less to sack, this distinguished, three-piece-suited, elderly figure (he was 60 when he started with *The Spectator*) who was known to have entertained so many leaders of the Left — Dalton, Cripps, Bevan, Gaitskell, Crossman, Jenkins — at his originally Norman manor, Hinton, in Oxfordshire. The house had once belonged to Henry Marten, a Leveller who signed Charles I's death warrant; as a reforming radical, Davenport liked to assert that he was Marten's reincarnation.

He had published his first book during the first world war, and entered journalism shortly afterwards, with encouragement from Maynard Keynes, who became something of a mentor and introduced him to leading Fabians. But Davenport, unlike many on the left, was not hoping for the collapse of capitalism. 'We Keynesians,' he commented, 'did not want to destroy the capitalist system, but to make it more efficient and more humane.' He wrote a column for the *Nation* before it was absorbed by the *New Statesman*, for which journal he continued to write for another 20 years, and he helped to found the XYZ Club in 1932, where City reformers met Labour leaders and discussed ideas for a National Investment Board and a Bank of England that was publicly accountable and not governed by someone like Montagu Norman.

Two letters in tribute to Davenport were published after he died: one from James Callaghan, who had just become ex-prime minister, the other from Harold Lever, who recalled that it was due to Davenport's financial backing that films of *Pygmalion* and *Major Barbara* were first made. He met his second wife Olga when she took the lead in the one play he wrote, *And So to Wed*, in 1946; and he was said to have once proposed marriage to Deborah Kerr.

Another old *Spectator* hand to die in the following year and, like Davenport, also a CBE, was George Hutchinson. His death from cancer, at the end of March 1980, came just weeks after two occasions which gave him great happiness. He received a Granada Television award for 'consistently distinguished services to journalism', and his book on Macmillan, *The Last Edwardian at No. 10*, was published. At the publication party, where only wine appeared to be on offer, a few guests discovered that the author's favourite tipple, whisky, could be obtained by invoking the name of the subject of the book. A large Harold Macmillan and soda soon became a popular order at the bar. In his appreciation of Hutchinson in *The Spectator*, the week after his death. Cosgrave described him as 'a mentor beyond price'.

By 1980 things at *The Spectator* were going rather well. Among new contributors who began to write regularly were the delightfully eccentric Roy Kerridge, a sub-Orwellian observer of life among the under-class, and Murray Sayle, who sent highly readable, if lengthy, reports from Japan, and occasionally digressed memorably on subjects such as his experiences with London prostitutes while working as a crime reporter for the *Sunday People*, and the Murdoch family's connection with Gallipoli (battle and film). Peter Jenkins, the *Guardian*'s political correspondent, took over the theatre, and Bryan Robertson returned to the arts pages, writing on theatre and ballet. Wheatcroft, whose idea it had been to recruit Jenkins, had put together quite an eclectic bunch of reviewers since he took on the literary editorship in 1977. But his tenure is perhaps best remembered for his patronage of two middle-European psychoanalysts, Hans Keller (primarily a music critic) and Thomas Szasz, whose writings and names were often mocked by other members of *The Spectator* and parodied in *Private Eye*. In 1979, in the guise of a review of Max Hastings's *Bomber Command*, Wheatcroft wrote a lengthy polemic against the RAF's area bombing of German cities during the last war, which produced one of the largest postbags from *Spectator* readers since Suez. Marnham became literary editor at the beginning of 1981, when Wheatcroft left to write a book on South Africa. While waiting impatiently to take up his duties, Marnham noticed that Wheatcroft had on his desk a telephone, very advanced in those days, which allowed certain numbers to be pre-programmed. He took it upon himself to reroute all Wheatcroft's most frequent calls to the private office number of Ingrams, who became increasingly irritated, when he picked up the telephone, to hear the voice of the outgoing literary editor of *The Spectator*. (On another occasion, which may have been due as much to a misunderstanding as to Marnham's propensity for playing jokes, Waugh agreed to go to Senegal, in Marnham's place, to give a lecture on press freedom, but was under the impression, until after his arrival in Dakar, that he was to talk on breast-feeding.)

With the names of Keller and Szasz still in mind, Chancellor said he wanted fewer eccentric reviewers of eccentric books. Marnham got rid of one long-time weekly reviewer, Benny Green, and introduced a number of new names in 1981: P.J. Kavanagh, Piers Paul Read, Eric Newby and the actress Diana Quick, who all produced very readable reviews. He did a second stint in charge of books during the second half of 1983.

Jenny Naipaul was unquestionably one of Chancellor's best appointments. She was a highly efficient, and tolerant, editor's secretary from 1975 until 1987 (halfway through Charles Moore's editorship), then became arts editor and, later, librarian. She was also married to Shiva Naipaul, the younger brother of V.S. (now Sir Vidia). In 1977, having published two novels and reviewed a few books for *The Spectator* (his first reviews were published by Hilary Spurling in 1969), Naipaul embarked on the journalism that would occupy much of his time over the next five years and would make him one of the outstanding writers of the Chancellor years. Naipaul travelled, first to Africa — his articles from Kenya, Tanzania and Zambia were incorporated in his book, *North of South* — then to Morocco, Iran, Portugal, India, the Seychelles and Australia. He wrote a memorable piece from Teheran on the inanities of Westernised Iranian life on the eve of revolution (which greatly upset the Shah's last ambassador in London, Parvis Radji), and in Australia he upset almost everyone of the 'progressive' tendency by repeatedly calling the Aborigines a primitive people. Taking part in a debate at Sussex University, Naipaul opposed the motion that the richer countries should transfer more of their resources to the poorer ones. Before the debate the majority in favour of the motion was expected to be about 2:1, and in his article describing the occasion he seemed almost pleased that, having spoken out against underdeveloped societies 'based on the underdeveloped personality', the majority for the motion rose to 83 per cent.

Naipaul was born in Trinidad of a Hindu family which had migrated from India in the 19th century. As Colin Thubron once wrote of him: 'With unsentimental outspokenness he dared to say things which a native-born Briton scarcely could.' One might accuse him of being wilful, aggressive, even perverse. But he was always entirely honest in his writings, if sometimes brutally so. As a genuine seeker after truth he was, in short, an archetypal *Spectator* contributor (he was also outstandingly good company).

When he angered black Africans, feminists and the politically correct, it was because he refused to patronise or condescend to those whom he was writing about. He thought it absurd and denigrating that countries as different as Ethiopia, India and Brazil should be lumped together by the term 'third world'. 'The longer I live,' Naipaul wrote in May 1985, 'the more convinced I become that one of the greatest honours we can confer on other people is to see them as they are.' Tragically, three months later he died of heart failure, aged 40. At the memorial meeting to celebrate Shiva's life, V.S. Naipaul spoke of his brother's 'prodigious development' in the last eight years. 'The welcome and freedom and fellowship he found on [*The Spectator*] answered his need; and he flourished.' A prize was founded in Shiva's memory, not for travel writing in the conventional sense but 'for the most acute and profound observation of a culture alien to the writer'. Hilary Mantel was the first winner; although the prize lapsed for a few years in the 1990s, it was revived and was worth £3,000 in 1998.

Xan Smiley, then editor of a newsletter, *Africa Confidential*, began writing for *The Spectator* from Rhodesia in 1976. Since Macleod's day the magazine had not been unduly censorious of Ian Smith's determination to hang on to power in Rhodesia; but Smiley persuaded Chancellor to think differently. The Rhodesian government, he said, was running an apartheid system, the guerrillas had no choice but to fight, and they were going to win. In contrast to newspapers such as the *Daily Telegraph*, he argued that sanctions should not be lifted, and that the war would last a great deal longer if they were. Smiley annoyed quite a number of Conservative readers, who thought of Smith, in the words of one correspondent, as 'the last branch of a fine old English oak' and who fondly imagined that the guerrillas could be contained or defeated. But Smiley travelled extensively in the country and knew the strength of the armed opposition, fired by Robert Mugabe's Marxist populism.

He continued to write with great perception after Bishop Muzorewa became prime minister in 1979. Taking the view that Muzorewa's internal settlement was worth a try, Smiley nevertheless urged, either in signed articles or in leaders written by him, that recognition should depend on the acceptance of several conditions, for example the removal of white blocking powers in a reorganised parliament, and the offer of new elections to include the parties backed by the guerrillas. These recommendations were in fact precisely those that were adopted before the elections which brought Mugabe, leader of the Zimbabwe African National Union, to power in March 1980. Smiley was hoping for a hung parliament in which Joshua Nkomo would hold sway. However, he thought that Mugabe was bound to win the largest number of seats, contrary to the expectations of Thatcher and Lord Carrington. He was well aware — which the Foreign Office seemingly was not — that voting was almost certain to be tribal, and that the Shona would give victory to Mugabe.

A number of old *Spectator* names came back to its pages during Chancellor's time: Inglis, Watkins, Peter Paterson, Grigg, Fairlie. (It is characteristic of *The Spectator* that every editor or political commentator who has been sacked or replaced — Taplin, Hamilton, Nigel Lawson, Gale, Chancellor, Waugh, Paterson, Macpherson — has written for it subsequently. Wilson Harris, having taken his Janus pseudonym off to *Time and Tide*, had agreed to write for *The Spectator* again shortly before he died.)

The political commentator from 1977 was Ferdinand Mount, who continued without interruption until 1982, then returned to write the political column again in 1986–87. He had previously been writing novels, and leaders for the *Daily Mail*, and he had worked for the Conservative Research Department. (He had also, in 1967, written a couple of pieces for *The Spectator* from New York.) In Moore's view, there was no more distinguished contributor to the magazine. As a writer of wit and elegance, as a spectator of the political scene, he was certainly in the class of Levin, Fairlie and Watkins. And as a balanced observer and an astute judge of character, whose views were sometimes firmly but never offensively expressed, he was outstanding. The feather-light touch of a descriptive first paragraph might lead on to the considered assessment of some minister and then, somewhat in the manner of a headmaster's report, to a severe ticking-off at the end. A wigging from Mount, however, was much better written than most school reports, and it was not be ignored. He began a column on James Callaghan when prime minister in 1978: 'Sunny spring morning. High wind bundling bishops along Millbank, full of coffee and biscuits from elevenses at Lambeth Palace…. Elderly party skips nimbly into gutter to avoid gaggle of silly foreign students, then skips equally nimbly back on to pavement, grey quiff blown up like a stormy sea-crest. Never seen a prime minister look better after two years in the job.' By the end of the article Mount was calling the government 'uniquely sluggish and second-rate' and saying that the problem was 'not the threat of Mr Benn but the actuality of Mr Callaghan'. After the trial of Thorpe, Mount memorably castigated him for being 'ruthless, evasive and deceitful' towards his parliamentary colleagues and for his shamelesss behaviour in standing for reelection while charged with conspiracy to murder. The softer, or more oblique, approach was no less telling: writing of Roy Hattersley's opportunism when, as Secretary of State for Prices and Consumer Protection, he had just announced the first single-figure inflation for five years and was visiting an Essex supermarket, Mount reported:

> Old ladies cornered by a stack of Bovril cubes or a wall of Kleenex are awed by the Minister's gracious inquiries about the price of sliced bread and pig's liver. Do prices seem to be a bit steadier? Mr Hattersley asks. Yes, well now that they come to think of it, prices do seem to be a bit steadier. Mr Hattersley clasps a packet of All-Bran with healing hands. He blesses a cling-wrapped cabbage.

Mount characterised Michael Foot, when he was elected Labour leader in November 1980, as 'a kind of licensed child. He is not expected to grow up, but rather is suffered by one and all to live in a solipsistic haze, surrounded by his dead father figures and the books he read 30 years ago.' By choosing Foot, he wrote, the Labour party had given evidence of an uncontrollable urge to enter its second childhood.

In the year that Thatcher won her first general election, the next prime minister but one had an article published in *The Spectator*. Anthony Blair, his name as published, had been called to the Bar in 1976; he did not become an MP until 1983. A friend from their student days at Oxford, James Hughes-Onslow (who was an occasional *Spectator* contributor), persuaded Blair that Chancellor would be receptive to his enlightened views; and so he submitted a piece on the inequalities suffered by immigrants under recent legislation, which was published on 18 August 1979. One further article by Blair was used the following year, and a third was rejected. When Blair and Cherie Booth were married in 1980, the then head of their barristers' chambers, Derry Irvine (appointed Lord Chancellor in 1997), referred in his speech at their Oxford wedding reception to the fact that

Blair had lately been seduced into writing for the right-wing press.

Circulation of *The Spectator* in 1980 was around 17,500 (a 35 per cent increase over 1978), but advertising revenue was still very modest, and Keswick was losing a six-figure sum each year. Having failed to get a parliamentary seat at the 1979 election, his interest in politics, and in *The Spectator*, began to wane. It used to be said that the influence wielded by the proprietor was equivalent to two seats in Parliament. But Keswick had wanted only to get into Parliament; he never sought to guide, or indeed to interfere in any way with, editorial policy. He might pass on to Chancellor occasional suggestions — there was some discussion about buying first publication rights to a David Frost interview with Richard Nixon — or he might express his dislike of some politician, but that was about it. Keswick was in fact the first proprietor of *The Spectator* not to make himself editor for at least part of the term of his ownership. So it was natural that he should be looked upon as a benevolent, patriarchal figure who had saved *The Spectator*, by buying it in 1975 and by appointing Chancellor as editor. In the magazine Chancellor himself paid tribute to his proprietor for having protected journalistic freedom, which had earned him 'the affection, loyalty and esteem of all kinds of unlikely people'. When he resolved to sell the magazine, Keswick was approached by Goldsmith, who would have paid a lot of money but would not have been a disinterested protector of journalistic freedom. He wanted to absorb *The Spectator* into his publication, *Now!*, which folded in September 1981. Keswick decided instead to accept an offer of £100,000 from a friend of his, the oil entrepreneur Algy Cluff, who formally became proprietor of *The Spectator* on St George's Day, 23 April 1981.

John Gordon (Algy) Cluff had founded Cluff Oil ten years before he took on *The Spectator*. He had a reputation as a successful speculative businessman — 'buccaneering' was the word often used to describe him in the press — who did a lot of drilling, from the North Sea to the South China Sea, without always finding oil. In the 1960s he had been a Grenadier Guards officer, serving in West Africa, Cyprus and Malaysia, and had contested a Manchester seat at the 1966 general election. But he did not buy *The Spectator* in order to acquire political influence, nor indeed with the intention of making money. His reasons were rather more cultural and, in a way, public-spirited. He wanted to add a new dimension to his life, and to have a connection with literary London. (For a time he co-owned, with Naim Attallah, the *Literary*

Review, Quarto and *Apollo.*) He greatly admired what Chancellor had done to *The Spectator* over the past five years, while Chancellor welcomed the injection of new enthusiasm which Cluff brought to his acquisition.

However, while Cluff made suggestions — for new columnists, for improving the appearance of the front cover and using photographs on some of the inside pages (an idea that was always resisted) — Chancellor took the novel decision, in June 1981, to abolish the weekly leading article. His reasoning, as he explained in the Notebook, was that *The Spectator* did not have a collective opinion about anything, that the leader represented merely one opinion, dignified by anonymity, and that he did not think *The Spectator* should be a preacher, assuming an authority and a certainty of opinion which it did not always possess. It was oddly endearing that while all newspapers and other journals of opinion seem to relish the chance to pontificate on every conceivable subject, the editor of *The Spectator* was saying, in his characteristically self-deprecating way, that he often had no strong opinion worthy of expression under the *Spectator* banner. A leader did occasionally appear — for instance at the end of July, when the Prince of Wales married Lady Diana Spencer — but it was not restored as a weekly feature until October 1982. One may guess that the decision to abandon the magazine's leading article, only two months after he had bought it, did not commend itself to the proprietor. (Nor was Cluff pleased when, at the end of 1981, he sent in an article on the future of Hong Kong and Chancellor published it as a letter.)

At the beginning of the new regime all seemed to be set fair. Chancellor retained complete editorial freedom and Cluff proclaimed himself 'a protector rather than an interventionist'. The two got on well enough, but there was not the easy understanding which Chancellor had enjoyed with his friend Keswick. At times Chancellor appeared almost not to want to establish friendly relations with the proprietor and his occasionally erratic behaviour did not help the relationship. In 1982–83 he was having a sort of mid-life crisis: his life became more disorganised than usual, he would sometimes fail to turn up for a *Spectator* lunch at Doughty Street, or even, on one occasion, for its annual summer party. At the beginning of 1983 he took a two-month sabbatical, travelling in the Middle East; and within a few weeks of his return he took a decision, to sack the literary editor, which would ultimately seal his fate.

The more immediate problems, however, were that there was a recession, the oil industry was badly hit and Cluff Oil's share price was falling. *The Spectator*'s loss for 1981 was around £300,000; savings had to be made and cost controls set up. It was fortunate that, within six months of Cluff's purchase of the magazine, he got a letter from James Knox applying for a job.

Knox combined both journalistic and business experience. He had written for *Antique Collector*, had started a magazine called *Natural World*, and had a master's diploma from the European Institute of Business Administration (INSEAD). Having joined as business manager in October 1981, he began by transferring the distribution of *The Spectator* (with some resistance from Chancellor) from *Private Eye* to the much larger and more professional Comag. Then he tackled the advertising, initially by sending free copies to potential advertisers (which, apart from bringing in advertising revenue over the longer term, was to result in the sponsorship by Highland Park malt whisky, from 1984, of the long-running and highly successful Parliamentarian of the Year awards lunch). Knox also spent some of his time visiting banks with Cluff in order to obtain funds for *The Spectator*. Since overdraft limits were geared to Cluff Oil's share price, the position was sometimes precarious, and on one occasion Marine Midland Bank decided, without any notice, to bounce the weekly batch of cheques. (Knox was able to put things right before any contributors' cheques were presented.)

None of this stopped Cluff from being always generous with his hospitality. Dinners were given and Chancellor was asked to stay at all three of his country houses, in Kent, Scotland and on an island in Poole Harbour. Cluff gave *The Spectator* a set of Beerbohm cartoons when Creighton demanded the return of some pictures which he said were his; and when *The Spectator* ran a 'treasure hunt', set by Booker over several weeks, Cluff donated one of his Lavery paintings, then worth at least £3,000, as first prize. The following year he gave a 1934 Daimler for another competition.

In the meantime *The Spectator* was making some useful friends. Graham Greene, a former cinema critic and literary editor of the magazine, was a great fan and wrote many letters to Chancellor from La Résidence des Fleurs in Antibes, where he spent most of his time. In February 1979: 'I can't bottle up my enthusiasm any longer. Surely Ferdinand Mount is the best parliamentary journalist since Taper. On the whole I think he is better than Taper was.' For a promotional advertising campaign Greene provided a fulsome tribute: '*The Spectator* is the most entertaining and best-written weekly in the English language.' But he was unimpressed by the prizes offered by Cluff in the two competitions. 'A second-rate picture by a second-rate artist' was his comment on the Lavery, while he ventured the opinion that 1934 was a bad year for Daimlers.

It was said that Greene had once won a *Spectator* competition with a parody of his own work. When a competition was set in 1980, asking for an extract from an imaginary Greene novel, the winner was Sebastian Eleigh, who turned out to be Greene's younger brother, Sir Hugh Greene, while in third place was Greene's sister. Greene's own entry, under the name of Colin Bates, was not judged to be among the best five chosen. But he used it, eight years later, as the opening passage of his novel, *The Captain and the Enemy*. (The setting and judging of the weekly competition had by 1980 been taken over by James Michie, poet, translator of Horace and Catullus and sometime co-director, with Graham Greene, of The Bodley Head. More than 900 competitions later, always under the pseudonym of Jaspistos, he was still thinking up fresh ideas in 1998.)

On his visits to London Greene would come quite frequently to the Thursday lunch at Doughty Street. On one occasion, in front of a senior Tory politician, he produced from his jacket pocket a postcard he had just received from Kim Philby in Moscow. On another, as he arrived in the ground-floor office, he was asked by the receptionist, 'Have you come about the carpet?' Later, Greene and Jeffrey Bernard became friendly and would lunch together in Antibes.

Editorial lunches at *The Spectator* were often highly entertaining occasions, and the best were usually those at which a clash of personalities occurred, or some embarrassment was caused. When Lord Longford was telling the lunch table how well he had got on with the Kray twins when he visited them in jail, Bernard made a memorable interruption. 'Don't be bloody naive,' he said dismissively. 'They're f...ing social climbers.' Paterson, who had good socialist credentials, once goaded Jessica Mitford by talking to her about 'blackamoors'. Another time he caused some consternation by bringing Alger Hiss to lunch. Beryl Bainbridge is remembered for having spent the latter part of one lunch sitting under the table, and Professor Richard Cobb for lifting his head from the table, where it had been resting for several minutes, to make a telling contribution to some literary debate which had been going on around him. He also once woke from a reverie at 4.30 to announce that he had better be going, as he had to catch the 3.15 train back to Oxford.

Convivial these occasions always were, although in Chancellor's day only wine was offered before and during lunch. Three exceptions were, however, permitted: Amis (whisky), Bernard (vodka) and Sam White (pink gin). One day the gin bottle was not on the tray when White arrived, and he was heard to growl, 'No gin — no lunch.' For some years the cooking was done by Jennifer Paterson, a magnificently extrovert personality who was later to become a cookery writer and television star (as one of the 'Two Fat Ladies'). Meat and game were what she most enjoyed cooking, and she tended not to be sympathetic to those who did not share her tastes. 'Why don't you like bunny, Kingsley?' she once asked him in her endearingly loud and jolly way, when he left his plate of rabbit stew. Another time she cooked roast pork on the day the Israeli ambassador was coming to lunch. When, during Moore's editorship, the Prince of Wales came to lunch, Jennifer Paterson produced a large halibut (which had to be sent down from Scotland, at a cost of £76), followed by guinea fowl. She presided over the kitchen from 1977 to 1988. Moore fired her for throwing plates out of the window when a junior member of staff got in her way while trying to make a cup of coffee. But she soon reinstated herself, and anyway was by then spending more time writing her *Spectator* cookery column.

An attaché from the Soviet embassy was once a guest at lunch. He was talking of having spent some time in Mongolia, while Jennifer Paterson was clearing the plates. 'Did you see much of my brother?' she suddenly interjected. The attaché's brow furrowed; he was irritated and uncomfortable, his expression seeming to say, 'Why this cook speak with me? Brother of cook? Is this some coded message?' The attaché could scarcely be blamed for not knowing that cook's brother had been British ambassador in Ulan Bator.

Unfortunately someone else was in the kitchen on the day that Spiro Agnew, the former US vice-president who had been forced to resign because of tax evasion charges, and the Australian comedian Barry Humphries were among the guests. Humphries, soberly dressed in a dark, pin-striped suit, conversed seriously with Agnew on such subjects as the future of NATO and Australia's involvement in the Vietnam war. Presumably the ex-vice-president had been briefed on Humphries's particular comic talents, but he cannot have been prepared for what happened next.

Chancellor knew that a change of clothes for Humphries had been delivered to the office, because he was due to go on somewhere straight after lunch, where he was to appear as Dame Edna Everage. Under pressure from Chancellor, he agreed to leave the dining-room during lunch and, having changed, return as the housewife superstar.

Ackroyd took him into his office where, having just published one of his first books, on the history of transvestism, he was fascinated to observe the metamorphosis taking place. When Dame Edna appeared in the dining-room the cheese was being passed round, and from that moment Agnew lost his appetite. He became very ill at ease. Who was this woman? And what happened to the Australian guy who was sitting here just now? 'We should be having a glass of ouzo together, Spiro,' Dame Edna cooed at the Greek immigrant greengrocer's son, putting a bare arm round his shoulder. The former vice-president was nonplussed and not enjoying himself. 'I would like to describe our meeting today as the Agnew and the Ecstasy,' she went on, as the rest of the table went on laughing.

A message then came from reception that an *Evening Standard* photographer was outside, hoping to get a picture of Agnew and Dame Edna together. The great tax-evader knew it was time to take evasive action. He mumbled his thanks and made off down the stairs at an impressive pace (the dining-room is on the third floor). Dame Edna followed, waving her handbag and calling lustily for Spiro to wait for her. But he managed to get out of the building and into his car, unmolested by Edna and unphotographed by the *Evening Standard*. It was a pity about the picture, but the general opinion was that it had been a very good lunch.

By 1981 a new discovery, John Springs, who presented himself at *The Spectator* with a portfolio of drawings and had a pronounced stammer, was producing some striking, thin-nibbed portrait caricatures for the cover. With Nicholas Garland now also doing front-cover drawings, and the use of a heavier, glossy paper for the cover, the magazine began to achieve more impact on the newsstands. Michael Heath and David Austin were the two regular cartoonists on the inside pages. Paul Johnson had begun a weekly press column in 1980, Tony Rudd was 'In the City' and Alan Gibson, a correspondent of the *Times*, was discoursing from time to time on cricket. In 1981 seven US immigration officials at Kennedy airport, New York, were identified as avid readers of the magazine; Fairlie left *The Spectator*'s pages to write for the *Times*; and J.A. Caesar (JAC), a former town clerk from Keighley, Yorkshire, retired after ten years as compiler of very tricky cross-words. Having dropped the definite article from its title on the magazine's cover, *The Spectator* was reinstated, at Cluff's insistence, in 1982.

Week after week, Chancellor's Notebook was one of the best things to be found in *The Spectator*. He became a master of this journalistic form, penning four or five sharply observed comments on matters of the day which, since the page was always written dangerously close to deadline, were often very topical. The marking of the 8,000th issue of *The Spectator* in November 1981 gave the editor the opportunity to be excessively modest, once again, about his achievements for the magazine over the previous six years. It tended, he wrote in his Notebook, 'to edit itself.... It is the writers who collectively give *The Spectator* its identity without much assistance from the editor.' Though 8,000 issues had been published since Robert Rintoul started *The Spectator* in 1828. announcing that 'the principal object of a newspaper is to convey intelligence' and that his journal would give 'a report of all the leading occurrences of the week', *The Spectator* in 1981 should rather have been celebrating its link with *The Spectator* of Addison and Steele in the early 18th century. The model for a typical *Spectator* article in the Chancellor era was an Addison essay, not a Rintoul report. A subject might be addressed from an unusual, even an apparently perverse, point of view, in the style not of an investigative reporter but of a discursive essayist. In the same issue Watkins complimented the magazine for the freedom it gave its contributors, and Peregrine Worsthorne commended their nonchalance, using a rapier to prick a balloon, as opposed to the *New Statesman*, which preferred to bring a sledgehammer to crack a nut. 'Alone among the political weeklies [*The Spectator*] has got its priorities right: the exposure of wrong thinking rather than wrong doing.' Worsthorne also seemed to approve *The Spectator*'s policy of not having leading articles advising the government what to do, of not adopting positions on the great issues of the day. This policy, of not having a policy, was to be put to the test less than five months later, when Argentina invaded the Falkland Islands.

During the first two weeks of April 1982, when Simon Courtauld, deputy

*David Austin and
Michael Heath were the
principal cartoonists
during Chancellor's
editorship.*

"Fancy coming out pacifist bashing?"

editor since George Hutchinson's death in 1980, was editing *The Spectator*, and while the task force was heading for the South Atlantic, there was reason to hope that a settlement would be reached. Mount called 'this last British Armada... a quixotic but necessary enterprise', and Waugh agreed that we were doing the right thing, even though it would end in abject humiliation for Britain. It was after Chancellor had returned from holiday in Tuscany, and war was getting much closer, that the jitters began. In line with his policy of opening *The Spectator*'s pages to the free expression of a variety of opinion, Chancellor published a piece by James Fenton who, in arguing the case against going to war over the Falklands, called the government's policy on the eve of battle 'frivolous, murderous, wicked', which many thought was a bit much. No change was made, for the duration of the war, to the practice of not having leading articles. However, a collective editorial line was, for once, adopted on the cover of the issue of 8 May, with the words: 'Time for a ceasefire'. This reflected both the view of Mount in his political column and of Chancellor who, on the morning that *The Spectator* went to press, decided to change the cover when news was received of the sinking of HMS *Sheffield* with the loss of 30 British lives.

Mount was, by this time, in an embarrassing position, finding himself publicly at odds with the person who was about to employ him. Before the Falklands conflict began he had accepted the offer of a job at No. 10 Downing Street, as head of the prime minister's policy unit. He thought he should give up the political commentary at once, but Chancellor persuaded him to continue for a few more weeks. Then General Galtieri invaded the Falklands. Over the next six weeks, when Mount in his column was counselling caution, settlement and cease-fire, Ian Gow was said to have asked Thatcher: 'Do you really want this man working for you, who loses his nerve the moment a few of our chaps get killed?' When Mount urged the government to negotiate a ceasefire, he was asked by Chancellor whether he was quite sure he wanted it published. The following week, 15 May, he wrote his last commentary (for the time being), in which he commended Francis Pym for the concessions he was offering Argentina, and then spent the next two years in Downing Street. It was never part of his job to advise Thatcher on foreign affairs, and to her credit she never mentioned the Falklands to him.

It was nearly four months before Colin Welch succeeded Mount as political commentator; in the interim the column was filled by a number of contributors, including Charles Moore, whose first appearance in *The Spectator* was during the war, on 15 May. Perhaps the best contribution to the Falklands conflict in *The Spectator* was the weekly military analysis of 'Patrick Desmond', a necessary pseudonym of John Keegan (since he was a lecturer at Sandhurst and employed by the Ministry of Defence), later to become defence editor of the *Daily Telegraph*. His future editor at the *Telegraph*, Max Hastings, was *The Spectator*'s man on the spot. Following a chance meeting in El Vino's the day before he sailed with the task force on the *Canberra*, Hastings was signed up to file for *The Spectator* as well as the *Evening Standard*. His last despatch, recounting his entry into Port Stanley on the final day of the conflict, was illustrated by Garland with a full-page cover drawing of the intrepid reporter riding towards the island capital on a sheep.

Had *The Spectator* had a good war? Some readers thought not, accusing it of having wobbled in its attitude to the recovery of the islands by force of arms. Amis wrote: 'Your coverage of the Falklands episode has cleared up one small point: whether you run a fairly responsible journal for the libertarian Right or a fairly entertaining magazine. You run a fairly entertaining magazine.' His complaint was that *The Spectator* had drifted about inconsistently on the tide of intellectual opinion. Chancellor responded that this was not entirely fair: 'What we did was to drift about on the tide of our own opinion.' He was never at all sure about the war; when it was over he wrote that 'a little rejoicing is now in order, but only a little'. The campaign had been 'risky and basically unnecessary'. Editorial opinion throughout was expressed through his Notebook; it did not really matter that there was no unsigned leader. *The Spectator* did carry some excellent stuff during those extraordinary weeks of spring and early summer in 1982. It was a pity, though, that Mount had to leave at half-time.

Waugh's view was that Galtieri's decision to invade the Falklands was provoked not so much by the Defence Secretary's decision to scrap HMS *Endurance*, the one armed Royal Navy vessel stationed in the South Atlantic, as by Thatcher's perverse and persistent refusal to give to Worsthorne the knighthood which was so obviously his due. More seriously, perhaps, Waugh went off on another tack during the war. His attention was engaged by a *Daily Mirror* reporter, John Pilger, who had been to Bangkok and bought an eight-year-old girl called Sunee, for £85, in order to highlight the so-called child slave trade in Thailand. Although the exploitation of child labour is widespread all over the Far East, the veteran left-wing reporter had chosen to indict one of the few Asian countries without a Communist or Soviet-backed government. When it emerged that Pilger and the *Mirror* had been hoaxed, that Sunee was in fact a Bangkok schoolgirl living with her mother, Waugh's joy was unconfined. In his column for 12 June 1982 he could not resist the suggestion that Pilger had knowingly been party to the hoax in order to discredit Thailand, and there followed months of lawyers' letters and threatened litigation, resulting finally in an agreed statement with each side paying its own costs. Waugh gave an undertaking not to libel Pilger in any subsequent reference to the 'Sunee story', but the case had one significant outcome that did not redound to Pilger's advantage. The verb 'to pilger' entered the language (mainly used by Waugh himself) and was dignified by an entry in the *Oxford Dictionary of New Words*. It is described as 'a critical or negative word' meaning, 'to treat a subject or present an investigation in a manner supposedly characteristic of the investigative journalist John Pilger, especially when this entails exposing human suffering or drawing conclusions which reflect badly on the actions of a powerful government or institution'. In 1984, in the last issue edited by Chancellor, a future *Spectator* editor, Frank Johnson, wrote of a manifestation of *le pilgerisme* in a French television series on Indochina. Waugh wrote in 1989, in relation to the sentence of death passed by Iran on the author of *The Satanic Verses*, of 'the price Rushdie must pay for pilgering'.

It is tempting to think of the Pilger episode, in 1982, as a diverting little incident, a lull in the fighting, between the Falklands and Beirut. Israel's invasion of Lebanon and its war against the PLO in Beirut were given stern treatment in *The Spectator*, notably by Desmond (Keegan) writing about Menachem Begin's terrorist tactics and the Israeli Defence Force's complicity in the massacre of Palestinians in refugee camps. Knowing of the magazine's long-standing pro-Arab, and sometimes anti-semitic, reputation, it was to Chancellor's credit that, when he took his sabbatical in early 1983, he should spend some time in Jerusalem.

Returning refreshed to the fray, he appointed Jock Bruce-Gardyne (lately Economic Secretary to the Treasury) as City columnist and Moore as political commentator in place of Welch. Welch had done the job for little more than six months and would in future write a weekly Centrepiece, giving scope to his literary talents beyond the confines of politics. Both Welch and Moore covered the June 1983 election, when readers were advised editorially, with the same sort of qualification as in 1979, to vote Conservative, even though to do so might involve 'holding their noses'.

Moore was introduced to Chancellor by Ferdy and Julia Mount. He was in his mid-twenties, working for the *Daily Telegraph* as a leader writer, and was described by Welch as 'pure gold'. Others would call him priggish, or prematurely mature, but it soon became clear that, despite reassuring moments of schoolboyish irresponsibility, he had leadership qualities. Moore was initially reluctant to leave the *Telegraph*, but Cluff's powers of persuasion won him over to *The Spectator*. A rather odd agreement seems to have been made between Moore and Chancellor, that after six months Moore would become joint editor, but before that period had expired he told Chancellor that such an arrangement would not work. Although Cluff never promised Moore the editorship, he had him marked down for the job when the time came. By his reaction to an amendment made by the literary editor, A.N. Wilson, to a book review in June 1983, Chancellor ensured that the time came sooner rather than later.

Andrew Wilson was aged 32, had already written and published eight books, and was known as one of the 'Young Fogeys' (a phrase coined, or at any rate first used in print, by Watkins in *The Spectator*). He rode a bicycle with old-fashioned handlebars and a basket at the front. He wore a waistcoat and sometimes a trilby; and he enjoyed drinking ginger beer. He had put together some lively books pages since he took on the job at the end of 1981 (Marnham having stood down in order to write a history of *Private Eye*). Wilson recruited Philip Larkin, Anita Brookner and Peter Quennell as reviewers, and he started a series, 'A Book in My Life', of which one of the most memorable was Angus Wilson's piece on H.J. Massingham's *The Harp and the Oak*. He also enjoyed occasionally making mischief. He had given Bel Mooney a biography of George Henry Lewes (Mr George Eliot) to review, and had compressed part of her first paragraph to read:

> Pushy, conceited, vulgar, over-energetic, and with one eye for the main chance: Lewes seems like a Victorian Clive James.

What Mooney had in fact written was:

> All the jibes at Lewes — that he was pushy, conceited, vulgar, over-energetic, and with an eye for the main chance — make him a welcome and refreshing relief from such dour Victorian valetudinarians as Carlyle and Herbert Spencer. Lively, a polymath, Lewes reads like an early incarnation of Clive James.

A significant change to the sense of the passage had been made, which could hardly be excused by saying that the review had to be cut due to space restrictions. Mooney and James were both understandably angry and Mooney wrote a letter which Wilson threw away. Chancellor took the view, though not immediately, that it was a sackable offence, and Wilson was dismissed. Some colleagues then accused Wilson of trying to make trouble; others attempted to intercede on his behalf. He was certainly very upset and contemplated an action for wrongful dismissal. Cluff, who had a high regard for Wilson and was on friendly terms with him, asked Chancellor to reconsider; but to no avail. Cluff did not easily accept Wilson's dismissal, and arranged to go on paying his salary for a while. Knox commented to Gavin Stamp (the architectural historian and another Young Fogey contributor to *The Spectator*) that he thought Chancellor would not last more than another six months.

It was not a bad guess. Seven months later, on 1 February 1984, Cluff took Chancellor to lunch at Chez Victor in Wardour Street and told him he would have to go. The news came as a shock to Chancellor, although not as a complete surprise, because he had already been told by at least two other journalists of the rumour that he was going to be fired. Cluff had been expressing his dissatisfaction with Chancellor to various people: it was not just that the sacking of Wilson had exasperated him, but that he considered the magazine to be lacking in political weight and Chancellor to be commercially irresponsible. He was also unhappy at the campaign that Chancellor had been running against the proposed flotation of Reuters as a public company. *The Spectator*'s circulation was by now close to 20,000 and its annual losses had been reduced to around £140,000, thanks in large part to Knox's success in attracting advertising (revenue had doubled in 1983) and in organising special promotions. But to Cluff it was still an unacceptable figure and, in short, he thought it was time for a change. He had a successor, Moore, but instead of appointing him at once, Cluff first offered the editorship to Germaine Greer, who told him that she was not the right person for the job (she did think, however, that she was the right person to be Mrs Cluff). Instead she recommended Ingrams, whom Cluff telephoned, to be told that he was quite happy to go on editing *Private Eye*.

Mount was unhappy at losing his editor, having only just come back to *The Spectator* the previous month as literary editor. (After Wilson's departure, John Gross agreed to take on the job, then changed his mind; Marnham returned to the literary editor's chair for six months.) Mount and other senior staff at Doughty Street had no difficulty in deciding that Moore must be made editor, and this course was urged on Cluff by Knox. Moore's appointment was announced, and an odd little episode was over. Those, such as Mount and Waugh, who had initially thought they should resign, decided to stay on (the decision was made for Waugh by the offer of more money). Courtauld left with Chancellor and went off to edit *The Field*; John McEwen resigned in sympathy with his old friend; and Ingrams was grateful for an excuse to give up his television column. Chancellor, who would soon become deputy editor of the *Sunday Telegraph*, was persuaded by Moore to continue as a regular contributor by writing about television.

It was inevitable that the involuntary departure of such a popular and successful editor should attract some adverse comment in the press. Besides, the manner of Chancellor's removal (which he said in the Notebook he was 'less than happy about') and of Moore's appointment was not well handled by Cluff. The formal announcement, that Chancellor and Cluff were parting by 'mutual agreement', led Chancellor to explain what this meant: Cluff had said it was time for Chancellor to go and he had agreed. In addition to many letters from Fleet Street colleagues, Callaghan, Lord Dacre and Daniel Farson wrote to commiserate and to congratulate him on what he had achieved for *The Spectator*. A letter typical of many came from Margot Walmsley at *Encounter*: 'This is tragic news — I can't bear to think of a *Spectator* not edited by you. You have made it the very best weekly in the world... we were grieved and shocked to hear the news.' Only, and predictably, Alastair Forbes struck a different note. While expressing some sympathy at Chancellor's demise, he wrote: 'What most surprised me about your hoisting by your own anti-personnel petard (as recently tested on poor Andrew Wilson) was your own surprise at it since it had been as widely expected as the fall in the value of the dollar and for quite as long.' * Chancellor edited his final issue — the 445th for which, as he wrote, he had been at least nominally responsible — on 24 March, a few days after a dinner had been given, on the Ides of March, at L'Escargot in Soho. Described on the menu as 'a celebration of the life and work of Alexander Chancellor and Simon Courtauld', the occasion was most memorable for the speeches made by at least half those present — Shiva Naipaul, Sayle, Waugh, Worsthorne, Gale, Taki, Bernard — some of whom jocularly expressed their fears for the future of the magazine under its new editor, also present at the dinner, Moore.

The Spectator, under Chancellor, had fulfilled an important role in journalism. It provided an intelligent, well-written, unpredictable yet always

---

*Another paragraph of the same letter, applauding the resignation of the 'ageing schoolboy' Ingrams as television critic and expressing the hope that Moore would not appoint 'another boy-clown to do an intelligent man's work', was quoted by Chancellor when he took over the television column the week after he had relinquished the editorship. This elicited a letter from Forbes rebuking Chancellor for having made unscrupulous use of private correspondence.

perceptive antidote to the Americanised, blanket coverage journalism increasingly being adopted by some of the broadsheet newspapers (and, incidentally, by the *New Statesman* under Bruce Page, lately of the *Sunday Times* Insight team). Many of *The Spectator*'s writers would continue under the new regime. Of the more light-hearted, though sometimes outrageously opinionated columnists — again, not to be found in the daily press — it was entirely appropriate that, in the last month of Chancellor's editorship, Bernard should produce one of his very best Low Life pieces:

Bye bye blackbird

It's been another rather silly week in the back garden of Soho. On Monday I met a black bird with thrush and, as I predicted in last week's column, the drama student didn't last long. Lingering over a pot of Earl Grey at the end of an afternoon seminar — included in the service charge — she casually dismissed King Lear as being an old man with woman troubles. I was so irritated I asked her to remove her toothbrush from my bathroom beer mug and make other arrangements for her future unhappiness. Such people come here in taxis but they leave in buses and it serves them right. Well, later that evening — back at the drawing board so to speak — in Kettners and sipping Cointreau, the poor man's pre-frontal lobotomy, these tired old eyes came to rest on this delightful looking black bird who omitted to tell me that she had thrush until I had actually signed her into the Great Portland Street Academy. I've put her on a crash course of natural yoghurt which rather messily had to be applied to the parts as well as swallowed and I've sworn her to celibacy until the start of the flat racing season which opens at Doncaster on 22 March, exactly one day after J.S. Bach's birthday. You could now call her a black bird in the bush and I fear I have none in the hand. The next morning I perked up a bit when the telephone rang and I heard the soft voice of my Dublin bookmaker. He told me that Capture Him, held in the highest esteem by his trainer Vincent O'Brien, must be backed when he comes to England in the spring and possibly for the 2,000 Guineas. But that's by the by and I only mention it since the information comes from the same source that gave us Bajan Sunshine for last year's Cesarewitch...

Which reminds me. The Inland Revenue finally got me to court last

Friday and they're going to tap my income at source for the next 13 months. I think I slipped up badly. I made the wretched collector an offer which he accepted with such alacrity that I knew immediately I'd gone over the top. Can you imagine writing something like 60 columns for practically nothing? So, if I sound a little churlish here until next year's Grand National you'll know it has nothing to do with thrush or drama students. I managed to needle the collector though. What these people don't like or understand after you've been pleading poverty in the dock is one's hailing a taxi outside the court instead of jumping on a bus. That's why they're tax collectors who'll never know the invigorating joys of treading water in the deep end without a life belt...

Just before I went into hospital — and this is a sordid story that warrants no detail — I collected a criminal record for kicking someone's car parked annoyingly on the pavement. A CID plain-clothes man arrested me in the Coach on a charge of criminal damage and took me to Vine Street where I was fingerprinted and photographed. But this is extraordinary. As we walked past the Swiss pub on our way to the nick the arresting detective said, 'You screwed the landlord's daughter here in 1976, didn't you?' Well, I was amazed. How anyone could have known what went on that Christmas Day after lunch on the saloon bar floor after the guvnor went upstairs for a nap I'll never know. But I liked the magistrate at Bow Street when I went up for the car kicking. He looked at my record and saw I'd been nicked last October for going over the top in the Raj of India restaurant and said, 'The last time it was rubber plants, Mr Bernard. Now it's cars. What next?' Well, you tell me, I thought. Probably a collector of taxes, possibly a drama student, maybe a black bird with the treble up of thrush, herpes and Aids. All I know is that when I leave this flat it gets bloody dangerous. No wonder vultures are nesting on the roof of the Coach and Horses.

3 March 1984

9

RIGHT IS RIGHT

'I suppose it will now fall into the hands of the New Right,' Lord Dacre, then Master of Peterhouse, wrote of *The Spectator* in 1984, in a letter to Alexander Chancellor. There were fears, too, expressed by Auberon Waugh at the farewell dinner for Chancellor and Courtauld, that the magazine would now become more political. In his first week as editor Charles Moore devoted his political column, which he would continue to write for another 18 months, to trying to allay these fears. As a 'partially political weekly,' he wrote, '*The Spectator* ought not to disdain politics, though it should not go on and on about it.' His task, as he saw it, was 'to engage in a difficult, but congenially conservative occupation — to preserve and, if possible, to build on what exists'.

Moore inherited not only some excellent writers, but prize-winning ones too. In 1984 Murray Sayle was acclaimed Writer of the Year by the Periodical Publishers Association (most notably for his riveting articles on the shooting down of a Korean airliner by a Soviet fighter in September 1983). Somerset Maugham Awards were given to Peter Ackroyd (for his novel *The Last Testament of Oscar Wilde*) and to Timothy Garton Ash, who had been writing a series of distinguished articles from eastern Europe, especially on the revolution in Poland. Christopher Hitchens began to write with greater regularity from Washington, and Christopher Fildes returned to *The Spectator* to write on finance and the City. He called his weekly column City and Suburban, reviving the appellation last used in the 1950s by John Betjeman, who died in May 1984. As an enthusiast of the Turf, Fildes was thinking rather of the City and Suburban Handicap, run during the Epsom spring meeting, and of his racing pseudonym, Captain Threadneedle, who would get a mention in the column from time to time. Andrew Gimson was made deputy editor, and *The Spectator* began publishing articles on wine and food.

While Moore was anxious to expand the magazine editorially, and James Knox to undertake much-needed promotion, they were constrained by the financial position. Although the loss of £143,000 for 1983 was a marked improvement on the two previous years, and the forecast loss for 1984 was a mere £50,000, the overdraft was rising relentlessly towards a level which Cluff could no longer sustain. Having formed a company, *The Spectator* (1828) Ltd in 1982, Cluff appointed directors, including Dennis Walters, MP, a pro-Arab friend of Ian Gilmour, and Charles Letts, based in Singapore, who were asked to subscribe for shares. He also tried to raise funds by issuing debentures (£5,000 repayable after five years) to companies which, instead of earning interest, would give them the right to two full-page advertisements a year to publicise their interim and annual results in *The Spectator*. But the idea met with little response.

Cluff was by now of the opinion that the future of *The Spectator* would be best secured in the hands of a publishing group. He was certainly not inclined to entertain an offer to buy the magazine which came from the Australian entrepreneur, Kerry Packer, whose legal adviser, Malcolm Turnbull, visited Moore at Doughty Street to reassure him that 'Kerry is not motivated only by greed — not all the time anyway'. By November 1984 (when Ludovic Kennedy was appointed to the board) the overdraft had gone over £300,000 and things were getting pretty desperate. Somewhat surprisingly, it was decided not to increase the cover price, which had been held at 75p since mid-1983. Cluff was in Australia on oil business when he was approached by John Fairfax Ltd, publishers of the *Sydney Morning Herald* and the *Melbourne Age*, who had heard that *The Spectator* might be for sale. The group's chief editorial executive, Max Suich, and general manager, Fred Brenchley, met Cluff at his hotel in Sydney, and two days later heads of agreement were signed in the airport lounge as Cluff was about to return to London. On 20 December *The Spectator*'s Christmas lunch was held at David Tang's brother's Chinese restaurant in Shaftesbury Avenue, but the board meeting scheduled for the same day did not take place. A month later, the ownership of *The Spectator* was transferred to John Fairfax Ltd, who paid off the overdraft at the Royal Bank of Scotland and additionally handed Cluff the sum of £815,000. Moore, hearing the news on his return from holiday in India, published a cartoon, by Michael Heath, showing a copy of *The Spectator* sticking out of a kangaroo's pouch. The sale was

John Fairfax Ltd received a Spectatorish welcome when it bought the magazine in January 1985.

concluded not a moment too soon. Knox had been obliged to hold up payment of the larger bills, juggling with creditors in order to keep the overdraft below its £350,000 limit. His first meeting at Doughty Street with Brenchley was interrupted by a message from downstairs that bailiffs had arrived to remove the photocopier.

Fairfax were also somewhat bemused to learn that they had inherited a regular contributor, *The Spectator*'s High Life correspondent, Taki, who was currently a guest of Her Majesty in Pentonville prison. He had been charged and found guilty the previous summer of being in possession of 21.4 grammes of cocaine for his own use, having been arrested at Heathrow after a flight from New York. One reader wrote in to ask if Taki had smuggled the cocaine with the intention of putting *The Spectator* on a sound financial footing or of offering it as first prize in the next *Spectator* competition. He offered to resign his column, but Moore said there was no need since Taki did not hold a position of responsibility and 'we expect our High Life correspondent to be high some of the time'. Before going to jail (he was there from mid-December 1984 until the end of February 1985) Taki suggested that he and Jeffrey Bernard should swap columns. While he had

spent the last three months in England and was about to consort with crim-
inals in prison, Bernard had been to Barbados and Paris and was about to
go cruising on the Mississippi. Taki returned to court (a civil action this
time) in 1986 for the hearing of a libel case brought against him and *The
Spectator* by an obscure but wealthy woman, Madame Rosemarie Marcie-
Riviere. The offending article was published during Cluff's time, in 1982,
and the case appeared to turn on whether or not she was expecting Taki to
come to one of her lunch parties. It should never have got to court: the
defendants were badly advised, and it was not surprising that they lost. The
plaintiff was awarded damages of £15,000, and Taki and Cluff shared the
total legal expenses equally, each paying £65,000. It was Cluff's last payment in respect of *The Spectator*, but by no means the end of his connection
with the magazine. He agreed with Fairfax to stay on as chairman, the position which he still holds today.

Brenchley's first thought was to replace Knox with a marketing manager
from the *Economist*. but he was dissuaded from this course by Moore, with
whom Knox had established a very successful working relationship. Knox
assumed the title of publisher and embarked on a spending programme
with Fairfax's enthusiastic support. For the first time *The Spectator* advertised itself on television, and a major subscription drive was started. Over
the next three years the number of annual subscriptions almost tripled: half
of them came from abroad, largely thanks to promotion and direct mailings
in Australia and the United States, and by 1987 total subscriptions exceeded
newsstand sales.

Fairfax also agreed to spend money on repairs to the Doughty Street
building and on reopening the basement, which enabled Knox to establish
and accommodate an advertising sales force of five people. Joanna Coles,
later to become a well-known journalist on the *Guardian*, and then the
Times, began as a telephone sales person at *The Spectator*, as did Philip
Marsden-Smedley, who dropped the Smedley when he became a successful
travel writer, and Mark Stuart-Grumbar, who was advertising manager.
Rory Knight Bruce, the first undergraduate editor of the *New Edinburgh
Review*, subsequently editor of Londoner's Diary on the *Evening Standard*
and a master of foxhounds, joined the team in 1985, overcoming Moore's
reluctance to take on yet another man with a double-barrelled surname.
Whatever their names, they were successful in bringing colour advertising

to *The Spectator* for the first time; at the back of the magazine the classifieds section was greatly expanded.

Moore encountered no resistance from Fairfax to his plans to increase the number of editorial pages and improve the appearance of the magazine. The introduction of radical design changes at the end of April 1985 caused an immediate outcry, but they were quickly modified the following week, and have remained substantially unaltered since. A glossy paper was adopted for the inside pages and, at Fairfax's instigation, colour covers became the norm towards the end of 1985. Price increases, from 75p to 90p in 1985, and to £1 less than a year later, seemed to have no harmful effect on circulation, which rose to 30,000 in 1986, overtaking the *New Statesman* for the first time.

In this healthy atmosphere Moore was able to expand. There was never any question of *The Spectator* losing its entertainment value: all the popular columns begun under Chancellor were retained, and to High and Low Life he added Home Life by Alice Thomas Ellis. A restaurant column, written by Nigella Lawson, was introduced, extending the wine and food coverage, and a bridge column by Lord Lever was suggested, although it did not materialise. Nor did the idea of bringing back the strip cartoon of Barry Mackenzie (which, written by Barry Humphries and drawn by Nicholas Garland, had run for years in *Private Eye*). However, Moore appointed as the first cartoon editor of *The Spectator* Michael Heath, who in turn recruited John Glashan from the *Observer* and several cartoonists from the ailing *Punch*. Henceforth a cartoon would appear on almost every page.

In spite of Waugh's warnings, Moore, not unnaturally for a political commentator, did want to make *The Spectator* more political, though he certainly had no intention of filling the front half of the magazine with political articles. During his first year, while he was still writing the political column, there was no leading article as such (a page of editorial, unsigned Notes appeared in addition to the signed Diary). What Moore did was to make *The Spectator* ideologically Thatcherite — under the previous editor it had been sceptical at best — while vigorously opposing some of the things for which the Iron Lady was responsible: in particular, the Anglo-Irish agreement of 1985 ('a fraudulent prospectus') and the Single European Act, which began with a solemn resolve to move forward to 'European Union'. *The Spectator* was concerned that under Margaret Thatcher Britain was becoming more involved in the European Community than ever before, and applauded her Bruges speech in 1988, in a leader headed 'Non!' She was commended for setting out the limits of her European ideal, and for being awkward in her dealings with Brussels. 'Her tone should be insistent, strident, tiresome, which, after all, is the sort of tone she is best at.' At the time of the 1987 general election the playwright David Hare, a token left-wing voice whom Moore became accustomed to wheeling on every five years, wrote an article deploring the prime minister's arrogance and her 'desperately shabby' government. In its pre-election leader *The Spectator* was censorious of her narrow philosophy and the fact that 'much of her support comes from a self-interest which is definitely unenlightened', while concluding nevertheless that the Conservatives under Thatcher had established a more recognisable moral position than had Labour.

Although the magazine was undoubtedly perceived to be more politically serious and to have moved to the right under Moore, the Tory party was never under any illusion, as it had been in the past, that it could lean on *The Spectator*. If Moore was disinclined to publish articles from the left, it was less for ideological reasons than for the fact that the left was so intellectually barren throughout the 1980s. He occasionally took to teasing Thatcher by publishing articles such as that by two psychiatrists, who wrote that among people suffering from dementia her name was better known than the Queen's and more often recalled than Harold Macmillan and Harold Wilson were in the 1960s. In a piece written in 1989 on Thatcher's character and the significance of her gender, Minette Marrin ended with a prescient warning:

> The questions facing her demand qualities she has not shown much of so far — a capacity for doubt, for unconventional responses, for compromise, letting be and the wider view. If she does not find these strengths, her great achievements may be eclipsed by the qualities that made them possible.

In the same year Waugh put it rather more bluntly, writing of 'the almost universal loathing in which Mrs Thatcher is now held in her own party and throughout the upper reaches of the country.... People have begun to see her obstinate determination to lead her party to defeat as the greatest obstacle to their future serenity.'

The left wing in *The Spectator* was most notably represented in the mid-1980s in the writings of Christopher Hitchens and Nicholas von Hoffman, who were for ever sniping at President Reagan. In spite of a number of complaints from readers, Moore, who was not well disposed towards America at the time, waited until 1987 before appointing the more even-handed Ambrose Evans-Pritchard as Washington correspondent in place of the other two. Evans-Pritchard had already been writing for *The Spectator* from Latin America for three years, and had been accused by Mark Almond of 'offensive left-wing twaddle' in his comments on the United States's failure to appreciate that the Sandinistas in Nicaragua constituted the only democratically elected Marxist government in the world. Evans-Pritchard would later be one of the first to predict the Sandinistas' fall from power.

He was one of three contemporaries of Moore at Cambridge whom Moore brought successfully into journalism. Gimson, deputy editor until 1987, did not initially appeal to the Australian proprietors, who thought him too young and inexperienced for the job. It was an understandable first impression: nicknamed 'Gymslip', with the fresh-faced appearance of a not very senior schoolboy, Gimson combined a disconcertingly high-pitched laugh. But his success, as a writer as well as Moore's deputy, led to his departure to the *Independent* and, later, to the *Daily Telegraph* as correspondent in Germany. Noel Malcolm, a Fellow of Gonville and Caius College, Cambridge, began writing a radio column for Moore, then became political columnist in succession to Ferdinand Mount in October 1987, the same month that Dominic Lawson arrived from the *Financial Times* to take over the deputy editorship from Gimson.

Stephen Robinson (subsequently the *Daily Telegraph*'s man in Washington and then foreign editor) wrote from South Africa and Northern Ireland; Michael Trend (later to become a *Telegraph* leader writer and Conservative MP for Slough) was an assistant editor. In 1988 Moore asked Craig Brown to write a humorous column, in the persona of Wallace Arnold, who was shown smoking a pipe and wearing a cap, wing collar and cravat. It was supposed to be a spoof on a certain type of *Spectator* reader. Arnold was a right-wing buffer, a bit of a club bore, given to boasting that he always knows what is going on. 'Afore ye go: Leaves from the commonplace book of Wallace Arnold' was the way the column was described; and it was by no means universally admired. Of several critical letters published,

David Astor called Wallace Arnold 'commonplace rubbish... boring, pompous and humourless'.

During Chancellor's time Anthony Daniels had been sending in unsolicited articles from the South Seas, where he practised as a doctor; and it was Moore who first spotted his talent for writing. He would also report from the Far East, Latin America and eastern Europe, and particularly from Africa, sometimes using the pseudonym of Edward Theberton, and always revealing some hidden truth about one of the more benighted countries of that continent. In the 1990s he took to writing a regular column, 'If Symptoms Persist...', under the name of Theodore Dalrymple, most frequently on his experiences as a prison doctor in the Midlands. His portrayals of prisoners caused considerable annoyance to the then Director of Prisons, Stephen Tumim.

The City coverage was strengthened by Jock Bruce-Gardyne contributing a fortnightly piece on the economy which, with Fildes's weekly offering, meant that the Chancellor of the Exchequer, Nigel Lawson, was being observed and judged in print by two of his former *Spectator* colleagues. A director of the Social Affairs Unit, Digby Anderson, was taken on to write a column called Imperative Cooking; and Moore's very bright wife, Caroline, was responsible for the literary Treasure Hunts. P.J. Kavanagh continued his gentle, reflective Postscript until 1986 — at its best when he was writing about the weather and the wildlife observed around his home in the Gloucestershire Cotswolds — then wrote a delightful monthly essay, 'Life and Letters', while also serving as poetry editor, appointed by Mount during his literary editorship. Mount resumed the political column, later becoming lead book reviewer, while Mark Amory began his stint as the longest-serving literary editor in *The Spectator*'s recent history. He joined in 1985 (on the same day that Christopher Howse was taken on as production editor) and was still at his desk in 1998 — and still ably assisted by Clare Asquith, great-granddaughter of the prime minister and sometime *Spectator* leader writer, who began looking after the books pages in 1976, and whose soft voice on the telephone has given solace to many ill-paid reviewers. Amory enlarged the circle of reviewers in the 1980s, with Anita Brookner and Bevis Hillier becoming new regulars, although his experimenting was not always successful. Graham Greene threatened to cancel his subscription when a review appeared by Barbara Cartland (her only one). In his first year Amory published an outstandingly rude review by A.N. Wilson of a book by Marina Warner, calling it 'mindless, prolix and pretentious' and her 'a bore and a charlatan'. Another former literary editor, Patrick Marnham, sprang to her defence the following week, averring that he had no doubt which of the two, author or reviewer, should properly be described as a charlatan. Moore never sought to impose a political line on the books pages, and did not seem concerned to learn that Amory was a founder member of the Social Democratic party.

Moore indulged his romantic side by publishing profiles of famous travellers such as Eric Newby, Patrick Leigh Fermor and Freya Stark, and also a series called 'Outsiders' and 'Survivors'. Some of these, such as Peter Kemp, who as soldier and then war reporter was drawn to the sound of gunfire for most of his extraordinary life, were also contributors to *The Spectator*. Hilary Mantel, the first winner of the Shiva Naipaul memorial prize, became cinema critic in 1987 when Peter Ackroyd gave up after almost eight years. In his final column he disappointed his many fans by saying that his sensibilities had become so blunted that he really could not face going to the cinema any more, and he was proud never to have had a quotation from one of his reviews used to adorn a cinema advertisement. Over the next ten years he went to see only three films.

The Young Fogeyish tendency at *The Spectator* confirmed its Anglo-Catholic credentials with the publication in 1986 of a book on the state of the Church of England, *The Church in Crisis*, by Moore, Wilson and Gavin Stamp. When religious affairs, in the form of a sermon from the Bishop of London, crept into *The Spectator*, Graham Greene was moved to inquire, 'Is piety now going to take the place of style?' On another occasion a correspondent commented on 'the conversion of *The Spectator* into a Vatican house journal' — a few years before Moore was himself converted to the Catholic faith. In 1989 he established a Thomas Cranmer school prize (together with the Prayer Book Society) for which competitors had to recite a collect, epistle and gospel from the Book of Common Prayer. The Prince of Wales, who was patron of the prize, and whose architectural vision of Britain was well received at *The Spectator*, delivered an address at the prizegiving at the City church of St James's, Garlickhythe, in which he said that the Prayer Book should be listed as a Grade I edifice.

Perhaps the most constructive Fogey undertaking was the campaign to save the red telephone boxes designed by Sir Giles Scott in the 1920s. All 76,000 of these much-loved kiosks, as they were more correctly known, were in effect condemned in 1985 by British Telecom's announcement that it was going to create 'a payphone service for the 21st century', replacing the kiosks with modern yellow-striped boxes of American design. The opposition was orchestrated by the Thirties Society and the conservation officers of a few local authorities, and given voice by Stamp in *The Spectator*, with the active support of its editor. Moore went to see the chairman of British Telecom, Sir George Jefferson, to try to get the policy reversed. Looking out of the BT office window at St Paul's Cathedral and a concrete block next to it, Moore told the chairman that there, to remind him every day, was the difference between the old and new telephone boxes. In 1986 the Department of the Environment did begin to give protection to a few early kiosks, and later this listing was expanded. 'No vandalism meted out to a kiosk by an individual has equalled that practised systematically by British Telecom,' Stamp wrote. When, ultimately, it was acknowledged that some traditional telephone boxes should be restored, rather than destroyed, because they were part of the heritage, the Thirties Society and *The Spectator* were entitled to feel modestly pleased at the outcome of the good fight they had fought.

The advent of a full-colour cover for *The Spectator* encouraged Moore to publish each week a 2,500-word 'cover story', which would on occasion be snapped up by the national newspapers. Fleet Street journalists had always enjoyed reading *The Spectator*, but now a more positive relationship came into being. *The Spectator* became a source of information and ideas to be followed up by the daily papers, and by the same token young writers cutting their teeth on the magazine were more liable than in the past to be lured away by the prospect of much higher earnings on a national newspaper. (The route from *Spectator* to *Telegraph* became a well-trodden one after the publications came under the same ownership in 1988. Before then, Max Hastings, newly appointed editor of the *Daily Telegraph*, had tried and failed to pinch Garton Ash, Mount and Gimson.) The first of the new-look cover stories, in March 1986, was a seminal, socio-economic article by Nicholas Coleridge on the life-styles of the new young rich of the City, which was set upon by Fleet Street. So, two years later, was Lawson's revelation that Britain was the largest importer of toxic waste.

The Spectator*'s
Levantine correspondent,
Charles Glass, was held
prisoner in Beirut for two
months in 1987.*

Moore also introduced a new section in the middle of the magazine, con-sisting of a long article which, while not exactly timeless, was not necessar-ily pegged to the news of the week. Such pieces of writing included memoirs, interviews, serialisations and travel articles. Kingsley Amis and John Mortimer were among the contributors; so was W.F. (Bill) Deedes, who drew on his memory and long years in journalism (since 1930) to write anniversary pieces along the lines of 'My Part in the Abdication Crisis', 'My Munich' and 'My Phoney War'. One week Alexandra Artley (Mrs Gavin Stamp) addressed the subject of 'green' books; environmentalism was becoming the new creed in the last years of the 1980s. Another week, Charles Glass, *The Spectator*'s correspondent in the Levant, wrote of how he had survived for two months while held prisoner by Hezbollah in Beirut. Glass, who was half-Lebanese and half-American, and worked for the American Broadcasting Company, was kidnapped in the summer of 1987. He was sustained by the strength of his Catholic faith; his English wife, Fiona, wrote a letter to the Pope (drafted by Moore) and was granted an audience in the Vatican. With great ingenuity Glass was finally able to break free of his ankle and wrist chains; by tying some of the links together with threads from his blindfold, he convinced his guards that the chains were tighter than they were and escaped from the room where he was shackled. Having entrusted himself to the care of the Syrian army (his wife had also written to President Assad), Glass returned to London via Damascus. The editor welcomed him back with an article headed 'Jail-breaking Glass', in which he recalled a previous occasion when he (Glass) had caused his wife anxiety by going missing for 12 hours. That time he had been spending a night on the tiles with Taki and Shiva Naipaul.

Excitement of a different kind was brewing in 1987 in Australia, in the boardroom of *The Spectator*'s owners, John Fairfax Ltd. Its chairman, James Fairfax, who took a benign but not very close interest in *The Spectator*, had a half-brother, Warwick, aged 26, who resolved, on the death of their father, to buy out the interests of the rest of the family. To do this he was obliged to sell off parts of the group. For a moment there was a real fear that *The Spectator* might, after all, fall into the hands of the dreaded predator, Packer, who bought Fairfax's magazine division plus two Canberra newspapers. But its one British magazine remained with the shrunken Fairfax when Warwick acquired control in October 1987. Moore and Knox had little confidence in their new proprietor, and even less after the stock market crash that same month. Warwick's Polish-born mother paid a visit to Doughty Street, and greeted Moore by saying, as if to reassure him: 'People think I married my husband for his money, but I am in fact a wealthy woman in my own right.' At the Tory party conference, also in October, Moore met Andrew Knight, chief executive of the Telegraph group, and asked him if Conrad Black would like to buy *The Spectator*.

The idea had not previously occurred to Black, but he was certainly interested in politics and political history as well as in business, and was prepared to pay £2.5 million for this political weekly. When Knox heard that Warwick Fairfax was in London, he went round to the Fairfax offices in Chancery Lane to tell him he could solve at least a minor part of his financial problems by accepting the offer without delay. The transfer took place in April 1988; the Fairfax group went into receivership at the end of 1990.

After six anxious months, the outcome for *The Spectator* was satisfactory. However, for the originally constituted company of John Fairfax Ltd, which had bought the magazine in 1985, it was a great disappointment. The Australians looked upon *The Spectator*, as one director put it, as their 'toe in the water', which would lead to further investment in British publishing. They approached Lord Hartwell (the then owner of both *Telegraph*s) but were rebuffed. When, however, his financial difficulties were becoming acute, in late 1985, he asked Fairfax for, in effect, a loan to the company via the Berry family, which would in time be exchanged for shares. By then 14 per cent of the Telegraph company was owned by Conrad Black, and his agreement with Hartwell, which gave Black first option on any further issue of shares, was such that Fairfax reluctantly decided it was legally precluded from investing in the Telegraph.

If the toe in the water of British journalism never became a foot, *The Spectator* nevertheless had reason to be grateful for that toe. Cluff had rightly concluded that if *The Spectator* was to grow and prosper, it must have the backing of a publishing group rather than a philanthropic individual. This had not happened to *The Spectator* before; Sir Evelyn Wrench, having issued the injunction to future proprietors that they should eliminate 'as far as reasonably possible questions of personal or commercial profit', may have stirred in his grave, but by 1985 *The Spectator* was almost ready for profit. Fairfax gave the magazine a serious business base: during its three years annual advertising revenue increased fourfold and circulation by 80 per cent; and *The Spectator*'s independence was not in any way compromised. The only risk of that came at the beginning of 1988 when negotiations were proceeding to sell *The Spectator* to Black. Rupert Murdoch thought of bidding for the magazine against the Telegraph group, and contacted Moore to inform him. With admirable candour Moore told Murdoch, in a letter, that his bid would not be welcome. 'Most of our contributors and many of our readers would be horrified at the idea of your buying *The Spectator*. They believe you are autocratic and that you have a bad effect on journalism of quality — they cite the *Times* as the chief example.' Murdoch went quietly.

Moore had also mentioned to Murdoch the potential problem of *The Spectator* retaining the freedom to attack the *Times* or the *Sun*, or indeed Murdoch himself, in a Murdoch-owned magazine. As if to demonstrate his continuing independence of any employer, Moore took it rather rashly upon himself, not long before he left *The Spectator*, to be critical in print, not so much of the *Telegraph* newspapers as of the proprietor himself.

While Black was in the process of acquiring control of the Telegraph in 1986, Moore had published a fairly unfriendly profile of him, which brought a long reply from Black, asserting that 'an absolute majority of the sentences in the piece were false' and, of one allegation, that 'every word, and every letter of every word of that statement are false'. He regretted that *The Spectator* should 'demean itself by recourse to scurrilous mudslinging'. Earlier that year Black had written to complain about an article by Hitchens which claimed that, following an operation for cancer, President Reagan was so incontinent that he would cause acute embarrassment in his forthcoming meeting with Mikhail Gorbachev. This was, Black wrote, 'nasty, macabre, vulgar and insolent claptrap'. (Hitchens did later admit that his remark was insensitive.)

Shortly before he left *The Spectator* Moore appeared to be in uncharacteristically reckless mood, or else still showing a not-so-overgrown schoolboy's contempt for authority. It was careless of him to allow the cartoonist Garland, in his book, *Not Many Dead*, to recall a dinner at Downing Street when Moore had cited a 'boring and pointless' monologue by Black on the subject of military uniforms. (Inevitably, Peregrine Worsthorne quoted this passage in his review of the book for *The Spectator*, which appeared in Moore's last week as editor.) Nor was it wise of him to tell the *Toronto Star* that Black had bought *The Spectator* in order to ingratiate himself with London society. Moore then chose to refer, in his Diary in January 1990, to his proprietor's two previously published letters, and to comment on his epistolary style. He compared it with 'some huge medieval siege engine', adding that it was full of sound and fury, but did not signify all that much. Moore also questioned whether it was right for the *Sunday Telegraph* to publish a hostile profile of Knight just after he had defected to the *Times* and had a public row with Black. Back came a letter from Black the following week, wondering why his editor felt the need to 'react to every subject involving the *Daily Telegraph* like a bantam rooster who feels his independence is threatened? He would do better to congratulate himself on having sought and found for *The Spectator* a proprietor who responds so equably to the minor irritations, such as this one, that *The Spectator* inflicts upon that person who ultimately, and more or less uncomplainingly, pays *The Spectator*'s losses and endures Mr Moore's condescensions.' Moore had made his point, and Black had given evidence of a sharper epistolary style; but there would be no more criticisms of the *Telegraph* group in *The Spectator*'s pages. It was not, however, to be the last letter Black would send to *The Spectator* for publication.

He had already written to say he had been 'disappointed by the lack of integrity and serious analysis in British... reporting of American affairs'. It was one of the lesser reasons he had bought the *Telegraph*, 'one of the few British publications whose reports on the United States are not habitually snobbish, envious and simplistic'. But in 1991 (when Dominic Lawson was editor) Black's disappointment at the negative attitude to President Bush of the *Daily Telegraph*'s, and *The Spectator*'s, Washington correspondent, Stephen Robinson, was such that he wrote to the magazine again. He recalled the 'demented ravings' of 'the unspeakable poseur, Hitchens' and regretted Robinson's 'unbalanced attack' on Bush and his enthusiasm for every Democrat who might stand against him in the 1992 presidential election. Having cautioned Lawson 'against reversion to the old *Spectator* practice of mere anti-Americanism' (he was referring to Moore's early years), Black then took him to task for publishing an 'error-riddled' cover story by Edward Whitley on the Reichmann brothers, the Canadian owners of Canary Wharf, and an unfriendly profile of Lord Carrington. 'Lord Carrington and Paul Reichmann would have the right to expect to be treated fairly by *The Spectator* even if they were not directors of the companies that ultimately owned it and friends of the proprietor. It is not normally the duty of the proprietor to distinguish between intelligent controversy and bile.'

This, surely, was sound and fury signifying something — a warning shot, at least, across the editor's bows. Just over a year later, however, following the election of Bill Clinton to the White House, Black wrote once more to the magazine. His letter contained apologies both to Robinson, who 'was not mistaken in taking the Democratic quest for the Presidency seriously', and to Whitley, who 'was essentially correct in his financial prognosis for Canary Wharf'. It was scarcely surprising that Lawson should head the letter, 'It takes a big man'.

The new board of directors, following the Telegraph takeover in 1988, included a couple of businessmen (Patrick Sheehy, Owen Green), a publisher (André Deutsch), Ludovic Kennedy and Ferdinand Mount. Norman Tebbit joined later, which prompted Kennedy's resignation. Sales were nudging 40,000 and the loss for 1988 of £450,000 (which included a lot of promotional expenditure) was halved the following year. The freehold of 56 Doughty Street was purchased for just over £500,000. Moore took advantage of the *Telegraph* connection by writing a 'View from Doughty Street' in the *Daily Telegraph* every Friday, which drew attention to some of the things in that week's issue.

1989 was to prove an important campaigning year for *The Spectator*. It had been critical of the joint agreement between Britain and China for the handover of Hong Kong when it was signed in 1984. Fearing for the future of Hong Kong Chinese under control from Peking, it had often cited the example of China's rape of Tibet. When the People's Liberation Army started massacring its people in Peking's Tiananmen Square in 1989, Moore reacted in the strongest terms. The cover of the 10 June issue carried an illustration of Britannia and the British lion bowing low to the East, with a single cover line: 'Our Betrayal of Hong Kong'. In a two-page leader he demanded that the government give right of abode in Britain to all 3.25 million UK passport holders in Hong Kong and at once establish fully representative democratic institutions in the colony. Failure to do this would mean that 'for the first time in our history, we have forced Britons to be slaves'; Thatcher 'will have presided over something worse than the betrayal of Czechoslovakia in 1938... over the most discreditable British policy of the 20th century'. It was a fine piece of idealistic haranguing; when, six months later, the government proposed allowing up to 225,000 Hong Kong citizens to come to Britain, one of the most vociferous opponents of such a 'vast wave of immigrants' was Tebbit, the newly appointed director of *The Spectator*.

The first intimation of Thatcher's mortality came with the resignation of a former *Spectator* editor, Nigel Lawson, from the Treasury. Fewer shockwaves had been caused the previous month at the party conference when Conservative associations were sanctioned for Northern Ireland; but it was something for which Moore had campaigned, and he once considered standing himself as a Tory for an Ulster constituency. (His father had stood as a Liberal candidate, against the Revd Ian Paisley, in 1970.)

The great event of the year was unquestionably the collapse of Communism. Garton Ash had written his first article for *The Spectator* on Albania in 1978. He had been in at the birth of Solidarity in 1980, and was taken on to the staff in 1981. He lived in Berlin (West and East), and in 1984 Moore made him the first foreign editor of *The Spectator*. (The job was originally offered to Marnham, who accepted and then changed his mind when he was offered a staff job in Paris by the *Independent*.) During his time in East Germany Garton Ash was, of course, closely observed by the state security service, Stasi. When, in 1992, he was shown his Stasi file (under the codename of Romeo), he found that *The Spectator* was referred to as Spekta, recalling the name of a sinister organisation in one of the James Bond stories.

In 1988 Garton Ash announced in *The Spectator* a scheme inviting readers to give half-price subscriptions to the magazine to individuals and institutions in Poland. Many of the articles were reprinted in underground periodicals. The idea was a great success: 184 subscriptions were sent in the first year and, in 1989-90, the number contributed by readers was 520. (The scheme was later extended to the rest of eastern Europe.)

Garton Ash reported from all over eastern Europe in 1989 as the end of Communism drew near. Many citizens of those countries thought he did much more than that. A Czech author, Karel Kyncl, would later write in the *Independent*: 'It is with minimal exaggeration that I state that, in the future, there will probably be streets in Warsaw, Prague and Budapest bearing the name of Timothy Garton Ash.' He was certainly one of the only Western journalists to be in Czechoslovakia in November when the whole fabric of Communism, secure for 20 years since the Prague Spring of 1968, collapsed in ten days.

TEN DAYS THAT STIRRED THE WORLD

It has been a year of peaceful revolutions in Central Europe, but this is the fastest, merriest of them all. What in Poland took years of hard struggle, in Hungary months, in East Germany weeks, has happened here in days.

Only the very beginning was neither fast nor merry. On Friday 17 November, some 50,000 people, mainly students, turned out for an officially permitted demonstration to mark the 50th anniversary of the murder of a Czech student by the Nazis. It was a long, joyful march, with the chants and slogans directed increasingly against the present rulers in Prague Castle, and it wound its way to the traditional forum for national manifestations: Wenceslas Square. Here, however, most of the demonstrators were surrounded and cut off by white-helmeted riot police and, for the first time, by red-bereted anti-terrorist squads. The crowd placed candles before them and tried to give them flowers. People knelt on the ground and raised their arms, chanting, 'We have bare hands.' But the police, and especially the red berets, beat them nonetheless: truncheoning men, women and children.

This was the spark that set Czechoslovakia alight. In the night from Friday to Saturday — with reports of one student dead, and many certainly in hospital — the students determined to go on strike. Then they decided to call for a nationwide general strike in a week's time. The universities were joined by the theatres, which had already been active in the defence of the playwright, opposition leader and now national hero, Vaclav Havel. On Sunday evening Havel himself called a meeting of all the main opposition groups, and members of the formerly puppet Socialist and People's Parties, in a theatre. They joined together in what they called a Civic Forum, demanding the resignation of the Party leaders directly responsible for the Warsaw Pact invasion in 1968, a special commission to investigate the 'massacre' of 17 November, the punishment of all those responsible for it, and the release of all prisoners of conscience.

Students, actors and intellectuals were thus the vanguard of this revolution. But, as in East Germany, the crucial difference was made by ordinary people coming out on to the streets: by People Power. For on Monday afternoon Wenceslas Square was filled by a huge crowd — 200,000 they say — supporting the students who spoke from beneath the equestrian statue of St Wenceslas, while behind it a banner on the huge and imposing national theatre declared 'the national theatre with the nation'. The moment had come. The most thoroughly Western of East Central European countries was demanding that its proper history should start again, as those of its neighbours, Hungary, Poland, Germany, already had. These children had shown them the way. As a friend explained to me, for 20 years people had kept quiet and knuckled under 'for the children's sake'. And now the police were beating even the children. 'Parents come with us,' said a banner on the Wenceslas statue, 'we are your children.' And so they did.

As in East Germany, when the Party leaders had woken up to what was happening, it was already too late. In Central Europe today, with Gorbachev in the Kremlin, the kind of violence needed to repress such masses of people appears simply not to be an available option. (But the prime minister, Adamec, subsequently emphasised that martial law would not be imposed, thus implying that the option had been seriously considered.) Once people saw the door to self-expression was open, they rushed through it with shouts of glee.

By midweek, the centre of Prague was plastered with improvised posters declaring 'Truth will prevail!' or 'Let the government resign!' or 'We support the general strike.' There were xeroxed photos of the prewar president, Thomas Garrigue Masaryk, and copies of the Civic Forum declaration (often computer-printed). Groups gathered in front of shop windows where televisions played over and over again a videotape of the 17 November events. Ever larger crowds gathered for the afternoon demonstrations in Wenceslas Square, waving their red, white and blue flags and chanting away as if this was the most usual thing in the world. Cars hooted in support as they drove across the top of the square, and small children gave V-for-Victory signs. Meanwhile, Adamec had his first meeting with representatives of the Civic Forum. The once puppet Socialist Party opened its newspaper, *Svobodné Slovo* (*The Free Word*), to fair reports of the protest movement, and its balcony, perfectly located halfway down Wenceslas Square, to the speakers organised by the Forum. Even the official radio and television began to report opposition demands.

On Friday came Dubcek. He looked as if he had stepped straight out of a black and white photograph from 1968. The same grey coat and paisley scarf, the same tentative smile, the same functionary's hat: all contributed to the illusion that we had just left a 20-year timewarp, with the clock that stopped in 1969 starting again in 1989. As we scuttled along the covered shopping arcades to reach the balcony, people simply gaped. It was as if the ghost of Winston Churchill were to be seen striding down the Burlington Arcade. But then he stepped out into the frosty evening air, illuminated by television spotlights, the crowd gave such a roar as I have never heard. 'DUBCEK! DUBCEK!' Many people mourn his ambiguous role after the Soviet invasion, and his failure to use the magic of his name to support the democratic opposition.

He has not changed with the times. His speeches still contain those wooden, prefabricated newspeak phrases. He still believes in socialism — that is, reformed communism — with a human face. The true leader of this movement is not Dubcek but Havel. But for the moment all that matters is that the legendary hero is really standing here, addressing a huge crowd on Wenceslas Square, while the emergency session of the Central Committee has, we are told, been removed to a distant suburb. They have fled. 'Dubcek to the castle!' cries the crowd: that is, Dubcek for President.

Later in the evening, Dubcek and Havel again share the stage. Literally so, for the Civic Forum has its headquarters in a theatre, called, appropriately enough, the Magic Lantern, and the press conference is held on a stage, complete with set. Dubcek and Havel are just telling us their different ideas about socialism when the conference is interrupted by the news that the whole Politburo and Central Committee secretariat have resigned. The theatre erupts in applause. Havel embraces Dubcek, and makes the V-for-Victory sign. Someone brings them champagne. Havel raises his glass and toasts 'A free Czechoslovakia!' For 20 years his work has been banned from Czechoslovak stages. But he has been saving it up. And this production will certainly go into the history books. Cry your eyes out, Bertolt Brecht.

... On Sunday morning, Adamec had a fully official meeting with a Civic Forum delegation led by Vaclav Havel. In the afternoon, there is yet another huge demonstration from the stadium, to which Adamec agrees to speak. 'Adamec, Adamec', chants the crowd, but when he calls for discipline, no more strikes, and economic rather than political change, the reception is as cold as the weather itself. All the greater is the enthusiasm for Havel and his concise description of the Civic Forum as a bridge from totalitarianism to democracy. 'Free elections' is again the cry.

The crowd has developed an extraordinary capacity to talk to the speakers, in rhythmic chant. 'Make way for the ambulance!' they chant, when one is needed, or 'Turn up the volume!' When a long list of political prisoners is read out they chant 'Stepan to prison!' (Miroslav Stepan is the much disliked Prague Party secretary, also held partly responsible for the 17 November action.) 'Perhaps we should give him a spade', says a voice from the platform, 'He'd steal it!' comes the almost immediate response from the crowd, half a million speaking as one. And then 'Here it comes!' And sure enough, there is a spade held aloft at the front of the crowd. 'Stepan, Stepan', they cry, as in a funeral chant, and then they take out their keys and ring them like Chinese bells.

... By the start of the general strike, at noon on Monday, it is already clear that it will be a success. The media, and above all the television, had given it extensive and mainly positive coverage. Many communists seem to have decided 'If you can't beat them, join them' — at least for the duration of the strike. Television reports of large, peaceful strike meetings all over the country had subtitles explaining that these reports were the television team's contribution to the strike.

... And now there is yet another demonstration on Wenceslas Square. Here an emerging star of the Civic Forum, Dr Vaclav Klaus, reads the text of the latest declaration, announcing the formation of a co-ordinating centre for Forum groups throughout the country. If Adamec is not ready to meet the Forum's demands, they will demand the government's resignation. 'Resignation!' chants the crowd. All this concerns only the transitional phase to the indispensable free elections.

... Just ten days ago, the police were truncheoning children on this very square. Czechoslovakia still seemed lost under the Brezhnevite ice of the last 20 years. Now the opposition, having organised a nationwide general strike, has just presented an alternative candidate for prime minister, and a programme for the end of communism in Czechoslovakia. And the people in the square applaud as if they would never have thought of anything else. 'That's it', they chant, 'That's it!'

... The first and, so to speak, heroic phase of the revolution is thus over. Symbolically, the Civic Forum now moves from its improvised quarters in the Magic Lantern to more normal offices provided by the City Council. These were perhaps not 'ten days that shook the world', but they were certainly ten days that delighted the world, changed the political face of Europe (for all of East Central Europe is now sailing towards democracy), and, above all, offered, as one of the earliest demonstration banners said, 'a chance for 15 million' Czechs and Slovaks. 'The heart of Europe cries for freedom', declared another home-made poster. The second phase that now opens bids fair to be one of tortuous, complex negotiation, with not a few divisions, ambiguities and compromises. The revolution inside the Communist Party itself has only just begun. This is no time or place for prediction. By the time you read this, four or five more extraordinary, unprecedented and unpredictable events will probably have occurred. The clocks have started again in Czechoslovakia, and they are racing to make up lost time.

2 December 1989

Before leaving *The Spectator* in 1990, Garton Ash won the David Watt memorial prize for his 'outstanding contributions towards the clarification of international and political issues'. He is now a senior research fellow at St Antony's College, Oxford.

By the beginning of 1990 both Moore and Knox had decided to leave. Knox went off to run an art investment company and, as Moore wrote in the Diary, in a generous tribute to his achievements for *The Spectator*, 'to return to authorship'. He had written a history of the Trinity Foot Beagles, and was about to embark on a biography of Robert Byron. Moore announced his own departure a week later, in mid-February, though not the reasons for it, which were also partly to do with authorship (he wanted to spend a few months writing a novel, as yet unpublished) and with becoming deputy editor of the *Daily Telegraph*. In his last week as editor, which was the week after the poll tax riots, he argued ingeniously in the leading article that the responsibility for them was not Thatcher's but the Labour party's, for having promoted 'the very dissatisfaction and resentment of which the recent riots were so terrible a manifestation'. Moore then took the opportunity to write a valedictory Diary, in which he said that his successor had asked him to write a column, beginning in the autumn. The new editor, with effect from April, was Dominic Lawson.

10

ANOTHER LAWSON EXPERIENCE

By 1990 *The Spectator* was once again a High Tory journal. Guided by the thinking of his mentor T.E. Utley, Charles Moore's *Spectator* also stood squarely behind the unity of the kingdom (especially including Northern Ireland) and the Book of Common Prayer. It was a worthy magazine, which only occasionally took itself too seriously. Whereas in those High Tory days of George Gale's editorship the tone of the magazine was often excessively strident or pompous, or both, 20 years on it was quite changed. The tolerance and worldliness of Alexander Chancellor's *Spectator* had been maintained; and for the future its lightness of touch would not be forfeited. Someone once wrote that *The Spectator* under Chancellor had been more of a cocktail party than a political party. If Moore gave the party a rather more serious political theme it was still a congenial gathering. Dominic Lawson preferred to host a surprise party which on occasion threatened to get out of hand.

Aged 33 when he became editor, Lawson was two months younger than Moore. They had been briefly at Eton together (but did not meet) before Lawson left to go to Westminster. Lawson, himself very good at chess, first came journalistically to Moore's attention with an article he had written while at Oxford on the lunacy of the best chess players, for a short-lived magazine called *Definite Article* which circulated in Oxford and Cambridge. He then worked at the *Financial Times*, as energy correspondent and Lex, until Moore appointed him his deputy in 1987, hoping that he would succeed him. Lawson had previously had a couple of walk-on parts in *The Spectator*. His editor father noted in the Diary in 1967 that it was from his schoolboy son that he had first learnt of the name of the head of MI6 (Sir

Dick White, father of Dominic's fellow pupil, Stephen — not a bad little scoop for a nine-year-old). When Nigel Lawson's ex-wife, Vanessa Ayer, died in 1985, Peregrine Worsthorne recalled her staying with Gale and his wife in Essex, accompanied by her 'four small children all perfectly dressed in old-fashioned clothes, the whole family looking as if they had stepped straight out of a Visconti film set'. This formerly pre-pubescent Viscontiesque figure wasted no time in making his mark when he took over the editorial chair at *The Spectator*. Lawson was determined that, under him, the magazine should cause a stir, and also become profitable. He was good at spotting and developing the potential of untypical *Spectator* contributors: Anne Applebaum, an American married to a Pole, Alasdair Palmer, an investigative television journalist, Leo McKinstry, a former Labour councillor and Martin Vander Weyer, a former investment banker. He was brisk, not to say brusque, in the way he went about the business of editing. A contributor to the Lawson *père Spectator* in the 1960s, who also wrote regularly for Lawson *fils* three decades later, said that both editors were demanding, combative — and rewarding to work for. After five years no one would say, as they did of Chancellor and Moore, that Dominic Lawson was a much-loved editor. But he was a very good one. Within three months of his arrival he was responsible for ending the career of a cabinet minister.

In interviews with politicians (Michael Heseltine and Chris Patten), Lawson had already evinced a talent for getting under their skin, if not unsettling them. At a lunch following the memorial service for Jock Bruce-Gardyne — *The Spectator* had published a tribute by Nigel Lawson and had republished Bruce-Gardyne's poignant thoughts on learning that he had a brain tumour – Dominic Lawson arranged an interview with the Environment Secretary, Nicholas Ridley. He would go to Ridley's house in Gloucestershire on a Sunday; they would have lunch and talk. Ridley had read from Viscount Grey of Fallodon's 'Fly Fishing' at the memorial service; little did he know that he was about to get himself well and truly hooked.

It was not until the tape recording of the interview with Ridley had been transcribed that Lawson began to realise that he was in possession of some pretty explosive material. He was to be accused later in some quarters of having taken unfair advantage of what had essentially been a private conversation over lunch. On the contrary: Ridley's comments, as published,

'Speaking for England' were the words beneath this cover drawing of 14 July 1990, but when Nicholas Ridley resigned two days later he was obliged to say that he was speaking only for himself.

were all taken from the tape recording which he knew was being made. At several points during their conversation he asked that the tape be switched off, because he was about to say something — for instance on the future sovereignty of the Falklands — which was at odds with government policy. But he was happy enough to be quoted on the subject of the future of Europe when he was, after all, only repeating the views of his prime minister. The trouble was that his Germanophobia (which, of course, Margaret Thatcher shared) caused him to get a bit carried away. The move towards monetary union, he said, was 'a German racket designed to take over the whole of Europe'. 'Being bossed by a German [the president of the Bundesbank] would cause absolute mayhem in this country, and rightly, I think.' Ridley was not in principle against giving up sovereignty, 'but not to this lot. You might just as well give it up to Adolf Hitler, frankly.' That was what did for Ridley: the drawing of comparisons between Herr Kohl and Herr Hitler. It inspired Nicholas Garland to do a devastating drawing for the front cover of the magazine. Lawson's idea had been an illustration of Ridley the country sportsman, raising his shotgun to fire at the German eagle overhead. But Garland's drawing was of a poster of Kohl on a street wall, on which a Hitler moustache and lick of black hair had been crudely daubed. Running away from the scene, paint pot and brush in his hands, was the figure of Ridley. (Two years later, and only a few weeks before Britain was forced out of the Exchange Rate Mechanism, Garland illustrated John Major's special relationship with Kohl by doing a cover drawing of him at his desk, with a huge portrait photograph of Kohl occupying half the desk and rising above him. The drawing inside showed the German chancellor with a tiny picture of Major in the far corner of his desk.)

Lawson had alerted Ridley's department to the imminent publication of something which might embarrass him (and, on request, he sent along a transcript of the interview after the article was published). He had also left the galley proofs in a briefcase at the house of Charles Wilson, a former editor of the *Times*, shortly before that week's issue went to press. Early on the morning of publication, the then editor of the *Times*, Simon Jenkins (later to become a *Spectator* columnist), rang Lawson and agreed to pay £5,000 for the right to reprint the article. When *The Spectator*'s parent company learnt, later in the day, that this political bombshell (which it had rapidly become) had been sold to the *Daily Telegraph*'s principal rival, it is scarcely an exaggeration say that all hell broke loose. Dan Colson, deputy-chairman and chief executive of the Telegraph group, rang Lawson to inform him that the *Telegraph* had first claim on all *Spectator* articles. Lawson replied that the *Telegraph* had offered to pay only £1,000 and that anyway he would prefer his article to be seen by readers of the *Times*. The upshot was that the *Telegraph* paid *The Spectator* £5,000 and the *Times* did not republish the article. (Lawson, who had joined *The Spectator* before Conrad Black bought it, thereafter became an employee of the Telegraph group.) Colson keeps in his office framed copies of two memoranda from the legal manager of the *Times*, both dated Thursday 12 July 1990. The first, timed at 3.50 p.m., confirms that the *Times* has exclusive rights to the Ridley article. The second, reversing his previous statement, is timed at 5 p.m. The *Sun*, without permission and in breach of copyright, did reproduce most of the interview; when Lawson complained, the editor of the *Sun*, Kelvin MacKenzie, sent a cheque for £2,000. (Additionally, Lawson very nearly made a tax-free £25,000 for himself, missing by one vote the award for European Journalist of the Year. He had the consolation, however, of being made Editor of the Year.)

Thatcher was miserable at the prospect of losing her Secretary of State for Trade and Industry, who was also a friend, but he had to go, and his resignation letter, talking of 'difficulties which my failure to use more measured words have caused', was published two days after *The Spectator*'s article. Such an outcome was neither intended nor expected by Lawson, although one may debate whether it should have been anticipated and, if so, whether some of Ridley's less measured words should have been published.

The prime minister rebuked Black, at a Downing Street dinner shortly afterwards, for having permitted *The Spectator* to do such a terrible thing; but he stood by his man. There were hard feelings expressed, of course, by some ministers, and especially by Ridley's wife. But after a couple of years had elapsed, during which Lawson *père* wrote a very critical review in *The Spectator* of Ridley's political memoirs, Ridley appeared in the magazine as a contributor, of two articles and a friendly review of a Spectator Annual. He expressed himself much moved by an army chaplain's account of a deserter awaiting execution during the first world war.

The issue of 14 July 1990, which contained the Ridley article, was technically sold out; an additional print run of 5,000 copies was arranged. As a result of this and other controversial interviews published that summer, both wholesale orders and subscriptions were soon showing healthy increases. No one was more delighted than *The Spectator*'s new publisher/managing director, Luis Dominguez.

Dominguez had an Argentinian family background and an English mother. He had spent much of his life in America, including 20 years with the *New Yorker* magazine. He was at *Harper's & Queen* when its former editor, Nicholas Coleridge, knowing that James Knox was leaving *The Spectator*, recommended Dominguez to succeed him. Knox and Dominguez met for lunch at Buck's Club; shortly afterwards Dominguez arranged to see Colson, who was intrigued to note his American accent and smooth appearance. He was immediately impressed when Dominguez handed him two apparently identical copies of *The Spectator*, the only difference being that one copy was much thicker than the other. Dominguez had pasted a number of luxury goods advertisements from the *New Yorker* into *The Spectator*; the potential was there for Colson to see. Dominguez got the job a month before Moore left Doughty Street. With his experience at the weekly *New Yorker*, he was ideally suited to take *The Spectator* commercially forward — or 'onward and upward' as he was so fond of saying. In a sense Moore had already begun, perhaps unconsciously, to 'New Yorkerise' *The Spectator*, using many more cartoons, a larger proportion of women writers, and introducing retail columns, such as wine and food. Dominguez saw no reason why *The Spectator* should not boldly go after advertising where it had never gone before, into what is known as the men's market. *GQ* magazine was being launched at this time, *Esquire* was being heavily promoted, and

Dominguez decided to pursue shops (Harvey Nichols, Aquascutum) and fashion designers and purveyors of 'fragrances' (Ralph Lauren, Versace, St Laurent, Givenchy) catering for men. It was strange territory for *The Spectator* to be entering; some thought it so alien that it should, in effect, be forbidden territory. But after a few months of presentations to advertisers, and once the paper quality had been improved to permit better reproduction of colour advertisements, the strategy began to work.

As an old *New Yorker* man Dominguez realised, of course, that there could be no collusion between editorial and advertising. So he had to take it on the chin when Versace withdrew its advertising in 1992 after Moore had written a highly critical article describing Versace's fashions as mixing 'the tones of a prostitute and an international arms dealer — lewd, aggressive, rootless, mercenary'. But there was a fellow feeling between him and Lawson which he could never have enjoyed with Moore. Dominguez had met Rosamond Monckton when she was doing public relations for the jewellers, Asprey. By the time she married Lawson (his second marriage) at the end of 1991, she was managing director of Tiffany's. Dominguez and Lawson may not have had much else in common, but they did have a shared interest in the luxury goods market.

They also had a mutual professional respect and generally did not intrude on each other's domains. Dominguez's advertising drive was so successful (revenue tripled over the next five years) that there were mumblings that *The Spectator* was getting too much of the 'wrong sort' of advertising. But Lawson was not concerned: he thought the advertisements made for a more handsome-looking magazine, he was ridding *The Spectator* of its Fogeyish image, and the circulation figures were continuing to rise. (Under Moore they had doubled, and during the years 1990–95 they would increase by a further 40 per cent to over 54,000. The ratio of editorial to advertising revenue, approximately 75:25 in 1990, had not materially changed by 1995.) Dominguez was resourceful, too, in promoting *The Spectator*: on radio (LBC and Classic FM), on posters in the London underground, showing mug-shots of not necessarily the best-looking contributors, through cartoon exhibitions at Dunhills and the sponsorship, with Allied Dunbar, of an annual political lecture (which, in recent years, has been given by Tony Blair, John Major and Gordon Brown). Syndication arrangements were made with newspapers in Hong Kong, South Africa, Canada and India.

Copies were carried on some British Airways flights, including Concorde, and a block of subscriptions was sold to Marlborough College, where a *Spectator* Society was founded. For the first time *The Spectator* became fashionable not just among the chattering classes but among business people and students both in London and in the country.

Lawson was making more waves during the summer of 1990. Two weeks before the Ridley article, he published what purported to be a conversation between the Queen Mother and A.N. Wilson. Since it took place at a private dinner party, given by Woodrow Wyatt, Wilson prepared himself for the resulting furore by acknowledging that 'it is probably the grossest impropriety to embarrass her, or her host, by repeating our conversation on that occasion'. What was published was otherwise fairly unexceptionable: while revealed as a literary lowbrow, the Queen Mother was described by Wilson as the only member of the royal family with any charm. But it was not expected that Lord Wyatt would remain silent. Wilson, he wrote in a letter to the editor, was 'boastfully shameless in being a scoundrel. But I hope you have enough decency to be ashamed of your participation in, and encouragement to, [his] squalid theft of an unauthorised "interview".' Nicholas Soames spluttered that Wilson had 'broken every convention of civilised society' and committed 'an absolutely fundamental breach of trust', while Lawson had 'condoned this deceit by printing such gossip and in so doing have greatly diminished the high reputation of your newspaper'. No one else bothered to write, though there were numerous expressions of outrage in the national newspapers, prompting another article from Wilson, asking, 'Why all the fuss?' It was , of course, a breach of convention to repeat the private remarks of a member of the royal family, but it was not inconsistent with the anarchist tradition of *The Spectator*. (And it was as nothing compared with the indiscretions committed by Wyatt in his memoirs, published after his death in 1998.) One correspondent asked the editor in July whether, having done his best to demolish the royal family and the government in the past few weeks, he would now turn his attention to the papacy. He left the Roman Catholic Church alone, but instead went after the judiciary, in the venerable shape of Lord Denning.

The former Master of the Rolls was in his 92nd year when Wilson interviewed him. He was given to reminiscing about England, in his endearing Hampshire drawl, and to damning all things, and people, European, includ-

Lord Denning's views on dealing with IRA suspects led to apologies from him and from The Spectator.

ing Sir Leon Brittan, whom he had known at the Bar and categorised as 'a German Jew'. Denning also appeared not to think much of the Irish, telling Wilson it would have been better for everyone if the Birmingham Six and Guildford Four had been hanged, and that, despite the findings of an inquiry that they had been wrongfully convicted, the Four were in fact guilty. *The Spectator*'s cover that week, drawn by the brilliant Peter Brookes, showed the elderly Denning walking in his garden with a gallows as a walking stick, above the cruelly witty headline, 'Hanging on'.

It was no way to treat a grand old man in the late evening of his life. The following week Lord Denning's name appeared alongside those of *The Spectator*, Lawson and Wilson, all apologising to the Guildford Four 'for making imputations against them and against their innocence'. Four months later Wilson wrote to *The Spectator* to apologise to Lord and Lady Denning for the distress which they had suffered as a result of the article. He referred to a request from Denning, before publication, to see the pages of the transcript in which he made remarks about the Guildford and Birmingham cases, and apologised for having sent Denning only three out of the four relevant pages. 'By an oversight I omitted to include one page' (the most embarrassing one). It was a shabby episode which left the reader in little doubt that both Wilson and *The Spectator* had behaved rather badly.

Lawson's first year continued on its exciting course, now influenced by great events. Thatcher chose to step down as prime minister on a Thursday morning, which is when *The Spectator* goes on sale in London. The cover showed her and Heseltine in a boxing ring, ready for the second round, and the leading article continued to give her the magazine's wholehearted back-ing in the ballot which was to take place the following Tuesday. Michael Heath's drawing for the Portrait of the Week got closest to anticipating what happened, showing the prime minister seated alone at a table, framed by a spotlight and staring at the pistol in front of her. By the following week's issue Major was in Downing Street. The Gulf war worked to *The Spectator*'s advantage, principally because it had signed up the BBC's man in Baghdad, John Simpson, whose copy would arrive on a cassette tape, courtesy of the BBC. One week Simpson reported that a cruise missile had shot down the street outside his hotel; this was memorably illustrated on the cover by Garland. Nicholas von Hoffman and Murray Sayle returned to the colours during the conflict, and John Keegan, defence editor of the *Daily Telegraph*, wrote a trenchant piece berating the BBC 'grandees' — in par-ticular, Jeremy Paxman and the Dimbleby brothers — for having caused needless anxiety to servicemen's families by refusing to acknowledge the obvious fact that the allies were always going to win the war without signif-icant loss of life. At Christmas 1990, three weeks before the war began, *The Spectator* devoted its leading article to its former Iranian correspondent, Roger Cooper, who was spending his fifth Christmas in jail in Teheran. Arrested on charges of spying — he was a fluent Farsi speaker whose under-standing of the country was at least the equal of any Westerner's — he had latterly been spending some of his time translating Ayatollah Khomeini's poetry, and was allowed to receive *The Spectator*. 'If it is too much to hope that Roger Cooper will be released at this season,' *The Spectator* wrote, 'we must pray that Iran may mark its own festival of renewal — New Year, at the time of the vernal equinox — with such a gesture, which is long over-due.' Cooper was freed at the beginning of April.

Black had not bought *The Spectator* in 1988 with the expectation of run-ning it at a profit. He was prepared to live, more or less indefinitely, with a small (around £100,000) deficit. But by 1992 the magazine was in danger (as some old *Spectator* hands put it) of becoming profitable for the first time in 30 years. Through Dominguez, *The Spectator* now had a closer relationship with the Telegraph group, which subsumed a proportion of the magazine's costs. Each week's issue was advertised, free of charge, in the *Daily Tele-graph*; and the parent company paid *The Spectator* for the right to republish Christopher Fildes's City and Suburban column every week. (The *Telegraph* was obliged to match the handsome payment which the *Evening Standard* had offered.) At the same time both advertising and circulation revenues were advancing strongly. But an ugly rumour which kept surfacing served to dampen the buoyant mood. It was feared that *The Spectator* would be removed from its Georgian town house to the Docklands and there enveloped within the monstrous plate-glass embrace of Canary Wharf, where the Telegraph group was housed. In fact, this option was never seriously considered, but Colson thought it served as a salutary reminder to *The Spectator* that it was financially dependent on the Telegraph.

However, its editorial independence was not at risk. Black has never envisaged intervening to require *The Spectator* to adopt, or desist from, a particular line. Instead, he has written occasional letters for publication, and he did on one occasion write an article taking issue with Ferdinand Mount's defence of the Church of England against the triumphalism of Catholic writers. Once *The Spectator* showed itself capable of showing a profit, Black looked on it less seriously: not so much an opinion-forming journal as an entertainingly provocative, intellectual gadfly which, while gadding about, was also being talked about. The only intervention required was usually in the area of 'heavy maintenance', in Colson's words, following some waywardness on the part of the editor or embarrassment caused by a contributor.

There was one such example in 1994, when Lawson published an article by William Cash on the influence of the new Jewish establishment in Hollywood. It had very little to say that was new, and it was not very interesting; but it did contain one or two gratuitously offensive phrases, such as 'Jewish cabal'. Lawson's Jewish antennae must have told him it would ruffle a few Jewish feathers, and it is reasonable to surmise that he could not resist the opportunity to do so. But there was no thought, in his mind, that the writer was motivated by anti-semitic tendencies. (When Anthony Lambton sent in an article on Lord Weidenfeld which Lawson judged to be anti-semitic, he refused to publish it.) Cash was merely a silly young man who, claiming friendship with Elizabeth Hurley, had never shown much maturity of judgment. Once his article had been drawn to the attention of the Hollywood bigwigs, their over-reaction was fairly predictable. 'We have a real problem here,' said Jack Valenti, chairman of the Motion Picture Association of America, to Black when he rang him to complain. His first thought was to take advertisements in the North American and British press accusing *The Spectator* of anti-semitism. Finally, after many letters critical of Cash's article had been published in *The Spectator*, Valenti weighed in with a letter about 'anti-semitic stereotypes' and 'racist cant'. His co-signatories included heads of film studios and the actors Sidney Poitier, Barbra Streisand, Kevin Costner, Kirk Douglas and Charlton Heston. Reference was made to the Inquisition in '13th-century Spain', prompting a letter which regretted that, since playing El Cid, Heston had forgotten that the Inquisition was not founded until the 15th century. When Black met Heston some time later and asked him why he had put his signature to that letter, Heston said his employers had told him to. Lawson argued, cleverly enough, that the reaction to Cash's article was symptomatic of a wave of political correctness in America. But there was a whiff of xenophobia (usually directed against Europeans) about some of the articles which Lawson published.

In seeking to be controversial, or at least to raise an eyebrow each week, Lawson also introduced a bit of sex into *The Spectator*. There was a piece by Harriet Sergeant on being seduced by a geisha; another, by Veronica Lodge (aka Anne Applebaum) on pornography, entitled 'Sex is Boring'; a long article on sexual activity in marriage; an interview with a Russian sex-change surgeon; and book reviews by Julie Burchill, on Shirley Conran and the lesbians Anaïs Nin and Jeanette Winterson. An article about the prurient obsession of the British press appeared in the same week that 36 references to sex were found in *The Spectator* by a correspondent from New Zealand. Rebecca Nicolson's piece, at the end of 1994, on the sexual overtones of the Englishwoman's love of horses was a contributory factor in the breakdown of relations between Worsthorne and Lawson. Worsthorne criticised the editor, both privately and in print, for having trivialised the magazine and broken confidences. Ultimately — having tried and failed to exclude Lawson from membership of the Beefsteak Club — he was obliged to resign from *The Spectator*'s board of directors.

Names from outside journalism were successfully introduced into the pages of *The Spectator*. Nigel Nicolson, father of Rebecca and son of Harold, who had written so well for the magazine in the 1940s, contributed a Long Life column; Alistair McAlpine, formerly treasurer of the Conservative party, wrote a monthly art column on the salerooms; Alec Guinness,

P.D. James and Jilly Cooper wrote Diaries (so, unfortunately, did Ruby Wax). The best new *Spectator* diarist was the playwright John Osborne, who in the last few years of his life frequently wrote what Paul Johnson described as 'the perfect diary paragraph, a little playlet in itself, with a magnificent curtain'. It was a great surprise to those at *The Spectator* who spoke to him on the telephone that he was a man of unfailing good manners, who often appeared to lack self-confidence. In his last Diary, for the 1994 Christmas issue, he referred to having been 'struck by yet another mystery ailment' and to the misfortune of having reached 65. 'I am haunted by thoughts of the things I may never do again, and I had hoped that some generous spirit would allow a moratorium on the Angry Old Men quips. But it was not to be.' He died on Christmas Eve.

There was a surprise factor about *The Spectator* which, more often than not, was liable to produce a frisson of excitement among the rapidly expanding readership. It might be a 'demolition job' by a book reviewer — James Buchan of Martin Amis, Kingsley Amis of Philip Larkin's biographer — or an article on the ending of the Prince and Princess of Wales's marriage. Armed with inside information, through his wife's friendship with Diana, that the Wales's were about to separate, Lawson commissioned Hugh Montgomery-Massingberd to write a piece which was published within hours of the announcement from Downing Street (this may have been brought forward when it was learnt what *The Spectator* was about to publish). It caused some consternation also at the *Daily Telegraph*, where Montgomery-Massingberd was employed as Obituaries editor, that he should deliver a scoop to *The Spectator*. (Relations between Lawson and the *Telegraph*'s editor, Max Hastings, were never very friendly. When he was made editor-in-chief of both the *Daily* and *Sunday* papers, Hastings sought to extend his jurisdiction to include *The Spectator* by telling Lawson to suppress an article by Simon Heffer accusing the Pakistani cricket team of cheating. After the matter of Hastings's authority had been raised at a *Spectator* board meeting, Colson told him to 'get back in his box'.)

Lawson's influence also had a modernising effect on *The Spectator*. Along with most other magazines, he adopted the practice of punning headlines on the cover ('Vile bobbies', 'The joy of sects'), which were usually more subtle than those employed by the glossy magazines. Marcus Berkmann wrote a column on pop music, and the glossy-magazine writer and briefly editor of *Harpers & Queen*, Vicki Woods, was a highly entertaining contributor, on subjects as diverse as the thatching of her cottage in Hampshire ('The thatcher years') and an encounter with Mike Tyson, the boxer convicted of rape ('Let'th jutht thiddown...'). One of Lawson's first appointments was of Frank Keating to write a weekly Spectator Sport, enabling him to take a number of unhurried and enjoyable strolls down memory lane. (He was succeeded by Simon Barnes when Keating's employers, the *Guardian*, became jealous that they were missing some of his best stuff.) On the same page Mary Killen had her 'agony aunt' column or, more accurately, her column of advice on etiquette, 'Dear Mary...' It was written in a style which she adapted from her reading of medical magazines, and it enjoyed a large following. Killen replaced one of her great friends, Craig Brown, who took his Wallace Arnold column off to the *Independent on Sunday*, threatening legal action when Lawson tried to hang on to the Wallace Arnold name by publishing a piece under the pseudonym (probably written by Moore). In addition to High, Low and Long Life columns, Lawson experimented, unsuccessfully, with Office Life and Half Life. And he dispensed with New Life, written by Zenga Longmore, the half-African half-sister of Roy Kerridge. Black had urged Lawson to get rid of her column as soon as he became editor; had he not made the suggestion, she would have been sacked much sooner.

William Dalrymple wrote from India, often on British survivals, architectural and human, and Ian Buruma was foreign editor for a year, in succession to Garton Ash. Buruma had worked for the *Far Eastern Economic Review* and spent six years in Japan. He filed for Moore from Hong Kong and Japan; then as foreign editor he wrote mostly on Europe and attended Hungary's first elections. In the arts section Rodney Milnes, after 20 memorable years as opera critic, handed over to Rupert Christiansen; Mark Steyn reviewed cinema, Ian Hislop and Martyn Harris television; and Ursula Buchan wrote on gardens. Giles Auty, appointed art critic by Moore, had become almost a lone voice against modernism and the modern arts establishment. He had trained as an artist and had taught at technical colleges. His *Spectator* writings, often polemical and politically incorrect, comparing the imposed culture of modernism with Marxism, struck a chord with the readership — though not, of course, with the likes of Nicholas Serota, director of the Tate Gallery, and Lord Palumbo. Auty was once ejected from the Royal Academy, and the BBC declined to ask him to expound his views. Finally, in frustration, he left for Sydney, Australia, where the word was carried in future to readers of the *Australian*. One of his greatest fans is said to be Rupert Murdoch's mother.

When he moved on to the *Sunday Telegraph*, Christopher Howse continued as author of the Portrait of the Week, and towards the end of Lawson's time began an amusing little column, under the pseudonym of Dot Wordsworth, on the use of language. Paul Johnson, having written a column on the press for ten years, not flinching from castigating Max Hastings for the *Daily Telegraph*'s lack of editorial direction, was invited by Lawson in 1991 to turn his attention each week to anything he liked or, more often, disliked. He continued hammering away at the excesses of the media and the need for a privacy law, and regularly railed at the incompetence of Major, always comparing him unfavourably with, as he saw him, Britain's new white hope, Tony Blair. More enjoyable, however, than these predictable rants were his disquisitions on the world of letters and painting, and descriptions of walking in the countryside or along the Grand Union Canal.

Simon Heffer, red-haired like Johnson, and sometimes thought to be almost as old as Johnson (he was, in fact, barely half his age), also had a passionate aversion to Major. During his three years as political commentator and deputy editor (1991–94), he seldom let up in his stream of invective against the Conservative prime minister. Having come from the *Daily Telegraph*, which was better disposed towards Major, he now grabbed at his new-found freedom. At the 1992 election, he wanted *The Spectator* to advise prospective Tory voters to stay at home. But Lawson would not go that far, so in his column Heffer wrote that the only good reason for voting Tory was to stop Michael Heseltine becoming prime minister. (The week after the election, at Heffer's instigation, John Patten, Education Secretary, wrote a cover article on good and evil: the Church's role in teaching the lessons of personal morality, the hope of redemption and the fear of eternal damnation. Within six months the government had so mismanaged the exchange rate, resulting in countless job losses, repossessed homes and bankrupt businesses, that there was good reason for its damnation and little hope of early redemption.)

While sharing Heffer's distaste for Major and for European Union,

Lawson was not, in fact, very interested in politics. But he was proud that *The Spectator* was the only publication which, from the beginning, stood against Britain's commitment to the Exchange Rate Mechanism. Journals such as the *Economist* and the *Daily Telegraph* continued to give their support to ERM almost until the end, when the government made its forced and humiliating exit from the mechanism in September 1992. (Lawson's ex-Chancellor father, while an advocate of Britain's membership of the ERM, thought we had joined at the wrong rate.) *The Spectator* correctly forecast that Major's responsibility for this debacle, and the fact that the Chancellor, Norman Lamont, did not immediately resign, spelt the beginning of the end for the Conservatives at the general election five years later. Word occasionally reached Heffer that the prime minister was upset by something he had written, which only encouraged him to pursue his man with even greater vigour. His column would have been more entertaining had he not been so obsessed with the need to unseat Major from the Tory leadership. Not long before he was summoned back to the *Daily Telegraph* in 1994, as deputy editor, to be replaced as political commentator by the *Telegraph*'s Boris Johnson, Heffer introduced to *The Spectator* one Alistair Campbell, then assistant editor (politics) of *Today* and subsequently Blair's truculent press secretary. In several interviews for *The Spectator* with Tory politicians — Sir Marcus Fox, Virginia Bottomley, David Hunt — Campbell proved successful at persuading them to 'go off message'.

Heffer's predecessor as political commentator, with broadly similar political views, was Noel Malcolm, whom Moore had appointed in 1987. His column, though always intellectually stimulating, did not give a vivid impression of the cut and thrust of Westminster politics. It was said that he did not often go to Westminster and mix with the members; he did not want to get his feet wet. Nor, when he became foreign editor in 1991, did he volunteer to go to Yugoslavia during the war to see for himself what was happening on the ground. He was, after all, a scholar and confined himself to armchair analysis — which, as a fluent speaker of Serbo-Croat (and several other central European languages) and subsequent author of acclaimed short histories of Bosnia and of Kosovo, he was well qualified to provide. (Simpson was, from time to time, Our Man in Sarajevo.) Malcolm was one of very few commentators to give warning, from 1991, that Serbia's war aims included the gradual destruction of Bosnia and its incorporation into a Greater Serbia. He lost no opportunity to berate the Foreign Secretary, Douglas Hurd, for calling the conflict a civil war and hastening Bosnia's destruction by his insistence on maintaining an arms embargo against that country. In the letters pages Malcolm would also give occasional history lessons to friends of Serbia such as Sir Alfred Sherman.

Applebaum became the fourth and, for the time being, last foreign editor of *The Spectator*. Like her three predecessors, she wrote mainly on central Europe — she had been based in Warsaw for the *Economist* and was the wife of Radek Sikorski, a contributor to *The Spectator* who later became Poland's deputy foreign minister — although she also spread her wings to America (the country of her birth) and Israel (the country of her faith). She wrote an excellent piece on the double standards of history, contrasting the differing attitudes to Hitler's mass murders and those perpetrated by Stalin. At the end of 1994 she had a hand in the unmasking of a *Guardian* journalist, Richard Gott, as a KGB 'agent of influence'. At the foot of the article were the words, 'Additional research in Moscow by Anne Applebaum', written expressly to persuade Gott, who might be tempted to sue for libel, that *The Spectator* had received confirmation of his activities from Russian sources. In fact, when she went to see a senior KGB officer, Mikhail Liubimov, he denied all knowledge of Gott. The principal credit for the scoop went to a reporter on *The Spectator* who usually wrote on social issues, Alasdair Palmer, whose principal contact for his revelation was a KGB defector, Oleg Gordievsky. Gott resigned, saying that he considered his meetings with KGB officers to be 'an enjoyable joke' (he also received money from them), and wrote to *The Spectator* three months later, seeking to justify his conduct by claiming that the KGB had been the principal organisation in the Soviet Union pressing for reforms. He also mentioned that he had written regularly for *The Spectator* in the 1960s. He in fact wrote three book reviews and one short piece on 'Mods'. (No less of a stir was caused four years later by allegations from a discredited former intelligence agent, published under parliamentary privilege, that Lawson had been on the MI6 payroll while editing *The Spectator*. The idea that he would pass on a good story to the government rather than publish it in his magazine was wildly improbable, though several ill-wishers longed to believe it.)

Charles Seaton died during the last year of Lawson's editorship. He had been at *The Spectator* for more than 40 years, as librarian, archivist and, as

Iain Macleod once described him, 'Lord High everything else'. He was sub-editor, proof-reader and editor of the competitions pages. For many years he set and judged the literary competition, and continued with his librarian's duties until he had passed his 80th birthday. Jenny Naipaul had gradually taken over some of his responsibilities, but Seaton was still looking after Raymond Keene's chess column in the week that he died. There were bits of the magazine which Seaton jealously guarded as his own property: during his 25-year association on the magazine with Nicholas Davenport, the City column was always handled by Seaton. Neither he nor Davenport would allow anyone else to check the copy and make minor amendments to it.

Seaton was a schoolmaster in north London when his old friend Walter Taplin, having recently been made editor of *The Spectator*, approached him in 1953 with the offer of a job. The indiscipline at the school was getting Seaton down, and he jumped at the chance to instal himself in the relative calm and isolation of a garret in Gower Street, surrounded by works of reference. Like many schoolmasters, Seaton was a kindly figure who could be brusque in his manner. He knew of this tendency and in later life regretted it. Iain Hamilton called him 'a fountain of knowledge and one who never failed to remind the rest of us that we were but human'. It was perhaps because of the impression he conveyed of magisterial omniscience that T.E. Utley remembered him as an old man when he was still in his early forties. He was, as Peter Fleming once called him in a Strix column, 'a fact-master' who not only was in possession of a vast store of knowledge but knew how to track down the most recondite facts, 'to go out into no man's land and bring back a prisoner'. Informed by Seaton that the 100th Strix column was coming up, Fleming decided to write about him. He caught Seaton perfectly in commenting that he was the sort of person to use 'such expressions as "of course" ("it was not, of course, until the following year that Paraguay decided to adhere to the Convention")... and "it is too often forgotten/sometimes overlooked/not generally realised" ("that the frontier agreement of 1920 was never ratified by either signatory")'. Nearly 40 years on, Seaton did not seem to have changed much. Indispensable and invaluable were the words most often used of him; indeed, his most invaluable legacy was the index which he compiled for each six-monthly volume of *The Spectator*, tabulated with unfailing accuracy under both subject headings and contributors' names.

The composition of *The Spectator*'s board of directors changed during Lawson's time. The 'wets' — Ludovic Kennedy, Ferdinand Mount, André Deutsch — departed, not necessarily for political reasons. They were replaced by Lord King (chairman of British Airways), Worsthorne and Fildes, who continued to write the most entertaining column in City journalism. Black joined the board in 1990, at the same time making Britain his principal residence, and his wife (Barbara Amiel) joined in 1993. Andrew Knight thought he could remain on the board having left the Telegraph for News International, but was soon disabused of that notion.

The Spectator declared (though not too loudly) a profit of £10,000 in 1992, and £230,000 the following year, the best in its history. By the second half of 1994 circulation had gone above 50,000, and in November it exceeded the previous best figure, of 53,600, achieved at the end of the second world war and including substantial bulk sales to forces overseas. When Lawson left towards the end of 1995, circulation stood at 55,000 and the pre-tax profit was well above £500,000. It was a remarkable achievement by both Lawson and Dominguez, and the previous proprietors could only gaze in wonderment at the figures. Even Sir Evelyn Wrench might have been impressed.

But he would have remarked on the Telegraph connection, asserting perhaps that, while it may not have materially compromised *The Spectator*'s independence, it did contribute to the magazine's profitability. And he might have disapproved of the way in which the Telegraph and *The Spectator* became entangled over the question of Lawson's successor.

By 1995 it was being suggested to Lawson that he might move to the *Daily Telegraph* as deputy to Hastings, with a view, presumably, to becoming editor of one of the newspapers in due course. Heffer was given to understand that he might then return to *The Spectator* as editor. But when Hastings retired (to employ Black's word) to the *Evening Standard*, speedy decisions were required. In the event Lawson was made editor of the *Sunday Telegraph*, Moore editor of the *Daily Telegraph*, and Frank Johnson, columnist and deputy editor of the *Sunday Telegraph*, became *The Spectator*'s editor, with effect from 1 November 1995. Heffer resigned and went to work for the *Daily Mail*.

In his last issue, which coincided with the death of Kingsley Amis (tributes from Anthony Powell, Keith Waterhouse, Alan Watkins et al.), Lawson commented that the last published words of not only Amis, but also John Osborne and A.J. Ayer, had appeared in *The Spectator*. He also said how proud he was that the magazine was now profitable rather than continually loss-making, because 'it means that no one can condescend towards you'. And he told the readers that they were in for a treat, because *The Spectator* was about to be edited by London's wittiest journalist. The following week Johnson repaid the compliment with a witticism from Alan Clark, who in his *Spectator* Diary referred to Lawson's 'loathsome sneering features, pastily glistening'. It was not a good beginning for the new editor.

11

A FROTHY FUTURE?

Frank Johnson had a hard act to follow. Sales of *The Spectator* had never been higher, the magazine had become profitable under Dominic Lawson for the first time in more than 30 years, and the 1995 profits figure was heading for £600,000. Several regular contributors — John Simpson, Kevin Myers, Anne Applebaum, Nigel Nicolson, Alasdair Palmer and, after three months, Auberon Waugh — left to join Lawson at the *Sunday Telegraph*. Johnson was not slow to appoint his own columnists, however. Bruce Anderson replaced Boris Johnson as political commentator, and the political editor of the BBC, Robin Oakley, began a weekly column on racing which, according to readership surveys, soon became one of the most popular in the magazine. Matthew Parris replaced Waugh, and Stephen Glover embarked on a column called Media Studies. Peter Jones, lecturer in classics at Newcastle University, was asked to write a short weekly piece entitled 'Ancient and modern', Michael Vestey began a radio column, and Michael Tanner, biographer of Wagner, became opera critic when Rupert Christiansen left for the *Daily Telegraph*. The *Express*'s opera critic, David Fingleton, was given the no less arduous job of restaurant critic, the *Telegraph*'s Alice Thomson was also asked to contribute a new restaurant column and Johnson reintroduced a regular Dance column, appointing Signor Giannandrea Poesio to write it. (While admiring Poesio's writings elsewhere, Johnson was initially uncertain whether the name Giannandrea indicated a male or female person. Jeremy Isaacs, then general director of the Royal Opera House, mistakenly thought the name was bogus and that the column was in fact written by Johnson.) A Country Life column was contributed by Leanda de Lisle (formerly of *Country Life*). Johnson's old colleague and friend, Peregrine Worsthorne, returned to *The Spectator*'s pages when his *bête noire*, Dominic Lawson, relieved him of his column at the *Sunday Telegraph*.

For someone whose interests were pre-eminently in politics, opera and ballet, Johnson had an unconventional background. The son of a pastry cook and confectioner in the East End of London, he attended a secondary school in Shoreditch, before joining the *Sunday Express* as a messenger boy at the age of 16. Following some years as a reporter for local and regional newspapers (when he became an avid reader of the political weeklies), he joined the political staff of the *Sun* before being appointed parliamentary sketch-writer for the *Daily Telegraph* in the 1970s. After a spell with Sir James Goldsmith's shortlived weekly magazine, *Now!*, he wrote the parliamentary sketch for the *Times*, confirming his reputation as one of Fleet Street's wittiest writers. However, like many humorous writers and actors, he was thought to have a complex personality. He did time as a correspondent in Paris and Bonn before joining the *Sunday Telegraph*, becoming its deputy editor, under Charles Moore, in 1994.

Johnson told a colleague that he intended his *Spectator* to be 'frothy': not trivial, but humorous, while having a serious purpose which would run through the whole of the magazine. His approach to the books pages differed from that of previous editors, who were happy to leave the choice of reviewers entirely to the literary editor. From the start of his editorship Johnson made it clear that he would decide to whom political books should be sent for review, thus establishing a closer political harmony between the front and back halves of the magazine than had existed for many years. He banned poetry from *The Spectator*, and dispensed with the services of P.J. Kavanagh, though he did introduce the publication of clerihews by James Michie. Favourable assessments of Napoleon were unlikely to find their way into *The Spectator*, not because Johnson held him in low esteem, but rather because he was known to be a military hero of the proprietor, Conrad Black.

Johnson did not want *The Spectator* to appear rabidly right-wing; his model as editor was the eclectic Alexander Chancellor rather than Johnson's friend, the ideological Moore, who edited *The Spectator* through much of Margaret Thatcher's decade. Johnson's *Spectator* was more overtly political than Chancellor's, though less so after the 1997 election. Foreign coverage was provided more regularly under Chancellor; Johnson's view was that, since the end of the cold war, 'abroad' was no longer as interesting or important. Irregular correspondents included Andrew Gimson from

Germany, Douglas Johnson, Professor Emeritus of French History at London University, on France (the two countries where Frank Johnson had previously worked), and Mark Steyn, doubling as the magazine's film critic, who wrote on American politics from New Hampshire, with a cynicism and a style reminiscent of *The Spectator*'s former Washington correspondent, Nicholas von Hoffman. Anne McElvoy, a former foreign correspondent for the *Times*, who had written for *The Spectator* in Dominic Lawson's time from Russia and Germany, became Johnson's deputy editor but left in August 1997, to be replaced by Petronella Wyatt, who had followed Johnson from the *Sunday Telegraph* to Doughty Street. Wyatt brought a younger and broader approach to the magazine. It was she who helped persuade Matthew Parris to become a regular columnist, brought in Joan Collins as a diarist, and introduced a diary from Tony Blair's sister-in-law, Lauren Booth, which caused a stir in New Labour circles. Wyatt also wrote a new column entitled Singular Life. At Stephen Glover's suggestion, Johnson put his name at the foot of the leader page each week, but later abandoned the practice (it had occasionally been adopted by Iain Macleod when he was editor). After Edward Heathcoat Amory's appointment as assistant editor, following McElvoy's departure, many of the leaders were written by him.

Anderson wrote well and was an astute observer of the Conservative party. He had been one of the first to predict that John Major would succeed Thatcher, and he nominated William Hague as Major's successor before most people had thought of him.

When Labour came to power with an overwhelming majority, Johnson was concerned that *The Spectator* should not be out of touch with this new phenomenon; sales figures might decline if it were. To his credit, having hunted around he made two discoveries, both of them new to journalism: Siôn Simon, who had been responsible for international media relations at Labour's Millbank election headquarters, and Derek Draper, lately Peter Mandelson's chief political adviser. Johnson's third discovery was Alice Miles, a former lobby correspondent with good New Labour contacts. Simon's first article, on Tony Blair's decision to take over the Tories' Millennium Dome project, was published on 23 August 1997; Draper first appeared in *The Spectator* three weeks later, on 13 September, writing about New Labour's threat to old monarchy. Simon and, to a lesser extent, Draper would continue to provide insights into the workings and the thinking of the new government. Between those two dates in 1997, however, something else happened: Diana, Princess of Wales, was killed in a car accident in a Paris underpass.

The Spectator of 16 August had a striking cover: it was of Diana's head and neck projecting from the bows of Mohamed al Fayed's boat, the *Jonikal*, with him on the bridge and his son Dodi, wearing dark glasses and an oily grin, on deck. Diana looks at once resolute and slightly apprehensive. Inside, Taki disclosed in his High Life column that he had had a telephone conversation with Diana that week. He had asked her whether she was planning to marry Dodi: 'Will you be wearing a chadar any time soon?', and she had said no. It was a good story, supported by a longer article from Robert Hardman, and an outstanding cover drawing, the first by a young illustrator, Jonathan Wateridge, another Johnson find, who in future would do the cover three times a month. After Diana's death, *The Spectator* was generally commended by readers for its measured response to the tragedy, though at least one correspondent found it 'snide and pompous'. By the autumn Johnson could feel fairly confident that, thanks to his New Labour contributors and to Diana, Princess of Wales, the danger of a post-election decline in sales had been averted.

Though Taki had worshipped Diana and had a pretty low opinion of the Prince of Wales, Johnson reversed the pro-Diana editorial line of his predecessor (she was godmother to Dominic Lawson's second child). In conversation Johnson once suggested forming a Carlist party, which came to the Prince of Wales's ears (probably via Santa Palmer-Tomkinson, who later married a *Spectator* contributor, Simon Sebag-Montefiore). The Prince was flattered, and a couple of years later agreed to write an article for *The Spectator* on the regeneration of cities and towns. An invitation was also extended to the Duchess of York to write the Diary, which was syndicated all over the world and which she devoted almost entirely to her holiday in Tuscany with 'my new friends, Sybilla and Gaddo della Gherardesca' — he later became her lover.

Five days after Diana died, so did Jeffrey Bernard, at the age of 65. To most people, and especially the medical profession, it was a miracle that he had lived so long. He was a diabetic, he had had a gangrenous leg off, and though he had latterly given up taking large doses of vodka and soda, he went on smoking (untipped cigarettes) until the end. (In 1996 Johnson had

Jeffrey Bernard might have preferred not to die within a few days of Diana, Princess of Wales, but his death attracted more publicity than those of Mother Teresa, Sir Georg Solti, Hans Eysenck and General Sir John Hackett in the same week.

sent him to Venice, possibly the most unsuitable place in the world for a man in a wheelchair, partly so that he could use the headline 'Jeff in Venice' on the cover.) During his last few months Bernard had to go three times a week to the Middlesex Hospital to be treated on a kidney dialysis machine, but it, and the ban on smoking at the hospital, made him so miserable that he finally decided he could take no more and would stay at home (a 14th-floor flat in Soho) until he died. Doctors told him that he might live another month, but in fact he survived only ten more days. On the day before his death he was visited by three women from *The Spectator*. One of them, the arts editor, Elizabeth Anderson (who presided over her pages with quiet assurance), reported in next week's *Spectator* that he made a few jokes, talked about Marlene Dietrich and said the editor was mad. At the end of his final column, published two weeks earlier, Bernard had been musing about one of his favourite places, Barbados, where he once got sunstroke and was sponged down with ice-cold water by a stunningly beautiful hotel manageress. Chancellor, who had brought him to *The Spectator*, and Peter O'Toole, who had played him in *Jeffrey Bernard is Unwell*, spoke at the funeral, and his ashes were interred beneath a beech tree at the end of the racehorse gallops, on the Berkshire downs above Lambourn where he had once lived.

Taki, his other half, in his appreciation of Bernard (written some years before), said that 'one of the hardest things for me… was having to write next to him, and invariably be compared to him. Without any false modesty, there was never any comparison.' Johnson announced that Bernard would not be replaced: 'Low Life dies with the writer who graced it.' Taki had written that he did not think High Life could work without Bernard alongside him. However, his column continued, seeming to get more intemperate than before. Shortly before Bernard's death Taki had caused some problems by insulting the Puerto Rican community of New York, calling them 'semi-savages' who had never made any positive contribution to their adopted country. There would have been no reaction had not the article been drawn to the attention of the mayor of New York, Rudolph Giuliani, who announced his fury at such racialist slurs, demanding that the editor resign or be sacked, and threatening sanctions against Conrad Black's American properties. When things calmed down, Paul Johnson wrote to say that, while Giuliani was an excellent mayor, he should have responded to Taki's column in the pages of *The Spectator*; and Frank Johnson congratulated him, a few months later, on being re-elected mayor for another term.

At the end of 1997 Harold Evans, former editor of the *Sunday Times* and recent ex-president of Random House, threatened legal action over an article commenting on the circumstances of his departure from the New York publishers. The matter was settled over three months later by Johnson agreeing to run a letter from Evans which, even after cutting, was tediously long. A full-page advertisement was placed between the letter's two columns, so that even fewer people would be likely to read it in full.

While taking responsibility for such problems, *The Spectator*'s long-serving, and at times long-suffering, chairman, Algy Cluff (who in 1998 had been doing the job for 17 years), had over the years assumed more often a headmasterly role, reprimanding an editor or contributor when necessary, whether for something which would have been better not published or, occasionally, for conduct unbecoming. Cluff presided over a board which comprised Conrad Black, Mrs Conrad Black (Barbara Amiel), Dan Colson, Lord King, Christopher Fildes, Sir Patrick Sheehy, Lord Tebbit and the magazine's new publisher, Kimberly Fortier.

Luis Dominguez had left in October 1996 to take up a job in Florida. Fortier, in her early thirties, came from California by way of New York, where she had trained in publishing. She had spent the previous nine years with the glossy magazine publishers, Condé Nast, becoming director of public relations and marketing. Though not by nature or background fitted for the idiosyncratic Englishness of *The Spectator*, she developed a rapport with the editor and his deputy — and she did the business. In 1997–98 *The Spectator*'s balance sheet was looking healthy: pre-tax profits rose above £800,000, advertising revenue was substantially increased and its sources broadened (cars and retail products were especially successful). Circulation stood at just over 57,000.

Elements of the modern world at the end of the millennium were beginning to impinge on *The Spectator*. Its food columnist and former cook, Jennifer Paterson, achieved television star status as one of the 'Two Fat Ladies'. And its biggest single-issue sale, probably since Iain Macleod's article in 1964 on the 'magic circle' which ensured Lord Home's succession to Macmillan, was recorded when a popular singing group, the Spice Girls, gave *The Spectator* their views on politics (Euro-sceptic and generally anti-Labour). Johnson had asked Sebag-Montefiore to interview Britain's leading pop star about political matters. When he learnt that this person was in fact five young females, he winced and told Sebag-Montefiore he was on no account to buy them lunch.

Under Fortier's influence, *The Spectator*'s Doughty Street house adopted a new look in 1998, with its 18th-century front door and fanlight painted bright red and, at its summer party to celebrate its 170th anniversary, a huge red bow festooning the facade. On the same evening lights were beamed on to the draped bookshelves of the literary editor's office, announcing that *The Spectator* now had its own website on the Internet. It was fast becoming the very model of a modern weekly magazine.

With profits approaching £1 million, it was also a continuing commercial success — no mean achievement when compared with the *New Yorker*, which lost almost £7 million in 1997. Several people deserve credit for *The Spectator*'s prosperity, none more than Charles Moore, who brought Dominic Lawson to the magazine and invited Conrad Black to buy it. And it was Algy Cluff who appreciated that *The Spectator*'s future could be secured only with the backing, and the financial discipline, of a publishing group.

Sir Evelyn Wrench, chairman for 40 years, had always been anxious to keep *The Spectator* away from press barons who might compromise its political independence. While this has not happened, it is unlikely, under its present ownership — Black's euro-political and economic views are fundamentally opposed to Gilmour's — that the magazine will return to the left-of-centre Conservatism of its earlier years. Wrench's concern that *The Spectator*'s proprietor should 'have regard to the importance of… eliminating as far as reasonably possible questions of personal or commercial profit' may be an unrealistic aspiration today. But now that profitability has been achieved (it would not have come so soon without the Telegraph's support), is it unreasonable to hope that the profit motive at *The Spectator* will never be paramount?

BIBLIOGRAPHY

Apart from *Spectator* anthologies, I have consulted the following:

Amis, Kingsley (ed.), *Harold's Years* (Quartet, 1967)

Beach Thomas, William, *The Story of The Spectator, 1828–1928* (Methuen, 1928)

Davenport, Nicholas, *Memoirs of a City Radical* (Weidenfeld & Nicolson, 1974)

Fairfax, James, *My Regards to Broadway* (Angus & Robertson, 1991)

Fisher, Nigel, *Iain Macleod* (André Deutsch, 1973)

Fleming, Peter, *The Gower Street Poltergeist* (Rupert Hart Davis, 1958)

Garton Ash, Timothy, *The File* (HarperCollins, 1997)

Glass, Charles, *Tribes with Flags* (Secker & Warburg, 1990)

Harris, Wilson, *Life So Far* (Jonathan Cape, 1954)

Inglis, Brian, *Downstart* (Chatto & Windus, 1990)

Moore, Charles, Wilson, A.N., Stamp, Gavin, *The Church in Crisis* (Hodder & Stoughton, 1986)

Mount, Ferdinand (ed.), *The Inquiring Eye, a Selection of the Writings of David Watt* (Penguin, 1988)

Shepherd, Robert, *Iain Macleod* (Hutchinson, 1994)

Watkins, Alan, *Brief Lives* (Hamish Hamilton, 1982)

Waugh, Auberon, *Will This Do?* (Century, 1991)

Wheatcroft, Geoffrey, *Absent Friends* (Hamish Hamilton, 1989)

Worsthorne, Peregrine, *Tricks of Memory* (Weidenfeld & Nicolson, 1993)

INDEX

I

I Loved Germany (Wrench), 10
Ibos, 127, 128
'If Symptoms Persist...', 211
Imperative Cooking, 211
In London, 169
In the City, 57, 69, 169, 193
Independent, 125, 210, 219, 220
Independent on Sunday, 238
Independent Television News, 167
India, 14, 184, 231, 238
Inglis, Brian
  dates as editor, xiv
  writes on books pages, 23
  appointed as assistant editor, 31
  and Suez, 47
  becomes deputy editor, 51
  introduces Consuming Interest column, 56
  and Nicholson's article, 57
  relationship with Gilmour, 62
  becomes editor, 63–4
  background, 64
  lacks interest in British politics, 64, 68
  characteristics as editor, 65
  decides not to support re-election of Conservatives (1959), 66–7
  and 'think piece' 70, 71
  difficulties with Gilmour, 73–5
  resigns, 76
  invited to become director, 78
  continues to write for *Spectator*, 78, 186
  supports Hamilton, 92, 95
  resigns from board of directors, 95
  brief mentions, 42, 53, 58, 61, 77, 79, 81, 92, 97, 98, 123, 124, 127, 141, 173
Inglis (formerly Woodeson), Ruth, 64, 73
Ingrams, Richard, 100, 167, 169, 171, 172, 176–7, 178, 179, 183, 200, 201
Inquiring Eye, The (ed. Mount), 83
Institute for the Study of Conflict, 97
Institute of Economic Affairs, 157
Institute of Pacific Relations, 4
International Labour Party, xiii
international liberalism, 22
Internet, 251
Investors Chronicle, 134
Iran, 184, 198, 234
  Shah of, 179, 184
Irish, the, 233 *see also* Northern Ireland/Ulster
Irish home rule, xii
Irish Times, 64
Irvine, Derry (later Lord Irvine, Lord Chancellor), 187
Isaacs, Sir Jeremy, 245

Isaacs, Sir Rufus, 44–5
Israel, 46–7, 48, 49, 71, 157, 166, 170, 179, 198, 241
Israeli Defence Force, 198
Italian Socialist party, 57
Italians, 57, 59
Italy, 10, 73 *see also* Rome; Venice

J

James, Clive, 199
James, P.D., 237
Jameson, Conrad, 124
Janes, H.S. ('Bertie'), 68, 77, 79, 86, 94, 95, 96, 97
Janus (pseudonym), 20, 186
Japan/Japanese, 70, 183, 238
Jardine Matheson, 160
Jaspistos (pseudonym), 191
Jay, Douglas, 159
Jay, Peter, 120
Jebb, Gladwyn (later Lord Gladwyn), 48
Jefferson, Sir George, 213
Jeffrey Bernard is Unwell, 249
Jenkins, Clive, 159
Jenkins, Peter, 183
Jenkins, Roy, 32, 38–9, 62, 67, 71, 155, 159, 182
Jenkins, Simon, 229
Jennings, Elizabeth, 24
Jesman, Czeslaw, 50
Jews, 8, 235–6
  anti-Jewish attitudes, 178–9, 235–6
Jinnah, Mohammed Ali, 14
Johannesburg, 34
John Bull's Schooldays, 70
John Fairfax Ltd, xiv, 205, 206, 207, 208, 215, 216
Johnson, Boris, 240, 245
Johnson, Douglas, 247
Johnson, Frank, xiv, 198, 243–51
Johnson, Paul, 126, 132, 165, 174, 193, 237, 239, 250
Jones, Jack, 158
Jones, Peter, 245
Joseph, Sir Keith, 84, 152, 155, 158
Juan Carlos, Prince, 70
Juliette's Weekly Frolic, 155–6

K

KGB, 12, 131, 170, 241
Kaufman, Gerald, 121
Kavanagh, P.J., 184, 211, 246
Keating, Frank, 238
Kee, Robert, 57, 62, 98
Keegan, John, 196, 198, 234
Keele University, 92